# The Infant Survival Guide

### Protecting Your Baby From the Dangers of Crib Death, Vaccines and Other Environmental Hazards

- by -

Lendon H. Smith, M.D.
with Joseph Hattersley, M.A.

SMART PUBLICATIONS™
PO BOX 4667
PETALUMA, CA 94955

707.763.3944 (FAX)
www. smart-publications.com

# The Infant Survival Guide
Protecting Your Baby From the Dangers of Crib Death, Vaccines and Other Environmental Hazards

*by Lendon H. Smith, M.D. with Joseph Hattersley, M.A.*

Published by:
Smart Publications™
PO Box 4667
Petaluma, CA 94955

fax: 707 763 3944
www. smart-publications.com

Library of Congress Catalog Card Number: 00-10990
First Printing 2000
Printed in the United States of America
First Edition

Library of Congress Cataloging in Publication Data
The Infant Survival Guide
Lendon H. Smith, M.D. with Joseph Hattersley, M.A.
Includes Index & References
1. Sudden Infant Death Syndrome
2. Crib Death
3. Vaccines
4. Infant

Preassigned LCCN: 00-10990

ISBN: 1-890572-12-8          $14.95          Softcover

## Warning- Disclaimer
Smart Publications has designed this book to provide information in regard to the subject matter covered. It is sold with the understanding that the publisher and the author(s) are not liable for the misconception or misuse of the information provided. Every effort has been made to make this book as complete and as accurate as possible. The purpose of this book is to educate. The author(s) and Smart Publications shall have neither liability nor responsibility to any person or entity with respect to any loss, damage, or injury caused or alleged to be caused directly or indirectly by the information contained in this book. The information presented herein is in no way intended as a substitute for medical counseling.

# Table of Contents

Chapter   One

# INTRODUCTION

We have chatted with many new or expectant mothers. Even though the odds are only one in 1,000 or less, we see the dread on their faces when the conversation turns to SIDS, caused by their fear of what might happen to their baby. In fact, this book was made possible by such fear. Following the earlier rejection of our original book proposal, publisher John Morgenthaler of Smart Publishing changed his mind. The Morgenthalers' baby was 6 months old; he and his wife were scared stiff about SIDS.

Every young mother will want this potentially life-saving, grief-sparing and health promoting information. We offer to you the definitive guide on how to avoid crib death.

SIDS, Sudden Infant Death syndrome, is a tragedy to any family. It is the loss without warning of a baby who usually had only minor health problems. Nothing is more upsetting to the parents, the doctors and friends than the death of an infant who seemed well formed and in good health. The baby is usually between 2 and 6 months of age, and his/her personality is just beginning to emerge. Laughter, squeaks of joy, solemn grimaces, moments of concentrated focus are all developing. Now, in a flash, all those promises of a joyful life are but empty dreams.

Over my 25 years of general pediatric practice, I never noted any one common thread in the histories of these babies. Most were active and robust; maybe they had a slight sneeze or sniffle but were never considered sickly. The parents were a mixture: some bright, some not so bright, but all seemed eager to rear a healthy child. The parents want answers. The kindly, friendly pediatrician can only stand there flat-footed and say "Duuuhh." It is embarrassing to us scientists.

Known almost exclusively in rich countries, SIDS is the leading cause of death in the first year of life. It is rare in developing countries where doctors don't yet attend childbirth, where mass vaccination programs have not been launched or chemicals placed in babies' bedding, drinking water has not been polluted with chlorine, fluoride and thousands of other chemicals. When all those features of "civilized" life are introduced, here comes crib death.

The SIDS rate in America has been estimated at about 0.75 per 1,000. It is more common in boys than girls (reasons are shown in Chapter 2). Also in Chapter 2 we delve briefly into the history of crib death, then tell of the discovery and proof of toxic mattress gases as its cause. We detail how influences such as electromagnetic fields and geopathic stresses affect risk.

Out of four million annual live births, that totals around 3,000 crib deaths a year or about eight now-avoidable SIDS tragedies every night. There are many more of these tragedies on weekend nights than other nights of the week. In Chapter 2 we elaborate on that and offer some reasons for it.

And now avoidable? This book presents what we believe to be the cause of crib death and how it can be prevented.

Everyone is familiar with the eye stinging of ozone in smog out-of-doors. But could gases kill babies indoors? Yes, they can. The cause of SIDS is toxic gases generated in the baby's mattress by fungi. And so we tell you in detail all you need to know about toxic gases that kill babies (Chapter 2), and what you can do to eliminate the risk.

Surprisingly, what the parents eat appears to have little effect on SIDS risk. But allergies increase risk, and we offer suggestions on how to avoid allergies. One of those ways is not to give children antibiotic drugs such as amoxycillin. The antibiotics themselves, used in a vain fight against usually viral rather than bacterial ear infections, promote allergies in a complex way, by destroying "friendly" gut organisms along with any "bad" ones, promoting development of antibiotic-resistant organisms and in other ways weakening immunity, Chapter 8.

Lots of books and articles provide advice on pregnancy (covered in Chapter 4), childbirth (Chapter 5) and nutrition (Chapter 8). Throughout, we emphasize the specific measures that will reduce the risk of gas poisoning. And we add information that could help parents avoid other serious problems, such as birth defects and lowered intelligence.

Conventional thinking assumes the cause of SIDS is unknown, that there are many risk factors and preventing it is hopeless. One can only lower the risk around the edges and offer sympathy afterward. By clinging too long to this mistaken belief, people concerned about SIDS are holding back its elimination.

In this book we propose a new paradigm (system of thought). (1) SIDS has one cause. We identify that cause, noting a very few exceptions. (2) And we tell you the method that has been 100 percent effective at preventing it. Hence the title: "The Infant Survival Guide."

What caused the huge postwar upsurge in SIDS deaths? Crib

---

A syndrome is the aggregate of symptoms associated with a disease condition (Oxford Dictionary, v. 2, 1976). In crib death the only symptom is death itself. The "syndrome" designation opened the door for well-paid specialists to investigate various "risk factors" for crib death while ignoring the actual cause. Their efforts have cost many millions of dollars.

SIDS was assumed to be multifactorial: several mechanisms can function, possibly more than one at the same time. No one of them may be enough to kill, but the combination kills. This way of attacking crib death is a cop-out and a failure.

The term "sudden" also doesn't apply. We show that various events make crib death totally foreseeable. Even the likely date can sometimes be predicted. SIDS risk begins about two weeks after birth; it is the leading cause of death in months 2 to 6. It reaches a peak in the third month, then declines rapidly and is rare after a year of age.

death had previously been rare, but it became common with the onset of food processing/adulteration, environmental degradation and mass vaccinations. After 1950 the governments of nearly all the industrialized countries (except Japan, see Chapter 2) required treatment of baby and child mattresses with fire-retardant chemicals. Phosphorus was later added to help preserve the mattress. Sadly, that well-meaning measure was counterproductive in two ways:

(1) It is well known that the number of baby deaths in residential blazes multiplied. Statistical evidence, unfortunately, is not available; and,

(2) American SIDS deaths ballooned 400-fold. The mechanism of death was identical in both types of tragedy. Fungi consume fire-retardant and preservative chemicals and emit neurotoxic gases. Below, we tell briefly of the mechanism. In Chapter 2 we elaborate on what it is that kills in both home conflagrations and SIDS. "The Infant Survival Guide" presents both the proven cause and, most important, the method to prevent it — which follows from knowledge of the cause.

Toxic gases arising from the baby's mattress cause nearly all crib deaths. Simple slip-on mattress covers called BabeSafe® have been 100 percent effective in preventing crib death, reports T. J. Sprott, Ph.D., of Auckland, New Zealand. Others have confirmed his claim. Sprott is the world's authority on crib death. In Chapter 2 we show how he became the authority he is.

Wrapping the mattress properly with a clear sheet of thick polyethylene plastic has been equally effective. In Measures, at the end of the book, we present instructions for mattress wrapping.

The truth about toxic gases was almost stumbled onto in the 1960s. Investigators recruited 2,000 mothers who had lost a baby to SIDS. Half, or 1,000, were instructed to elevate the head end of their new baby's crib an inch or two; the other 1,000 kept the crib level. Among the babies sleeping in slanted cribs there were zero crib deaths; among those in level beds, two — about the average expected at that time per 1,000.

Those conducting the test, reported by a metropolitan newspaper, could not explain the result. Now we know. Slanting the crib allowed those heavier-than-air toxic gases to flow to the foot end and fall harmless to the floor. That's still a usable plan until BabeSafe® or proper mattress wrapping is obtained, and at times when it might not be feasible, such as while traveling.

Pediatricians often tend to be overspecialized and know little of how toxic gases can arise from babies' mattresses containing phosphorus, arsenic and antimony.

Vaccines increase risk of SIDS among babies who are not protected from the toxic mattress gases. They do this both immediately and in a delayed fashion by inciting toxic gas-promoting fevers and longer-term illnesses.

Vaccinations also create shortened, poorer-quality lives. Chapter 6 fully supports and documents that statement and offers ways to protect your child from this life- and health-threatening situation.

Weakened immunity as well as allergies increase the risk of SIDS through lowering the baby's ability to tolerate a given concentration of toxic gas. And as we explain in Chapter 2, the fevers of frequent infections increase gas concentrations. We discuss allergies and weakened immunity in Chapter 8 along with their probable causes.

Other agencies and professional groups increase risk of crib death. In Chapter 9 we discuss the EPA's (Environmental Protection Agency) phobia about ultraviolet light (UV). In fact, moderate direct outdoor exposure to sunlight is required for good health, both mental and physical. It will help avoid crib death.

The EPA and the surgeon general — ignoring scientific research published since 1945 — also increase risk of lung cancer by urging costly measures to lower radon gas in homes. The risk of lung cancer (and presumably SIDS) is related to radon. But the correlation is negative: Higher radon correlates with lower risk.

Dentists also promote crib death indirectly through their use of mercury fillings and root canals. The risk is particularly high if the mother has fillings installed or removed while she is pregnant.

**Technical Note:** Dr. A.M. Barrett in 1953 first described and defined SIDS. It is defined as an unexpected infant death, after which thorough autopsy and examination of the death scene and circumstances at time of death reveal no identifiable cause of death.

Eighty-four percent of SIDS babies have been found with a wide range of recognizable symptoms that an educated parent or pediatrician might well have heeded — but not sufficient to make the parents expect death.

Inflammation in the upper respiratory tract has been found in over 90 percent of SIDS autopsies. Warren Guntheroth, M.D., recognized as an authority on SIDS, wrote, "This has convinced most of us that mild virus infections play some role, perhaps in increasing the probability of a prolonged apneic episode."

Apnea is repetitive pauses in breathing. We show that apneas themselves do not cause SIDS; instead it is toxic gases. Cases that are carefully investigated, including autopsies, but which remain unresolved, may be designated as "undetermined" or "unexplained." And so some of the seeming drop in incidence could result from the use of this new definition.

The incidence of SIDS in the United States has decreased to below one case per 1,000 live births (1997). Highly specialized pathologists are finding defects in the brain and conduction system of the heart in SIDS cases. Rare metabolic diseases and infanticide are also being detected more often. SIDS is a diagnosis of exclusion, so the more we know, the less likely SIDS will remain the cause of death.

Chapter Two

# TOXIC GASES:
# THE SINGLE CAUSE OF
# NEARLY ALL CRIB DEATHS

E nough for definitions and general principles. It's time now to examine precisely what it is that kills babies in what is labeled SIDS. This chapter will be a relief: It will show parents how to achieve what appears to be 100 percent protection against crib death. But the chapter is a shock, too. For it raises (although it does not answer) the question, Why has this potentially life-saving, grief-preventing information not been made generally known to the public? We detail the cover-up of this information in our technical summary of the book in *Townsend Letter for Doctors and Patients,* July 2000. This can be referenced on the internet in Joseph Hattersley's web site located at: www.angelfire.com/wa/jhattersley/content.html.

Before World War II, unexplained infant deaths did happen, although they were unusual. But after 1950, governments of the United States, Britain and nearly all the other industrialized countries (except Japan, see later) required treatment of baby and child mattresses with fire-retardant chemicals. Sadly, this well-intentioned measure was counterproductive in two ways.

Close observers know that the number of baby deaths in home fires grew substantially.[1] Unfortunately, supporting statistics are not available.

American "SIDS" deaths ballooned 400-fold. The mechanism of death was identical in both types of tragedy. What is that mechanism? A common, ordinarily harmless household fungus *(Scopulariopsis brevicaulis)* and certain microorganisms consume fire-retardant arsenic[2] and antimony, preservative phosphorus, and an impurity in the mattress plasticizer (softener).

While doing this, they emit the heavier-than-air, nearly odorless neurotoxic gases phosphine (PH3), arsine (AsH3) and stibine (SbH3). These gases are an alarming 1,000 times more poisonous than carbon monoxide, which can kill a person in a closed garage with a running car engine. They are about as toxic as Sarin, used in the Iran-Iraq war of the 1980s and in the terrorist subway poisoning in Tokyo in 1995.

---

*"In probably the worst environmental disaster of the 20th century, toxic gases emitted from mattresses or other bedding have killed about one million victims of SIDS worldwide."*

---

Gas generation starts when mattress and bedding warm to body temperature in contact with the baby's body. Perspiration, dribble, urine, vomit and — this, we shall see, is critical — high (alkaline) pH enable the fungus to grow and produce gases rapidly. If a baby breathes these gases even in minute quantity for a prolonged time, they can interrupt the choline/acetylcholine transfer of nervous impulses from the brain to the heart and lungs. As shown in scientific literature, that shuts down the central nervous system; the heartbeat and breathing stop.[3,4]

In Chapter 1 we told how the mechanism was almost discovered in the 1960s but not explained. And in a technical section later, we tell of a proposed alternative mechanism to explain how the toxic gases cause death. In probably the worst environmental disaster of the 20th century, toxic gases emitted from mattresses or other bedding have killed about one million victims of SIDS worldwide. Most of these gases (phosphine is an exception, details later) settle in a thin, nearly odorless layer on the baby's crib.

So the parents know nothing of the danger until their discovery, typically the next morning, that their baby is dead. A few deaths occur no more than 10 minutes after the parent leaves the baby alone.[5] One of the results of the death is the guilt reaction.[6] Every parent of a baby, or parent-to-be, is wondering, "Will my child become a statistic? Will he/she have to die because of something I did or did not do?" Older children would develop a headache and call for help; for physiological reasons, adults are not put at risk by such gas generation.

In a related matter that promotes a lot of news items, in SIDS and near-miss babies, inhalation of the toxic gases often causes small red blotches under the skin known as petechiae. Technical scientific documents fully explain this.[7] These also often appear shortly after vaccinations.[8] In a dozen cases cited by Viera Scheibner, Ph.D., author of *VACCINATION: 100 Years of Orthodox Research Shows that Vaccines Represent a Medical Assault on the Immune System*. Blackheath, NSW 2785, Australia: Australian Print Group, 1993,[9] vaccine damage has been so severe it gives the appearance of physical shaking. As a result, parents have been accused of smothering or murdering babies, some have been deprived of their children or imprisoned.[10] Some babies have in fact been fatally injured by shaking, in what is dubbed "Shaken-baby syndrome."

To prevent crib death caused by inhalation of the deadly gases, an appropriate barrier is needed between mattress and baby. An inexpensive slip-on mattress cover called BabeSafe® came to market in New Zealand in 1996. Among 100,000 babies sleeping on the product in New Zealand[11] and elsewhere, not one crib death has been reported.[12,13]

Parents achieve equally successful prevention by wrapping the entire mattress with thick, clear polyethylene plastic sheeting. Directions are given at the end of this book.

Until BabeSafe® is obtained, or when its use might not be feasible such as while traveling (even wrapping a motel mattress might not be practicable), a parent can elevate the head end of the crib an inch or two. This will let any of these heavier-than-air gases that may have collected, flow to the foot end — and fall to the floor. (A bassinet with impervious sides would trap gases.) A rolled towel just south of baby's rump prevents sliding. Also be sure the baby sleeps face up.

Throughout the book, readers will notice frequent mention of studies made in New Zealand and Australia. The former has always had a high rate of SIDS, and crib death has long been a serious problem among Australian Aborigines. In both cases, toxic gases appear to result from the ubiquitous fungi-consuming arsenic and other substances present in items such as sheepskins and tea tree bark. The fungi are found everywhere. See below.

The 100-percent success of BabeSafe®, together with Peter Mitchell's finding of doubled and redoubled SIDS risk in a mother's second and later babies (Figure 1.), appears to refute all other explanations of SIDS. In the remainder of this book we show how each risk factor either raises the concentration of toxic gas or lowers the baby's ability to tolerate a given concentration, or both.

Who discovered such toxic gases? And what is the proof of our statements about them? The fungal generation of arsines has been known for well over 100 years. Before the day of plastic and other synthetic mattress materials, it killed thousands of children in Europe in the 1800s. The Italian analytical chemist B. Gosio discovered its cause in 1892.[14,15]

T. James Sprott, Ph.D., proposed the toxic gas hypothesis of SIDS in 1986.[16] Sprott is a New Zealand consulting chemist and forensic scientist. His success, notably in certain criminal cases, earned him great fame and respect in New Zealand. Barry A. Richardson, a British consulting scientist and expert in materials degradation who has published more than 200 papers in peer-reviewed scientific journals, outlined the connection to crib death

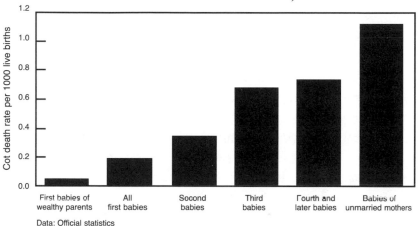

**Figure 1.** Crib death rates for first and later babies and babies of unmarried mothers: Britain, 1992. From T.J. Sprott, *"The Cot Death Cover-up"?* Penguin-NZ, 1996. Used by permission of Penguin-NZ.

in the early 1990s in two journal articles.[17,18] Sprott corroborated and strengthened the argument in 1996 in his compelling (I couldn't put it down) book, *"The Cot Death Cover-up?"*[19]

In Britain, in 1991 Peter Mitchell — not a professional researcher but one who was deeply concerned about crib death — made a landmark discovery. Patiently summarizing records of hundreds of cases, he found that SIDS risk doubles from the first to the second baby, and nearly doubles again from the second to the third (Figure 1).[20] A 1996 study found the risk substantially higher still in fourth and later babies. Others had noticed higher risk in babies born later but couldn't explain it.

The fungal spores are established in the mattress during prior use and so gas production starts sooner and in greater volume. Infants of poor single parents, with used mattresses and bedding and high stresses of daily living, have seven times greater SIDS risk than wealthy parents' babies.

Similarly, in Taiwan from 1988 to 1992, babies born second to fourth were 70 percent more likely to die of SIDS than the first Risk for fifth or later babies was up 130 percent.[21] The authors of the article didn't know about toxic gases and so they couldn't understand their findings. These statistics, which almost certainly apply to countries such as the United States and Canada, can be explained only by the toxic gas hypothesis.

Output of the gases from babies' mattresses, and, consequently, the number of SIDS deaths, declined rapidly in Britain after Richardson dramatized the problem on BBC television in June 1989 in "The Cook Report." More than 60,000 worried British parents phoned in. Parents bought new mattresses without the potential for toxic gas creation or properly wrapped old ones. Manufacturers quietly began to remove the chemicals, which fire safety regulations had required.

SIDS had long been increasing in Britain. It reached a new peak in 1986-1988 after the amount of preservative phosphorus put into baby mattresses was increased.[22] The new ongoing, first-ever decline in Britain's SIDS rate, shown in Figure 2, accelerated in December 1991 after publicity urging parents to put babies to sleep face up.[23] (Many SIDS victims are known to have rolled from side to prone.[24])

The toxic gas hypothesis explains the nearly worldwide drop in crib deaths that followed.[25] See Figure 2. Incidence in Britain (0.7 per thousand live births) is now 70 percent lower than 1986-88, when it was 2.3 per 1,000. It is slightly below the rate of about 0.75 per 1,000 (totaling about 3,000 a year) in America.

---

Many deaths in the first month after DPT (diphtheria/pertussis (whooping cough)/tetanus) vaccination are inaccurately called "SIDS." No count is kept. Including them, the total SIDS death toll is higher. Babies die after DPT because, unprotected against toxic gases, the fevers generated by vaccines increase generation of the gases. This happens both immediately and at predictable intervals afterward. Also, the infections reduce babies' tolerance of any given concentration of gases. For a more detailed discussion, see Chapter 6.

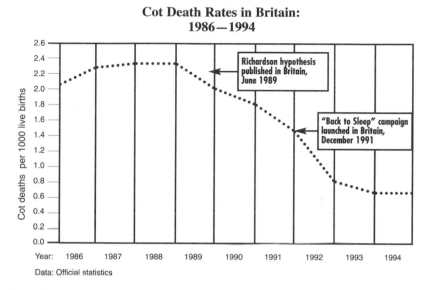

**Cot Death Rates in Britain:
1986—1994**

Data: Official statistics

**Figure Two.** Crib Death Rates in Britain: 1986-1994. From T.J. Sprott, *"The Cot Death Cover-up?"* Penguin-NZ, 1996. Used by permission of Penguin-NZ.

The British Limerick Commission rejected the toxic gas hypothesis.[26] Yet, when read carefully, according to Sprott and Michael Fitzpatrick, M.D.,[27] the tests reported in the Limerick Commission's analysis clearly confirm the hypothesis[28] — as demonstrated by the success of mattress wrapping and BabeSafe®: not one crib death.[29] [30] However, the commission's final report, which is all that citizens and physicians read did not accurately state those findings.

Ample further evidence supports the toxic gas explanation. After "near-misses," monitoring of breathing and heartbeat confirms the described sequence of events. And in SIDS autopsies, evidence of lasting cerebral hypoxia (severe lack of oxygen in the brain) both before and after birth corroborates the mechanism.[31] Discussion to follow clarifies how hypoxia relates to SIDS, in particular in our proposed additional mechanism of toxic gas death.

Hypoxia promotes formation of tiny, electrically imbalanced particles known as free radicals. A free radical is an atom that has an unpaired electron in its outer ring: As a result, free radicals (also called oxidants) are unbalanced and highly reactive. They dart about the body damaging cells. Any molecule they meet in turn becomes a free radical.[32] This can start a chain reaction that could destroy tissues at random.

Other free radicals reach us through toxins in the air, water, and food, or are generated inside our bodies as part of our defensive response to infection or other stress. In excess, they promote diseases of all kinds and aging.[33,34] An antioxidant molecule donates an electron so as to quench a free radical.

---

A proposed additional mechanism of toxic gas death. Repeated, at times severe, episodes of hypoxemia (insufficient aeration of arterial blood) or asphyxia, or both, occur in infants who are at increased risk for SIDS.[35,36] Cyanosis, blue color of lips and nail beds, which is very common in SIDS victims, results from lack of enough oxygen.[37,38]

---

*Webster's New World Dictionary* defines hypoxia as an abnormal condition resulting from a decrease in oxygen supplied to or utilized by body tissues. Research-oriented Derrick Lonsdale, M.D., labels it hypo-oxidative metabolism; it kills tissues. "Any cell (except erythrocytes, red blood cells) made hypoxic for a sufficient period is irreversibly injured."[39]

"Regarding injury to the brain, neuroscientists use the terms hypoxia and ischemia interchangeably. (Ischemia is a lack of oxygen-carrying blood flow in an organ or tissue.) In local ischemia, cells in the center of the ischemic zone are damaged most rapidly; cells in the surrounding area (the ischemic penumbra) receive some oxygen from other blood vessels and thus are less hypoxic."[40]

The killing of tissue leading to SIDS can take the form of apoptosis, i.e. programmed cell suicide, or "cellular hara-kiri,"[41] which is commonly associated with diseases of aging. Apoptosis does greater damage at higher body temperatures;[42] that fits our proposal, below, that inhalation of toxic gases — concentration of which is higher with a fever — initiates apoptosis leading to crib death. Cells at the center of the hypoxic area can die, instead, by necrosis, i.e., rupturing and spilling the cellular contents into the extracellular fluid.[43]

Karen A. Waters, M.D., and her colleagues at Montreal Children's Hospital found neuronal apoptotic cells in 79 percent of 29 SIDS victims they examined. They found none in the control cases.[44] Apoptosis in 2 percent to 3 percent of neurons can signify a cell regression rate of 25 percent per day.[45] They found apoptosis in more than 20 percent of such cells, implying rapid cell death.

Waters continues, "In SIDS victims, neuronal loss has been reported in the brainstem arcuate nucleus,[46] a region thought to be involved in control of respiration…and we found significant neuronal apoptosis in the nucleus of the tractus solitarius, a region involved in autonomic and respiratory control [i.e. in making breathing an 'automatic' process not requiring conscious control.]

"Repeated episodes of hypoxemia first lead to confirmed neuronal apoptosis in select vulnerable brain regions. Then comes the disappearance of a significant number of cells, and eventually impaired function."[47]

1) Inhalation of ammonia from the baby's feces can aggravate hypoxia/hypoxemia. Ammonia combines with and inactivates carbon dioxide; the baby needs free $CO_2$ to trigger the breathing reflex.[48] Apoptosis, interestingly, also serves an important homeostatic, i.e. health-promoting function during central nervous system development.[49]

---

**Technical Note:** Smoke residues from American cigarettes are "laced with sugar and dupe the gut into expecting food, triggering insulin release."[55] Japanese and South African cigarettes, among others, do not contain sugar and toxic additives.[56,57] The late internist/cardiologist Moses M. Suzman, M.D., of Johannesburg (Chapter 7) confirmed the statement about South African cigarettes and said that South African blacks do not develop lung cancer, despite heavily smoking unfiltered cigarettes.[58]

2) The body tissues of crib death babies and the mattresses on which they died contain high concentrations of antimony, the source of stibine gas,[50] whereas bodies of babies who died of other causes and non-SIDS inducing mattresses contain little or no detectable antimony.[51] Remnants of phosphorus and arsenic are present in the body naturally, and so tracking them is not meaningful.[52]

3) The hair of living babies contains 10 to 100 times more antimony than their parents' hair, demonstrating that they have been exposed to gas generated from their mattresses.[53] And about 95 percent of 200 consecutive SIDS babies in a 1989 test sample died on used mattresses.[54] Most of these statements cite Dr. Jim Sprott's book and his periodical *Cot Life 2000*, which is available on the Internet at his web site: www.cotlife2000.com.

4) The decline in SIDS in Britain, described above and shown in Figure 2, itself strongly supports the toxic gas explanation.

---

*"But crib death was virtually nonexistent because chemicals that fungi could convert into toxic gases weren't added to mattresses until after the war."*

---

5) Smoking was much more common in Britain in the 1930s and 1940's than now. But crib death was virtually nonexistent because chemicals that fungi could convert into toxic gases weren't added to mattresses until after the war. See also below.

We ask our readers' patience in considering the technical material that follows. We believe it is so important we must include it. Protection against toxic mattress gases appears to eliminate SIDS risk, but that fact does not eradicate vaccine damage short of death (Chapter 6). By inactivating certain enzymes, cigarette smoke residues induce peroxidation (formation of excess hydrogen peroxide) in the baby's blood plasma,[59,60] or the cadmium in cigarette smoke catalyzes, i.e., facilitates oxidation in the babies' lung tissue when there is a deficiency of vitamin E and selenium.[61] Either mechanism can make babies more susceptible to gaseous death if the mattress is generating the gases.[62 63]

Maternal smoking associates itself with higher SIDS risk for infants who share with parents beds that are not properly protected. The relative risk was 9.25 (95 percent confidence intervals 2.31 to 34.02).[64] Interpretation: Babies of mothers who smoked were over nine times more likely to be victims of SIDS than those of nonsmoking mothers. Confidence intervals are a statistical matter.

Tobacco smoke may affect the neuroregulation of breathing, which could result in apneic spells (repeated pauses in breathing), and so increase risk of sudden infant death to a baby who is not protected against toxic gases.[65,66] "In contrast with mainstream smoke, environmental (passive) smoke contains greater amounts of ammonia, benzene, carbon monoxide, nicotine and carcinogens such as 2-naphthylamine n-nitrosamine.[67]"

The damage probably is greater for women who are also on birth-control pills.[68] Tobacco-derived compounds enter a woman's cervix,[69] where they may cause cancer (but see chapter nine), or into a fetus, where they may cause respiratory problems or genetic damage that will predispose the child to cancer. The baby is inclined to low birth weight and respiratory problems, both of which increase SIDS risk. And Alexander Schauss, Ph.D., warns that such children may not get enough zinc, as the cadmium in cigarettes prevents zinc absorption. See also Chapter 4.

Other matters may increase a baby's susceptibility to a given toxic gas concentration. Examples include preterm birth, environmental toxins including pesticides, nutritional deficits creating hypothyroid condition among others, antibiotics, alcohol and depressive condition of the mother.

Poor nutrition has not been proved to increase SIDS risk. But poor nutrition and anything else that can increase fevers still might. In 1600, there was no evidence that germs were dangerous — but that did not prove they were harmless. However, proof of any nutritional theory of SIDS would require: 1) collection of tissue samples from SIDS babies and from infants who died of known causes. Then, (2) consistently lower iodine (or thiamine) would have to be found in the SIDS autopsies. After that, (3) a mechanism would have to be proposed and supported. (4) Most difficult: In light of Peter Mitchell's findings given earlier and shown graphically in Figure 1, crib death risk caused by such nutrient deficiency would have to be consistently twice as high in a mother's second baby and twice as high again for her third baby. In fact, most families maintain about constant nutritional practices throughout their child-rearing years (child rearing to include not only birth but also childhood). 5) And the reason for insufficiency of a nutrient to cause such upward steps in risk would have to be proposed and supported.

Poor nutrition tends to accompany low-income status, and that leads to continued use of fungus-infected bedding.

The toxic gas explanation casts new light on poorly understood aspects of these unmitigated family tragedies. Crib death is most common in industrialized countries where baby mattresses contain any of the three elements: phosphorus, arsenic, and antimony. In countries such as Japan, Hong Kong and the Pacific islands, beds are either chemicals-free cotton or simple woven floor mats.[70] Fungi such as *S. brevicaulis* are everywhere.[71] But without fire-retardant chemicals to consume, they create no toxic gases. Preservatives and fire retardants in Japan use safe boron; SIDS is slowly rising there as parents adopt Western-style mattresses and bedding.[72]

Toxic gases arise from sheepskins and other "natural" bedding such as tea-tree bark fibers, which are widely used throughout Australia and New Zealand. The New Zealand Cot Death Study, 1987 to 1990, found that half of all crib deaths occurred on sheepskin.[73] Depending on the soil on which the sheep graze, their skins can contain high concentrations of phosphorus, arsenic and/or antimony. Tea-tree bark normally contains phosphorus, since the trees excrete toxins into their bark.[74]

Anything that raises the temperature of the bed promotes toxic gas generation. A rise from 98.6° F to 104° F can increase gas generation 10-fold or more.[75] In one study, 68 percent of SIDS victims had symptoms of respiratory infection, which can produce fevers, versus 32 percent of controls.[76] Researchers Carpenter and Shaddick found SIDS most common in babies who had symptoms of respiratory disease in the two weeks before death.[77] High room temperature and swaddling the baby as now recommended by authorities[78] (see below) also promote more gas generation.

---

"Back to Sleep" practices have produced a new problem of malformed heads.[81] The number reported has increased six-fold.[82] On-back sleeping gives some babies a flattened back of the skull and a bulged front.

This "epidemic" of misshapen skulls has triggered an "epidemic of misdiagnoses."[83] Pediatric surgeons misdiagnosing the misshapen skulls as craniosyntosis — a rare condition, in which the bones of the skull fuse too soon — have performed thousands of surgeries, sawing off the top and back of a baby's skull. Instead, a skillful practitioner can handle most such conditions nonsurgically — possibly by a headband or by simply alternating sleeping positions.[84]

---

The facts outlined above will surprise the "experts," who for years shouted "Back to Sleep." Sleeping face up, a baby is less likely to inhale heavier-than-air toxic gases generated in the mattress. But phosphine, which is derived from preservative phosphorus, is only slightly heavier than air. So a baby can die from inhaling that gas despite sleeping face up.[79] Babies have died of SIDS in almost any position; one died in his mother's arms.[80] Our interpretation: She picked up her baby after he was already dying from gas exposure.

A reason for not sleeping on the back has been to avoid aspiration of gastric contents — spitting up and inhaling it. But a proper forensic autopsy would disclose that and so would elimi-nate[85] diagnosis of SIDS, which requires failure to find a cause.

In 1995, Anne-Louise Ponsonby, Ph.D., reported that sleeping on the back or side with a quilt increased SIDS risk nearly four-fold — supposedly through smothering. Blankets and pillows "can mold to baby's face."[86] So the authorities reversed field again; they now say to remove bedding from infant sleeping areas and dress the baby warmly.[87]

Such overwrapping could multiply SIDS tragedies in two ways. (1) Smothering is extremely rare among babies, including those put to sleep face down. Head turning in sleep is develop-mentally regulated even in prematurely born babies; they rarely assume a face down position.[88] But many quilts contain phospho-rus or antimony or both, and most quilts are seldom washed. So they can be infested with the same gas-generating fungi discussed earlier, increasing risk in that way. (2) Also, blankets can trap toxic gases.[89]

Other factors. Sprott emphasizes that rebreathing of carbon dioxide does not cause SIDS. "All babies exhale a similar amount of CO2 regardless of whether they are first, second or later babies. Therefore, the rising rate of cot death from one sibling to the next refutes the theory that rebreathing of CO2 causes crib death."[90] CO2 is in fact an important trigger of respiration,[91,92,93] helping the baby to minimize risk of apnea/hypopnea.

SIDS incidence is double in the parts of Austria above 700 meters (just over 2,100 feet) altitude compared to those under 500 meters.[94] And in Sweden, outdoor temperatures below the annual mean of 5.9° C (42.6° F) — primarily in October-February, and much more in unusually cold years — in combination with a sud-den decrease in temperature, are associated with SIDS.[95] At cold-er temperatures, due to either altitude or weather, parents wrap their babies more firmly, increasing risk of generation and trap-ping of gas, probably explaining the finding.[96] The Swedish report also mentions hyperthermia as a potential SIDS cause, but with-out the toxic-gas mechanism, which explains it.[97]

Related to that, Martin L. Pall, Ph.D., biochemist at Washington State University, wrote in a letter: "It has always seemed to me that crib death may be the opposite of high-altitude insomnia. In high-altitude insomnia, the lack of sufficient oxygen makes sleep difficult. This may be a protective mechanism that prevents crib death from happening. A person who wakes up when hypoxic will not die of crib death. If this is so, there may be factors that influence these two phenomena in opposite ways —possibly both genetic and environmental factors. Again, if this notion has any validity, there may be hints in the literature on high-altitude insomnia that may give information on how to avoid crib death or at least on which infants may be at greatest risk."[98] We could reinterpret that last phrase as "potentially raising or lowering a baby's ability to survive a given concentration of toxic gases."

---

*"In millions of families, parents and babies sleep together on chemical-free cotton or woven floor mats"*

---

Bed sharing with parents is the typical sleeping arrangement in countries like Bangladesh. SIDS is about one-50th as common in such underdeveloped countries as in rich industrial countries. In millions of families, parents and babies sleep together on chemical-free cotton or woven floor mats.

But in Western countries, adults' mattresses can contain the same chemicals and fungi as their children's and can thus generate the same toxic gases.[99]

Pediatrician/author William Sears, M.D., suggests bed sharing as one of several protective measures against SIDS.[100] That suggestion is based on research by anthropologist James McKenna, Ph.D., formerly at Pomona College, and others. A much larger part of brain and nervous system development occurs after birth in humans than in other animals. Baby, facing mother through the night, unconsciously coordinates his breathing to some extent with her breathing, including brief arousals. And baby sleeps less in deep stages three and four, in which arousal is more diffi-cult.[101,102] Also, having nourishment available "on demand" through the night promotes success in breastfeeding. Interestingly, Mrs. Sears and others report that nighttime nursing does not inter-fere with a restful sleep for baby or mother.

---

*"Baby, facing mother through the night, unconsciously coordinates his breathing to some extent with her breathing, including brief arousals."*

---

Sears also suggests the mother carry her baby in a sling, main-taining bodily contact throughout the infant's waking hours, as is the practice in such countries as Bangladesh and among "primi-tive" tribes in the Amazon. That practice promotes development of a bonding relationship with the mother and better social adjust-ment later in life. Confirming the value of touching the baby, a study compared what is called Kangaroo-mother care (KMC) in which the new baby is strapped upright to the mother's chest, skin to skin, versus a system of restricted parental access. In the KMC group, the breastfeeding rate was higher and there were fewer infections; babies and their mothers were released from hospital 1.1 days earlier. This kind of care, however, cost much more.[103,104]

After about the first month of life, infections promote SIDS through fevers leading to more rapid toxic gas generation.

We recommend Sears' book for a wealth of background infor-mation. He projects the enumerated measures could lower SIDS risk by about 50 percent.[105] (The value of breastfeeding in avoid-ing crib death has yet to be proved.) But we would like to help parents lower SIDS risk by 100 percent, i.e., to zero.

SIDS deaths occur in bed sharing,[106] often called co-sleeping, for three primary reasons. Studies have excluded asphyxiation by a parent rolling onto the baby.

1) Bed sharing offers no assurance if the baby always sleeps over the same part of the mattress, unless that part is protected against toxic gases, following instructions from Sprott, which are reproduced at the end of this book. Adult mattresses can contain the same chemicals and fungi as babies' and children's mattresses, and can thus generate the same toxic gases.

2) Electromagnetic fields (EMFs) from electric blankets and other electrical devices such as TVs in the bedroom have been shown to increase SIDS incidence — even when turned off — if they are connected to household circuits.[107,108,109] They are a factor even in an adjacent room if close to the wall. John N. Ott, ScD. Hon., helped a family whose son had intractable learning and behavior problems. A turned-off color TV in an adjoining room was eight inches from the boy's head all night. After that TV was disconnected from house circuits, the boy's learning and behavior returned to normal.[110]

Stress,[111,112] which acts to deplete vitamin B6, is high and rising not only in the workplace and domestic life but also notably from myriad growing sources of electromagnetic radiations, wrote Dr. Robert Becker. Those come at us from electric wires and lights, radars, microwave ovens, computers and VCRs, on and on. (Eating food cooked in a microwave oven is a separate minefield. See Chapter 4.) The stresses from EMRs in the world are probably greater than those experienced during past periods of the Earth's reversal of polarity, which were associated with massive extinctions of species, he said.

The adult brain is 10 to 100 times more sensitive in sleep than when awake;[113] a baby's brain is more sensitive still, by an unknown, possibly large multiple.[114] Extremely low EMFs and ELFs have also been designated possible carcinogens[115] (substances capable of initiating a cancer).

An electric blanket that is connected to the house wiring exposes the body, and especially the brain, all night to a magnetic field 1,800 times that of a heart pacemaker; if turned on, it is 18,000 times stronger.[116] This penetrates about 6 to 7 inches, probably including the embryonic or fetal brain. As a result, a new study by Yale researchers found that women who used an electric blanket during early pregnancy were 74 percent more likely to have a miscarriage[117] and four times more likely to cause brain tumors in their babies,[118] than women who did not sleep under an electric blanket during early pregnancy.

---

*"... a new study by Yale researchers found that women who used an electric blanket during early pregnancy were 74 percent more likely to have a miscarriage, and four times more likely to cause brain tumors in their babies...."*

---

These exposures reduce pineal-gland secretion of cancer-protective (and multiple sclerosis-protective) melatonin — as do aspirin and other nonsteroidal anti-inflammatory drugs (NSAIDs).[119] The pineal gland is a part of the brain. An adequate supply of melatonin also helps resist several other diseases and aging.[120,121,122,123,124,125] An operating electric blanket also emits fumes.

Another problem is poorly insulated or otherwise incorrect electric wiring, as well as electric cables in floors and walls with little or no shielding.[126] If the electricity enters the house on the wall outside a room, that room should not be used as a bedroom; any person within 1.5 meters (about 5 feet) of such a cable is subjected all night to chronic EMF exposure. Even electric clocks at bedside create a very high magnetic field; this subjects the sleeper to an EMF equivalent to that near a power line. As with electric blankets, such magnetic fields have been linked to high incidence of brain tumors. An electric clock six feet away is out of harm's range.[127]

The pulse frequency of a magnetic field determines whether it is harmful. The electric current used in American homes is 60 cycles per second. Normal frequencies of the human brain during waking hours range from eight to 20 cycles per second; in sleep the frequencies may drop to as low as two per second. According to John Zimmerman, Ph.D., the higher ones present in artificial electric currents may disturb the brain's natural resonant frequencies and in time lead to cellular fatigue.[128]

That 60 cycles per second quickly cuts off the brain's production of melatonin.[129] "Melatonin controls the immune system and regulates hormones in the body such as serotonin, dopamine, noradrenaline, the stress hormone prolactin, and the sleep hormone called somatotropin. Many electrically affected people exhibit the symptoms of chronic fatigue syndrome (CFS) and wake up in the morning feeling exhausted."[130] The magnetic component can also deplete the body's enzymes, weaken the immune system and cause proliferation of free radicals.[131,132]

We certainly can't stop using electricity, but we need to use it safely.[133]

(3) Also, many waterbeds are made of polyvinyl chloride, a soft plastic, which always contains phosphorus and antimony — the sources, respectively, of toxic phosphine and stibine gases. They are heated, promoting toxic gas generation. And they, too, expose the sleeping mother and baby all night to EMFs.[134]

In sum, any of these influences weaken the baby's, as well as the mother's, immune system.[135,136] Weaker infantile immune system means more fevers, which promote toxic gas generation. And EMFs probably also lower a baby's tolerance of a given concentration of gases. There is no evidence that EMFs themselves cause crib death. They simply expose an unprotected sleeping baby to enhanced risk of death from the one known cause of SIDS: toxic mattress gases.

Geopathic stresses, which are taken more seriously in China and Europe than in America, increase incidence of crib death. Electromagnetic radiations rising constantly through the earth are normally benign and promote good health. But on lines at the surface — extending upward through higher levels of buildings — where these rays have passed through underground water channels, metal or oil deposits, caverns, tunnels, etc. (other sources are listed in books on the subject) the stresses can be very dangerous.[137,138] Although only about 12 inches wide, such stress lines are estimated to cover perhaps 2 percent of the Earth's surface.

The radiations coming up from the earth all the time are electromagnetic; water channels and tunnels, for example, interrupt them forming what students of the field call "rays."

Among more than 25,000 sick European people who were surveyed, 95 percent of those with cancer or AIDS, a high proportion of patients with multiple sclerosis, 95 percent of 3,000 learning-disabled children[139] — and 80 percent of babies who died of crib death — had a single factor in common: geopathic stress.[140,141] This information merits serious study by the teaching profession as well as medical researchers.

A specialist told, in an article in *International Journal of Alternative & Complementary Medicine* in 1994, what the instruments are and how to use them. He measured and mapped stress lines in a particular building. All the people whose desks were located on a stress line — on the first, second floor or whatever — were sick a lot. And women working on such a line reported few pregnancies. He reported that cats love geopathic stress lines, and dogs hate them. One might learn by watching where tabby curls up and stays a lot, and seeing if the dog studiously avoids that/those spot/s.

Geopathic stress makes an unprotected baby more susceptible to toxic gas poisoning by (1) stimulating physical chemicals that cascade within the brain;[142,143] (2) potentially causing mutations in the cells and damaging the baby's genetic code, known as DNA; or (3) interfering with the melatonin/nitric oxide system in the baby's brain, which controls the cardiovascular system.[144] The electromagnetic stresses are very tiny; the infant brain, but not an adult brain, appears to lift their amplitude in a paroxysmal discharge.[145]

Any of these mechanisms can weaken immunity. This can lead to fevers, promoting gas generation in the beds of babies who are not protected against gases, and "may explain clusters of infant deaths over large geographical areas, occurring during or shortly after successive days of geomagnetic pulsations."[146]

Also, micropulsations may increase on weekends due to decrease in the cultural use of power frequencies[147] (on weekends, far fewer electric motors in factories are running). The pulsations derive from natural sources; those from industrial activity seem to modulate or vary the strength of natural pulses. The previously mysterious 42 percent higher incidence of crib deaths on Saturdays and Sundays than on weekdays[148] appears to be explained.

A baby whose bed is on an earth stress line will seem unusually crotchety or constantly creep to one corner of the crib, or both. Ann-Louise Ponsonby and her associates, in a four-year study of crib deaths in Tasmania (the jewel island hanging from Australia), found that "an infant who usually moved a lot during sleep" brought a relative SIDS risk of I.7. That means such an infant was 70 perocnt muie likely to die of SIDS.[149] A baby sleeping on a geopathic stress line would move a lot.

There is a simple home method of dowsing for, i.e. detecting stress lines in any building. But even that isn't needed. Simply take the crib to another part of the house, even to another side of the same room. Cats love geopathic stress lines, and dogs hate them. One might watch where tabby curls up and stays a lot, and see if the dog avoids those spots.[150,151]

What about residential fires? We noted that a 5-degree climb in temperature of the bedding can increase gas generation 10-fold. But in a house blaze the mercury can climb hundreds of degrees. Gas generation could increase much more in a fire; how much higher the concentration of gas would rise depends on the ability of the fungi to survive high temperatures.

And as we said earlier, SIDS is unusual in Japan, where preservatives and fire retardants use boron. Can't American mattress-makers substitute safe boron for the three materials from which fungi generate dangerous gases? In Chapter 3 we tell of two medical doctors, on opposite sides of the world, who eliminated crib death from their patients' families using principally vitamin C.

Chapter Three

# HOW TWO DOCTORS
# STAMPED OUT CRIB DEATH

T wo medical doctors, on opposite sides of the globe and unknown to each other, eliminated infant mortality including crib death from their patients' families, each for about 25 years. Drs. Frederick R. Klenner and Archie Kalokerinos accomplished this feat using principally vitamin C (ascorbic acid). The therapy cost only pennies a day. No baby on either of the two doctors' vitamin C regimens is known to have died.[1]

How does prevention with vitamin C tie into the toxic gas explanation of crib death? As discussed in Chapter 2, toxic gases arise from sheepskins and other natural bedding widely used in Australia and elsewhere.[2] Dr. T. James Sprott emphasizes that alkalinity in the baby's bed enables the ubiquitous fungi to grow rapidly and produce toxic gases in volume. But the urine, vomit, dribble and sweat of the baby ingesting ascorbic acid are acidic. "That acidity," he shows, "offsets or reverses the alkalinity in the baby's crib, preventing generation of toxic gases."[3] So this is a chemical, not a nutritional, preventive.

Klenner, M.D., of Reidsville, N. C., rid his patients' families of infant mortality including SIDS from the late 1940s into the 1970s. Why did he choose vitamin C? Except for guinea pigs and primates including humans, all mammals generate vitamin C in their livers. A mouse, a dog or an elephant might normally create

3 to 13 grams per 70 kilograms (154 pounds) of body weight. When stressed they may generate 100 to 1,000 times more.[4]

In fact, animal livers make the entire vitamin C complex; ascorbic acid, one important segment of the complex, is commonly mislabeled "vitamin C."

Humans suffer from a genetic defect. Millions of years ago, a common ancestor of the primates (monkeys, apes, all of us) lost the ability to make vitamin C. Irwin Stone, Ph.D., worked out what appears to have happened.[5] Because they got plenty of vitamin C in their daily diet, including raw meat,[6] those early ancestors of ours no longer needed the internal biochemical machinery to generate the vitamin. By mutation a new strain arose, lacking that equipment; this new strain gradually displaced individuals whose livers still used energy to make ascorbate. The story for guinea pigs is the same.[7]

---

*"Because they got plenty of vitamin C in their daily diet, including raw meat, those early ancestors of ours no longer needed the internal biochemical machinery to generate the vitamin."*

---

In the words of John T.A. Ely, Ph.D., health researcher at the University of Washington in Seattle, "Humans suffer all diseases and disabilities because of their inability to do that [generate vitamin C internally]."[8] (Ely's important paper appeared at the perfect moment to help us in writing this chapter.) Klenner simply did for his patients what most animals do for themselves.

Here's a note on the vitamin C complex. Emanuel Cheraskin, M.D., D. M.D., studied vitamin C for 35 years. He summarized its importance this way: "Taking vitamin C without bioflavonoids is like clapping with one hand." How much bioflavonoids? He suggested about 50/50. Thus, when eating an orange one needs to eat white pulp about equal in weight to the flesh itself.

On the back cover of Cheraskin's book, *"Vitamin C. Who Needs It?"*[9] George R. Schwartz, M.D., writes, "If vitamin C were a new prescription pharmaceutical, I'm sure physicians would be inundated by advertisements promoting its use in selected patients."

In his SIDS prevention program, Klenner asked mothers to take growing amounts of synthetic, i.e., manufactured ascorbic acid (AA) during pregnancy. In his study of 3,009 pregnancies he found that the stress of the condition pushes the need for AA up to 10 or 15 grams (15,000 milligrams) daily. "The fetus," he wrote, "is a parasite draining available nutrients from the mother."

In the first trimester mothers took 4 grams a day, 6 grams in the second trimester and 8 to 10 grams daily in the third trimester. He obtained excellent results with these large amounts in women who had had trouble carrying a pregnancy to completion. All the babies were robust, and there were none of the now "normal" complications of pregnancy and childbirth.[10]

If a transfusion was needed during pregnancy or at any other time, to each pint of blood to be infused Klenner added 10 grams of sodium ascorbate, which is closely related to AA (we'll call it NaA; Na is the chemical symbol for sodium). The Japanese have long done this; as a result, said researchers F. Morishige, Ph.D., and A. Murata, M.D., there is no hepatitis from transfusions in Japan.[11] In America, post-transfusion hepatitis continues to be an embarrassing problem.

When each mother entered the maternity ward, Klenner also gave her an injection of sodium ascorbate. It has long been known that women who do not take an ascorbate supplement show a dangerous fall in plasma ascorbate from about 1.0 milligram per deciliter to around 0.35 mg/dL when delivering her baby. C. Javert, M.D., and H.J. Stander, M.D., showed more than 50 years ago that "Those levels are associated with serious diseases or death in the newborn."[12] Could one of those be labeled a crib death?

Using AA and NaA in massive quantities orally, intravenously (IV) and sometimes intramuscularly (IM), Klenner cured measles, mumps, chicken pox, adenovirus, herpes, encephalitis, even polio, before the introduction of Salk and Sabin vaccines.[13,14]

Patients with nearly all these conditions usually regained normal health after a few days of his treatment. He treated many patients in hospital only with vitamin C, giving it IV or IM for an extended period where necessary. He did add calcium gluconates.[15]

In viral diseases, where antibiotic drugs are powerless, the ascorbate therapy is invincible. Like other nutrients such as garlic, ascorbate does not recognize resistant organisms. It is color blind. Against bacterial diseases, he found, AA/NaA works well in tandem with an antibiotic. Robert Cathcart III, M.D., confirmed this.[16]

The therapy synergistically destroys the very organisms that are resistant to the antibiotic being used. *And so the puzzle of drug-resistant organisms was resolved 50 years ago.* This is important to parents. At the least, infection with an unconquered resistant superbug could make a baby more SIDS-susceptible and afflict the mother for the rest of her life.

In surgery, just as in childbirth, ascorbate given intravenously or topically (see below) enabled quick recovery.[17] Illustrating the power of intravenous ascorbate — a young patient came down with mononucleosis, which Klenner regarded as a 50-gram disease. One could cure it by taking 50 grams of ascorbic acid per day. The girl's church gave her the last rites.

"But the mother took things into her own hands when the attending physician, who felt death was inevitable, refused to give ascorbic acid. Into each bottle of IV fluid she secretly and quickly 'tapped in' 20-30 grams. The patient, he reported, made an uneventful [!] recovery."[18] Inexcusably, modern medicine condemns AA/NaA as useless without trial. Quoting Ely again, "The intellectual paralysis induced by the incompetence identified by the late Linus Pauling,[19] winner of two Nobel Prizes, makes the whole world suffer deadly epidemics, even polio and deaths in virology labs."[20]

Not only do some patients get hepatitis from transfusions; some needlessly suffer or die of bacterial diseases caused by resistant organisms — when antibiotics combined with ascorbate would bring about a cure. After giving birth, mothers immediately began to breastfeed without any delay for preliminary washing, wiping, and testing — and they took about 10 grams of AA daily. Snuggling up close and seeking nourishment, hearing the familiar thumping of mother's heart, baby started to bond with her. Infants slept in whatever position they chose.

---

*"Because babies are born low or lacking in antibodies to infectious diseases, immunity-strengthening colostrum and breast milk build up the new person's health that lasts throughout life."*

---

Because babies are born low or lacking in antibodies to infectious diseases, immunity-strengthening colostrum and breast milk build up the new person's health that lasts throughout life. Nursing promotes the mother's wellbeing too. If she appropriately nourishes herself, using much more than that one supplement, "breast is best" by a country mile. And so begins the TLC (tender loving care) that babies so much need. Without it they would be far more SIDS-susceptible. In American foundling homes early in the 20th century, no one touched the babies. Every single one died.

The health of both mother and child was so much better than otherwise expected, Klenner wrote, that "failure to use this modality [AA/NaA — including the injection when entering the maternity ward — and immediate breastfeeding] in all pregnancies borders on malpractice."[21]

Today's ob/gyns are finally catching up with Klenner's techniques in supervised childbirth, which he perfected more than 50 years ago. But as we have shown above, the ascorbate injection when the mother entered maternity and her continued ingestion of AA were also critical. Without it, remember, ascorbate levels in the baby can fall so low as to threaten "serious diseases or death in the newborn."[22] What health-restoring miracles could today's ob/gyns render by following Klenner's lead?

Mothers can use a perfectly safe, effective substitute for the ascorbate injection when entering the maternity ward or at any other time. Since few if any ob/gyns are likely to inject ascorbate before delivering her baby, any mother can build the level in her blood to about where the injection would put it.

One can apply almost any nutrient to any convenient part of the skin with the totally nontoxic, inexpensive solvent DMSO (dimethyl sulfoxide) to increase the nutrient's penetration into the circulation. DMSO itself, available in health food stores, offers powerful healing features.[23] Klenner long used the technique, as does Jonathan Wright, M.D., a leading present-day "integrative" practitioner in Kent, Wash.[24] (Integrative doctors seek to use the best of both conventional medicine and a variety of alternative therapies.)

The mother will in that way utilize information that her doctors do not share; she is decades ahead of them. If that makes her nervous — she follows good precedent. Jeffrey S. Bland, Ph.D., creator of Functional Medicine Update, which we cite throughout our book, told a moving story. At one time he experienced an episode of schizophrenic symptoms. The doctors wanted to keep him in the hospital for observation. But he too was decades ahead of the doctors: and so his wife smuggled into the hospital niacin (vitamin B3), vitamins B6 and C. Using high doses of those, using techniques long ago developed by Abram Hoffer, M.D., Ph.D., and associates,[25] he cured himself and resumed his brilliant career. To the doctors his cure was impossible. Hoffer cures 95 percent of "acute" (new) schizophrenics whom he treats. But mainline psychiatry is not interested.[26]

Make a paste of C crystals or ground-up AA tablets in a little DMSO, mixing in other elements of the vitamin C complex, if available. Better, grind up vitamin C-complex tablets (see Resources). As soon as labor begins, apply this seemingly magical paste liberally and frequently, both at home and on the way to the hospital. One can even have a spouse or friend smuggle it into the hospital to apply before going into the delivery room. (In a birth attended by a midwife, use of this technique will be well accepted.) Unless the mother is allergic to DMSO, which is rare, this simple trick is utterly without risk (see also Measures).

Why is it so safe? (1) It avoids the stomach and the rest of the sometimes-troublesome digestive system. (2) Other mammals, we will recall, build up internal ascorbate when they are stressed, to 100 or even 1,000 times normal. The result is healing and resistance to disease, the opposite of harm. The same must be true of humans.

Doctor and family will be amazed at how well mother and baby will thrive, and how few problems appear compared with friends' birth experiences. (Do not swallow DMSO, except for the more expensive pharmaceutical grade and under the direction of a knowledgeable practitioner.)

The technique works equally well for a child or an adult whose stomach, for whatever reason, cannot tolerate ascorbic acid. In fact, anyone who isn't allergic to DMSO can use the technique to improve tolerance of any surgery and to speed recovery afterward. For frail elderly patients this could well prevent death, Cathcart found.

If ascorbic acid alone stops SIDS, need we do anything else? The two doctors used other nutritional elements along with AA. Moreover, dietary habits and environments have greatly worsened, and this deterioration continues. However, AA should still reverse the alkalinity required by fungi to generate toxic gases.

Pioneering practitioners today improve the system by using the entire vitamin C complex, which we saw that animals synthesize in their livers. Doctors use this technique both in daily supplements and in the DMSO-mixed paste on the skin. This points us in the direction to take when a virus or other organism attacks a child in one of the common childhood diseases — or when it hits an adult. Further nutrients such as magnesium, vitamins A[27] and B6 also strengthen immunity. Homeopathic remedies, too, can often help.[28,29]

---

We need to remind readers that ascorbic acid still is safe, as well as effective. In 1998, certain British scientists wrote in a letter to the editor of the respected scientific journal Nature that 500 milligrams a day of vitamin C, by acting as a pro-oxidant, promotes cancer.[30]

Bruce Ames, Ph.D., Balz Frei, Ph.D., and Mark Levine, M.D., who are recognized as authorities, and a subsequent test showed that conclusion is wrong. The finding may have resulted from the laboratory technique.[31,32] Was it a purposeful red herring?

In fact, "vitamin C comes to the rescue by volunteering its own electrons," wrote Robert F. Cathcart III, M.D., "sacrificing itself to spare other molecules.[33]

Vitamin C," he continues, "is one of nature's antibiotics to rev up the action of white blood cells."[34]

Remember, too, that those scientists publishing in Nature used "vitamin C" only as synthetic ascorbic acid. This substance in large quantity can indeed be harmful, particularly with iron, whose absorption it promotes. Researchers find that tough cancers such as leukemia, prostate and breast cancers may stock up on ascorbic acid to protect themselves against oxidative therapies such as radiation and chemotherapy.[35]

Knowing the risks of ascorbic acid with iron (Chapter 4), Klenner and, later, Kalokerinos gave mothers no iron before, during or after pregnancy unless tests showed a deficiency.

Oral AA in quantity can be harmful unless it is accompanied by bioflavonoids to form the vitamin C complex, ideally fermented in yeast. Throughout this book, we emphasize the desirability of supplementing many nutrients to work together as a team, rather than heavy amounts of any one or two.

---

What does vitamin C really have to do with crib death? A review of the research on the subject published from 1970 to 1981,[36] carrying 142 references, found "no evidence of vitamin C deficiency" in SIDS autopsies. But the pathologists looked at the recommended dietary allowance (RDA) and ignored the evidence. Under their microscopes they saw inflammation, presence of minor viral infections, clusters of macrophages (scavenger immune cells) in alveoli (tiny lung air sacs) and excessive secretion of mucus in the larynx. Observers found evidence of repetitive apneic episodes leading to hypoxia during the babies' short lives.[37]

Hypoxia, often accompanying minimal viral infection, could occur before, during and after birth. Ascorbate deficiency could easily explain hypoxia, except during birth, as well as the inflammation that can cause it.[38] (In Chapter 2 we discuss the possible role of hypoxia in toxic gas crib death.)

All those observations scream "deficient vitamin C." The bodies of SIDS victims, like those of people dead of heart attacks and like the brains of patients killed by Alzheimer's disease, are devoid of all nutrients. The findings match the great Hans Selye's nonspecific (or general adaptation) stress syndrome.[39]

---

Klenner proposed a second theory of SIDS causation. He believed that a respiratory virus in a baby with a truncated immune system might spread all over the body in minutes, winding up in the brain as encephalitis, accompanied by pneumonia and diaphragmatic spasm.[40]

Klenner proposed a third theory of crib death. "They die by suffocation, but by way of a syndrome similar to that found in cephalic tetanus toxemia culminating in diaphragmatic spasm, with dyspnea and finally asphyxia."[41] Such suffocation would differ from that proposed and rejected in Chapter 2.

Possibly this doctor didn't know toxic gases could cause SIDS, Anyway, babies in his care were not exposed to such gases, thanks to their intake of ascorbate.

---

Now for a bit of perspective. In 1753, James Lind showed how to prevent and cure clinical scurvy using citrus, which contain the vitamin C complex. But 100,000 British Navy sailors dropped dead of scurvy, even while working — sudden death — until all the old "experts" had died and were replaced by new-thinkers, who chose to make the sailors "limeys." The British Merchant Marine waited 118 years after that before following Lind's lesson.[42,43]

The adult RDA of AA is only 60 milligrams. Ingestion of that amount suffices to prevent clinical symptoms of scurvy and allows "a margin of safety," which is all the RDAs were designed to do. Providing most people with RDA quantities of several vitamins and minerals through fortification of processed foods, misleadingly advertised as "enrichment," has largely cleared rich-country populations of the symptoms of severe deficiency diseases. Among these were beriberi (from critically deficient thiamine, vitamin B1, and from moisture-spoiled rice and maize[44]), pellagra (deficiency of niacin, vitamin B3), kwashiorkor (seriously deficient dietary protein), xerophthalmia (vitamin A) and rickets (vitamin D), as well as scurvy.

---

*"Linus Pauling and others found that adults who ingest only 60 milligrams of vitamin C daily tend to develop heart attacks, cancer and other degenerative diseases."*

---

Linus Pauling and others found that adults who ingest only 60 milligrams of vitamin C daily tend to develop heart attacks, cancer and other degenerative diseases.[45] The mother consuming as little as 60 milligrams would elevate her baby's risk of scurvy SIDS. Raising the RDA for vitamin C to 200 mg/day has been proposed.[46]

Archie Kalokerinos, M.D., eliminated infant mortality including crib death among his Aboriginal and white patients in "outback" New South Wales, Australia, from 1967 to 1992. This achievement is particularly noteworthy for he worked with people living in conditions similar to certain Native American populations in our Southwest, where high infant mortality is the rule.

The Aborigines Kalokerinos served scratch out a living in abject poverty in a harsh environment, subsisting largely on powdered milk, jam, white bread and sausage. They are constantly close to scorbutic, i.e., in danger of death from scurvy. For that diet contains almost no vitamin C and is deficient in many other needed nutrients. Sudden ascorbate depletion — usually precipitated by vaccinations (see Chapter 6) can cause the heart to quit pumping in what is called SIDS.[47,48,49]

In 1967 Kalokerinos began to use ascorbate. He picked up the idea of using vitamin C earlier in his career when a child dying of scurvy dramatically recovered before his eyes after an ascorbate injection. This seeming miracle was adopted into his practice.

Mothers gave their babies 100 milligrams (mg) of ascorbic acid daily per month of age to 10 months as a preventive, always in divided quantities. One hundred mg a day the first month, 200 mg/day the second month and so on. After 10 months of age, one gram a day per year of age was recommended. (For babies who were not breast-fed, Klenner earlier used this same oral ascorbic-acid supplementation schedule.) Instinctual body language tells the infant the slight sour taste of vitamin C crystals mixed into formula or other food is good.

If doctors objected that so much oral ascorbate might cause diarrhea, Kalokerinos reminded them that that is less serious than death; and mothers can vary the quantity. Native adult Fijians, untouched by Western dietary influences, ingest 1,000 to 8,000 milligrams a day in their food.[50]

---

Frederick Klenner, M.D., originated the technique of vitamin C bowel tolerance, and Robert F. Cathcart III, M.D., perfected it.[52] Stir up ascorbic acid in water and drink the sour stuff, to a quantity just short of diarrhea. The amount needed differs for each person and each instance. Lower the quantity gradually as symptoms improve. If they do not improve rather quickly, see a physician. See also Measures.

A mother can in that way eliminate SIDS-promoting infections both before and after giving birth. This simple therapy, strengthened by supporting nutrients, can also ease a youngster through childhood illnesses such as mumps and whooping cough. Compare this to application of AA to the skin with DMSO; some people use both methods. Even as a preemptive strike, say, if one gets chilled. And homeopathic remedies can help greatly.

Here's an example. Suppose a pediatrician warns a mother that 100 mg/day per month of age is "too much" vitamin C. If she follows the advice and a crib death follows, might that physician be found criminally liable?

Kalokerinos gave sick children intravenous sodium ascorbate, adjusting the quantity according to the severity of illness. An Aboriginal child who had been vaccinated and wasn't on the nutrient regimen was brought to him near death. Her pulse and breathing were barely detectable. He injected sodium ascorbate; 20 minutes later she sat up and began to drink hungrily from her bottle.[51]

Uncorrected, her vaccine-induced ascorbate deficiency and depleted immune system would have killed her. Older ill children were given oral bowel tolerance ascorbate.

Kalokerinos reported, and Weston Price confirmed (chapter four), that Australian Aborigines enjoyed superb health until white men brought their nutrient-depleted, additive-laden foods. The natives had no resistance to these diseases — and their vaccines. He was certain the Aborigines also have an immunological fault, which heightens their susceptibility.[53]

After white doctors began to "immunize" Aboriginal babies, in the Northern Territory of Australia infant mortality approached 500 per 1,000 in some areas. It reached that level in Collaranebri in "outback" New South Wales, where Kalokerinos established his practice — whence the title of his first book, "Every Second Child." A high proportion of those fatalities were called "cot deaths," the term used instead of "crib death" in most of the world.

Most Aboriginal babies had constant colds and many had ear infections; in their case, the latter resulted from immune deficiency rather than from milk sensitivities badly treated using antibiotics as in America. See Chapter 8. (The Aborigines have never had cattle.) Their mothers' milk, like their "solid" food, was extremely low in vitamin C, so their body ascorbate stores were constantly depleted.

"Some would die within hours," he wrote, "from acute vitamin C deficiency precipitated by "immunizations." Others would suffer immunological insults and die later from 'pneumonia,' 'gastroenteritis' or 'malnutrition.' If some babies survived, they would be lined up again within a month for another "immunization." If some survived even this, they would be lined up again. Then there would be booster shots for measles and polio. Little wonder they died. The wonder is that any survived."[54]

---

*"If some babies survived, they would be lined up again within a month for another 'immunization.' If some survived even this, they would be lined up again."*

---

To save their babies from that fate, Kalokerinos had the mothers, both Aboriginal and Caucasian, feed 100 milligrams of ascorbic acid, "vitamin C," in divided amounts daily per month of age. In case of brief diarrhea, which is cleansing, not harmful, they slightly lowered the quantity. But this is critically important — they did not stop using it. His patients also supplemented their babies' highly deficient diet by giving them one milligram a day of zinc per month of age, a multivitamin/mineral supplement and a tablet for essential fatty acids. For destitute families, this doctor bought supplements in bulk.

And he made unscheduled home visits to check compliance, testing the ascorbate content of baby's urine and mother's breast milk with an accurate dipstick device. If 8 to 10 milligrams isn't excreted per deciliter of urine or secreted per deciliter of mother's milk, Kalokerinos found, the baby is at extreme risk of SIDS.[55] (A deciliter is one-tenth of a liter; a liter is 1.0567 quarts.)

Ascorbate detected in the urine doesn't prove the nutrient is being wasted any more than water in the urine proves that the water we drink is wasted. In fact, a person excreting zero ascorbate is on the verge of death from scurvy. Part of every human's intake of many, if not all, nutrients are lost in urine. But like water, they serve essential functions on their way through.

Simpler nutrient deficits can precipitate breathing disruptions, and the vitamin program stops these, too. A white mother who had refused vaccinations found her baby's apneas ended on Kalokerinos' program. Because other doctors were skeptical, she stopped; the child's apneas reappeared and ceased again when she put him back on the nutrients.[56]

Using this regimen, Kalokerinos eliminated infant mortality including crib death among his patients' families until he retired in 1992. He long enjoyed close cooperation with his partner, Glen Dettman, Ph.D. They maintained a decades-long partnership until Glen's death in 1994 to a heart attack.

What is the situation among poor people in the Australian Outback since Kalokerinos retired? Children who are vaccinated and treated with antibiotics and other conventional medicines are dying as before.[57]

But certain doctors around Australia prevent SIDS, hypopneas/apneas, attention deficits, and other "side effects" of vaccination by dosing children with ascorbic acid for two weeks before, on the day of and for two weeks after vaccinations.[58] In Chapter 4 we discuss steps that parents can take before and during pregnancy to minimize risk of crib death and other unwanted outcomes.

Chapter   Four

# BEFORE AND DURING PREGNANCY

M uch that parents can do before and during pregnancy might raise or lower risk of crib death. The mechanism, as discussed in Chapter 2, involves variations in a baby's tolerance of a given concentration of toxic mattress gases. And as stated there, fevers can promote faster gas generation. Proper nutritional and other practices can also lower risk of birth defects, lowered intelligence and a multitude of other problems. To begin with, let's discuss good practices before pregnancy.

In the 1930s, Weston Price, D.D.S., visited, studied and photographed members of 14 primitive communities around the world. All the groups Price studied provided special foods to prospective parents, to both mother and father before conception, to women during their pregnancy and to growing children. They practiced the spacing of babies so mothers could replenish nutrient stores for subsequent children. [Price did not study their child-spacing methods.] Above all, they imparted their nutritional wisdom to the young, thereby ensuring the health of future generations. In sharp contrast, modern parents approach childbearing in a carefree manner and indulge their children in refined and highly sweetened foods from infancy.[1]

The Paleolithic human or "cave man" diet was not low in fat.[2] Throughout the world, primitive peoples sought out and consumed fat from fish and shellfish, birds, insects, reptiles, dogs, sheep, eggs, nuts, milk products, whatever protein was available. Interestingly, the middle-ear infections that are so common in Western cultures and obesity are rare in "native" societies.[3] It is not surprising that for people eating and living healthfully, their babies didn't experience many health problems our children suffer through.

Raising a healthy child requires preconception planning at least for a few months, but it is better if for the lifetime of both prospective parents. "Animal breeders know this. We take better care of our livestock than we do of ourselves!"[4]

The prospective father would be wise to take a high-quality multiple vitamin and mineral capsule. Lendon Smith writes in *"How to Raise a Healthy Child"*:

> "The semen of all fathers of babies with congenital anomalies [defects and other abnormal conditions at birth] showed a high degree of malformed sperm, low count and poor motility."[5]
>
> Developing excellent health before conception eliminated SIDS deaths in a medium-sized sample, compared to a nonparticipating group.
>
> "The prudent couple who are planning to conceive a baby should avoid any food that is not whole and take supplements that will help their bodies detoxify harmful substances they are unknowingly eating and breathing."[6]

Each dollar spent prenatally on health promotion could save $3.50 in special education and Medicaid costs in the child's later life.[7] Starting off and continuing with poor nutritional habits, people end up needing government assistance with their prescription drugs.

---

Reviewing from Chapter 2, Yale researchers found that women who used an electric blanket during early pregnancy were 74 percent more likely to have a miscarriage[8] and four times more likely to cause brain tumors in their babies,[9] than women who did not sleep under an electric blanket during early pregnancy.

Avoiding premature delivery could prevent a lifetime of physical, intellectual and psychological problems[8a,10] and higher mortality.[10a] Low birth-weight babies (less than 5.5 pounds) have poorer immunity and so are more SIDS-prone. Their tolerance of a given concentration of toxic gases is weakened; and fevers that may result promote more rapid gas production if the baby is not protected against toxic gases as discussed in Chapter 2. Prenatal infections increase risk of low birth weight, as do iron supplements taken without iron deficiency (see later in this chapter).

In a study in King County, Wash., from January 1965 to September 1968, the SIDS rate overall was 2.32 per 1,000 live births.[11] Among babies who weighed 3.5 to 4 pounds at birth the rate was 13.27 per 1,000; between 7.5 and 8.5 lb. at birth, 1.55 per 1,000. (Those figures would be lower now; the relationships remain, though.) "At age 12 years or more, the effects of low birth weight were still apparent. Intelligence was down, emotional disturbances and educational difficulties were present," Dunny says.[12]

Intelligence is supposed to be genetically determined; yet infants born with low birth weight, which may result from malnutrition, have IQs on the average five points below normal-birth weight children.[13]

Care after low-birthweight births averaged $86,000 and led to $2.6 billion medical expenses in 1995.[14] Studies from the United States and Europe reveal that these babies have a 35 percent higher risk, as adults, of coronary death and a six-fold higher risk of diabetes or impaired glucose metabolism. Low birth weight also promotes increased numbers of mutations and obstructive lung diseases in adulthood.[15,15a] Very low birth weight (less than 3.5 lb.) also strongly promotes cerebral palsy and mental retardation.[16]

To minimize risk of low birth weight, about 30 pounds total weight gain in pregnancy is ideal. Very little (3-5 pounds) is needed in the first trimester when the embryo is tiny; some suggest a pound a week weight gain after the first trimester.[17] Infants born to obese women who gained little weight during pregnancy had a high death rate. An obese mother would be wise to lose before but not during the pregnancy.[18]

The immune system may become sensitized to allergens before birth. And allergies/food sensitivities — promoted by low body temperature and the presence of parasites, which prosper at lower temperatures[19] — might increase risk of crib death by inciting ear infections (Chapter 8). Accompanying fevers would bring about higher toxic gas generation.

Not eating the same food more often than every four days may keep the fetus from developing food sensitivities. Attempts to prevent the development of allergy may need to be started from early infancy into early pregnancy or even before conception. And that includes the paternal diet.[20,21]

Avoiding birth defects: It has been clearly demonstrated in the laboratory animal, pet animal and agriculture that 98 percent of all birth defects are not "genetic" in nature, but in fact result from nutritional deficiencies of the egg, sperm, embryo and fetus and can be prevented by preconception nutrition. The animal industry has all but eliminated tragic and expensive birth defects by supplying high quality preconception and gestational nutrition to breeding animals, according to Dunny's book.[22]

---

*"In ugly contrast, of every 10 American children one is born with low birth weight, and six of every 100 are born with "minor" or "major" physical malformations."*

---

In ugly contrast, of every 10 American children one is born with low birth weight, and six of every 100 are born with "minor" or "major" physical malformations. *One in four* is born with some degree of learning and/or mental deficiency. Zinc deficiency contributes to all these (see later).[23]

Weston Price[24] and Francis Pottenger[25] showed "abundant evidence for the nutritional method of avoiding structural and mental damage and achieving full genetic potential." Pottenger showed that abnormalities long considered genetic could be reversed by improved nutrition in the same or in subsequent generations. (See also Chapter 8.)

Mineral deficiencies during pregnancy can cause malformations in the baby. E.J. Underwood, Ph.D., wrote,[26] and other investigators have confirmed, "It is now known from animal experiments that maternal manganese deficiency during embryonic development produces a variety of irreversible congenital malformations including multiple skeletal and joint structural changes, as well as a variety of structural defects of the skull and the otoliths [those relate to ear crystals], resulting in ataxia [difficulty coordinating muscular movements], loss of equilibrium, and tremors."[27,28,29]

Particularly during the first trimester, an expectant mother needs to avoid foods and drinks that might cause birth defects. Researcher Margie Profet showed that a little pregnancy illness could help the mother know what food and drink to avoid.[30] In fact, nausea in the first trimester is associated with improved pregnancy outcomes.[31,32] Although excessive pregnancy illness can be dangerous, counseling and other techniques to try to prevent any such illness at all are counterproductive. We suggest they might increase risk of SIDS, as well as likelihood of birth defects.

Yet pregnancy sickness is in part physiological. Lendon Smith, M.D., wrote:[33]

"A lack of vitamin C and magnesium can cause the nausea of early pregnancy. And if a woman is not getting enough of the B vitamins in that first trimester, notably B6, her baby may not get the right building blocks to make a well-developed dental arch and palate. Stop the vomiting so the baby gets the nutrients.

"Take B6, zinc, vitamin K and ginger root; also snack every two to three hours including 4 a.m. to keep the blood sugar from falling too low. The metabolism of the pregnant woman is so great that if she does not eat for eight hours, she has used up her glycogen stores and starts to burn fat for fuel, leading to acidosis. (Glycogen is a partially soluble, starch-like substance produced in animal tissues, especially liver and muscles, and changed into a simple sugar as the body needs it.) Fatty acids then metabolize to acetone and acetoacetic acid, causing nausea. To counter the acidosis, the body vomits stomach acid to balance pH, the acid/alkaline status."

A mother who properly nourishes herself with plenty of the vitamins and minerals naturally occurring in fresh, raw foods will deliver a baby strong in immune response, free of infections and, if she breastfeeds, also free of colic. An easy, relatively painless birth is an extra bonus. And she is far less apt to suffer from postpartum depression, tooth degeneration, unreliable vision and other assorted symptoms that have been wrongly ascribed to psychological problems.[33a]"

To adapt diet to one's blood type, we recommend the methods of pioneering Peter d'Adamo, M.D.[34]; see Sources of Information. About needed vitamin supplements, see later.

However, a vegan (total-vegetarian) diet is not advisable, particularly during pregnancy and lactation. It could risk neurological and intellectual damage to the baby from deficiency of vitamin B12. No food of plant origin contains any of that vitamin, and so a B12 supplement is advisable. Serum measurement of B12 is grossly inaccurate; at least homocysteine (HC) and methylmalonic acid should be tested.[35] Vitamin B6 level may be low, as well.[36]

Elevated HC can be serious for baby as well as mother: It increases risk of catastrophic clotting and of arterial damage. This can increase risk not only of adult heart attack, stroke, arthritis, Alzheimer's disease and cancer — but also Down syndrome (Chapter 5), and perhaps heart attack SIDS (Chapter 7).

In a comparison, vegetarian mothers gave birth to babies with lower birth weight, head circumference, and length than omnivorous mothers, who eat a wide variety of foods including meat. After adjusting for maternal height, duration of gestation, parity (number of pregnancies), gender of infants and smoking habits, the vegetarian babies had less DHA in their plasma and cord arteries than omnivore babies.[37]

We caution against extremely low fat or pure vegetarian diets at all times, as well as during pregnancy. Not only vitamin B12 but also DHA and EPA (See omega-3, later) were missing from the diet of vegetarians, and in their plasma and cord artery phospholipids.[38] Dietary analysis of the food eaten by a group of vegans and vegetarians found they were consuming well above the RDAs of various vitamins. But among minerals, zinc came in at 96 percent of RDA and selenium at a desperately low 46 percent of its none-too-high RDA.[39]

Repeated studies have shown that low selenium promotes both cancer and heart disease. A map of U.S. showing low soil selenium matches ones showing areas of high cancer and heart attack incidence. And the soil content of selenium can vary from place to place by a factor of 100.[40]

Pregnancy requires twice as much protein as other times; the edema that precedes dangerous eclampsia is due to low-protein diet. (Preeclampsia can be made less likely by ingesting adequate vitamins C and E.[41]) Low protein will prevent formation of important brain cells. This can never be made up later and may affect the child's cerebral and endocrine (hormone system) functions in adulthood, as the brain influences the endocrine system.[42]

In another comparison, protein deprivation during pregnancy and in the baby's first six months led to children with IQs at age 4 all of 16 points below the average of those born to women on more normal diets.[43]

Findings in this area have been carefully excluded from textbooks, wrote Lendon Smith, M.D., "because they contradicted the dominant belief that intelligence is genetically determined. Poverty and accompanying poor nutrition seems to be the cause of many diseases we had thought were due solely to heredity. Clinging excessively to a dominant paradigm harmed progress."[44]

Cellular biologist Bruce H. Lipton, Ph.D., wrote,[45]

"Talking and singing to the baby while it is still in the womb has been proved beneficial to its later mental and physical well being. The mother passes information to the fetus during pregnancy concerning the status of the environment. The mother's emotions, such as fear, anger, love, hope among others, can biochemically alter the genetic expression of her offspring. Physiological responses to environmental signals include regulation of the nervous system, endocrine organs and the cardiovascular, respiratory, digestive and excretory functions.

"Although the developing child is unaware of the details evoking the mother's emotional response, it is aware of the emotions' physiological consequences and sensations. And so, while developing in the safety and confinement of the uterus, the child is provided a preview of the environment defined by the parent's perception and behavior. It is specifically chronic, or continuously held emotions that are detrimental during pregnancy. However, the behavioral consequences of children exposed to negative or destructive attitudes during their prenatal development can be psychologically reversed, once the issues are recognized."

---

*"If they are ignored and left to shift*
*for themselves with an occasional*
*bottle of milk thrown at them, babies*
*will turn off the world, get sick, and die."*

---

Continuing that theme, Dr. Smith reported from his many years' experience as an active pediatrician:[46]

"Babies need to be touched, massaged, fondled, sung to, smiled at, loved and accepted. If they are ignored and left to shift for themselves with an occasional bottle of milk thrown at them, babies will turn off the world, get sick, and die. The lack of pleasant, loving stimuli may be a factor to explain some cases of SIDS. Maybe the nervous system did not have all the necessary connections to respond to spells of apnea."

Other precautions: Nitrates and nitrites in cured, nutritionally dead[47] meats and magnesium salts in canned peas in the mother's diet during pregnancy were associated with risk of anencephaly — the neural tube defect, born without a normally formed brain. Anencephaly happens most often in low-income families.[48] Adequate protein in cheese and milk seems to be protective.

Herons and chickens that had been exposed to dioxin during gestation had unusually large left brains; high doses changed the forebrain, which is critical to motor function and integrated thinking.[49] Such structural brain deformities seem consistent with reports of cognitive problems in children exposed in the womb to dioxin-like compounds.[50]

- Sprays and foggers are sometimes used to rid homes of fleas and ticks. Children exposed in utero to these products were twice as likely to develop a brain tumor as those not so exposed.[51]

- Burning incense in the house during pregnancy exposes the fetus, and the mother, to high levels of carcinogenic nitroso-compounds and benzopyrene, and is associated with childhood leukemia, according to research published in the Journal of the National Cancer Institute.[52]

Could sprays and dioxin-like compounds contribute to crib death?

Dextromethorphan, the major ingredient in most over-the-counter cough medicines, causes birth defects and fetal death in chick embryos exposed to concentrations comparable to those typically taken by humans. The researchers believe a single dose can cause a birth defect and a miscarriage.[53]

Excess consumption of potatoes during, or even in the last few weeks before pregnancy, increased the number of neural tube defects.[54] And some herbs that are ordinarily considered safe including aloe, comfrey, echinacea, ginseng, and valerian may be toxic for some women during the first trimester when the tiny embryo forms limbs and organs.[55]

Be aware of that. Yet, in general, herbs are orders of magnitude less toxic than patent drugs. Furthermore, herbs and other botanical medications have a very wide therapeutic window of opportunity and patent drugs very narrow. A little too much of many a drug can cause serious side effects and lead to hospitalization.

Outside of pregnancy and for the entire family, many gain benefit using botanical medicines, guided by a qualified practitioner. Entire clinical organizations integrate functioning of botanical, nutritional, pharmaceutical drugs and a variety of other kinds of practice. Rather than "a pill for every ill," they use the least toxic therapy first and seek to treat the whole patient — body, mind and more.[56] An order of magnitude means 10-fold; two orders of magnitude = 100-fold, etc.

A fetus detoxifies caffeine very slowly. After 100 hours, more than four days, half of it is still there.[57] Caffeine and brews containing it worsen chances of SIDS-risky premature birth. They do this by interfering with regulation of fetal oxygen levels. The mother's habitual overbreathing can worsen this; see Chapter 9.

*"And other substances in coffee besides caffeine may*
*adversely affect*
*physiology, specifically during*
*embryonic and fetal development."*

Besides caffeine, cola drinks contain excessive phosphates, which interfere with the body's utilization of calcium, on top of their high content of nutrient-draining, immunity-weakening sugar. Cola drinks also increase long-term risk of kidney stone formation[58] and contain dangerous excitotoxins[59] (see sidebar). Too much caffeine, in whatever form, can also cause spontaneous abortions,[60] miscarriages — and panic attacks. See sidebar below.

New Zealand researchers found that mothers who consumed 400 milligrams or more of caffeine a day — the equivalent of four cups or more of coffee — while pregnant increased their baby's risk of SIDS by 65 percent[61] (see later.).

Caffeine washes vitally needed nutrients including calcium and magnesium out in the urine through its diuretic action. Coffee and tea inhibit absorption of non-heme iron by about 40 percent and 70 percent, respectively[63] (see later). And other substances in coffee besides caffeine may adversely affect physiology, specifically during embryonic and fetal development.

Caffeine consumed during pregnancy readily crosses the so-called blood-brain barrier. In animal tests it has been associated in utero or early postnatal exposure with decreased brain weight, alterations in brain development and in learning and memory. Studies in humans are conflicting. Decaffeinated coffee introduces other chemicals into the system that may be worse than the caffeine they remove. Total abstinence from both is strongly recommended.[64,65] IUGR (intrauterine growth retardation, also called microcephaly), which is promoted by caffeine, increases risk of SIDS.

The odds ratio for miscarriage related to consumption of three or more cups of decaffeinated coffee daily during the first trimester was 2.4. Mothers who drank three cups of decaffeinated coffee a day in early pregnancy were 2.4 times more likely to experience spontaneous abortion than abstainers.

---

Sherry A. Rogers, M.D., helps patients end years of panic attacks by using a magnesium supplement,[66] which may also lower SIDS risk. Others reduce panic attacks by lowering intake of sugar—including, in particular, fructose—refined carbohydrates, caffeine and alcohol.[67] Alcohol increases estrogen levels[68] and may be full of pesticides and fungicides.[69]

The increase in heartbeat from drinking pasteurized and homogenized cow milk can put some people into panic.[70] It is helpful to avoid toxins including addictive aspartame (NutraSweet™ and others[71]), and to learn not to hyperventilate[72] (see Chapter 9).

---

Diet colas are particularly bad. Animal tests show the excitotoxic amino acids (EAA) that they contain appear to cross the placental barrier and the still-forming blood brain barrier of human fetuses and newborns. A pregnant or nursing mother eating a bowl of commercial soup and drinking a diet cola can generate, in the tiny developing brain of her fetus or newborn, an E-toxin concentration of 200 milligrams per kilogram of body weight. That influences the way the new brain is formed and can cause irreversible brain damage.[73] It could do vast other damage to the fetus, too. Who is to say it couldn't increase risk of SIDS?

---

It is important to seek out vitamin supplements made from food; over 99 percent of vitamin products on the market are synthesized from petroleum and other raw materials. That includes many so-called "natural" vitamins. The real thing is well worth the higher cost. (See Sources.)

Most readily available vitamin products are absorbed poorly, if at all. Vitamin tablets are typically bound with DCP, a chemical that does not break down well in the body; nurses chat about "bedpan bullets." Use capsules, soft-gels or in some cases loose powder. Be wary of cut-rate sales. And avoid timed-release formulas.[86]

It is best to consult a skilled nutritionist or practitioner, who can test your blood and determine individual needs. Because of biochemical individuality, one person's requirements may differ radically from another's.[87,88] See Sources of Information.Warning: Very high, unbalanced intakes of isolated synthetic antioxidants such as ascorbic acid (Chapter 3), tocopherol-type vitamin E and beta-carotene can appear to promote cancer, although not to a statistically significant degree.[89,90,91] In the beta-carotene trial in Finland, the people assigned to take the vitamin had smoked one year longer than those on the placebo; since cancer develops slowly, that would probably more than account for the slight excess.[92]

Throughout this book we suggest food-based supplements forming a team, rather than one or two single supplements in quantity.

---

Fat-soluble vitamins, which can accumulate in the liver, must be used, but with care. Vitamin A is essential to an embryo to develop normally; but too much, especially before the seventh week of gestation, can cause birth defects.[93,94] It is easy to get 5,000 IU (international units) of vitamin A in multivitamins. The threshold for defects seems to be 10,000 IU per day, particularly before the seventh week.[94a] Vitamin D, too, is extremely important but can be overdosed; natural vitamin E is hard to overdo as part of a balanced supplements program.

Young children cannot easily convert beta-carotene into needed vitamin A; infants do not make the conversion at all.[95] The human body can never convert beta-carotene into a dangerous amount of vitamin A. Vitamin A also has long-forgotten anti-infective power; cod-liver oil, which also contains natural-form vitamin D, was long part of the morning routine for millions of children in America and Europe.[96] Its power against infection has been fully confirmed in controlled trials. So it can logically be incorporated into the home infection preventive (see Measures). For more on vitamin A, see below.

> Enzymes in raw food are specialized amino acid fragments serving much the function of the spark plugs in a car. Enzymes catalyze, i.e., make possible every reaction in our bodies. Professionally prepared enzyme supplements can greatly benefit health. They enable our bodies to use plants' multiple nutrients, which processing and cooking discard or destroy along with their enzymes.[97,98] (See Chapter 8 and Sources.)

Fetal alcohol syndrome is very well known, but not its fundamental cause. A study published in the New England Journal of Medicine showed that women do not have as much alcohol dehydrogenase, the enzyme necessary to metabolize alcohol, in their stomach lining as men.[99] "That is why we generally cannot drink as much as our male counterparts," wrote environmental medicine pioneer and practitioner Sherry A. Rogers, M.D.[100] Risk of disease was twice as high in women as in men for any given level of intake.[101] "The threshold seems to be 30 grams of ethanol per day, particularly when drinks are taken both with and without food."

From Dr. Smith we learn that even moderate drinking (less than two cocktails or glasses of wine or beer a day) had palpable effects — both physical and psychological — on the children. Alcohol is especially bad during the first trimester when limbs, organs and tissues are forming, usually before a woman knows she is pregnant.[102]

One can minimize liver toxicity from alcohol by taking niacinamide; but do not use a slow-release form.

> Even fermented soy, which is supposedly better than unfermented, is not recommended for anyone[103] and particularly not for pregnant mothers and newborns.[104,105] In particular we caution against isolated fractions of soy phytoestrogens; these can be expected to perform worse, even, than whole soy food. They are powerfully denatured in manufacture[106] and are promoted with exaggerated claims.[107]

Pregnancy requires extra vitamins and minerals because of accelerated urinary losses. Specific deficiencies often include magnesium, potassium, chromium and vitamin B6.[108,109] Particularly during pregnancy and breastfeeding, the mother should supplement her diet with individually appropriate amounts of ascorbic acid (vitamin C) with bioflavonoids (see Chapter 3) or — far better — vitamin C complex (see Resources and Measures). The natural forms are far better than "bioflavonoids" tablets.

Carefully selected vitamin supplements are perfectly safe during pregnancy, wrote leading orthomolecular psychiatrist Abram Hoffer, M.D., Ph.D.[110]

> "Orthomolecular" means trying to adjust substances that are normally found in the body into the relationships that are optimal for the biochemically individual patient. Orthomolecular psychiatrists tend to use large quantities of nutrients such as niacin, vitamin B6 and vitamin C. They seek to eliminate foods, substances, and inhalants in the patient's life that cause adverse reactions such as allergies and sensitivities. They use psychoactive drugs far less than mainline psychiatrists, if at all, and phase them out as soon as possible.[112] (See also Chapter 3.)

"The results are clear. I cannot recall in the past 40 years a single female patient of mine on vitamins giving birth to a child with a congenital defect. Their doctors had told my patients that they must stop all their vitamins while pregnant. They looked upon vitamins as toxic drugs."[110]

---

*"The results are clear. I cannot recall in the past 40 years a single female patient of mine on vitamins giving birth to a child with a congenital defect."*

---

Joel Wallach, D.V.M., N.D., and Ma Lan, N.D., wrote that many birth defects result from allopathic medical doctors giving vitamin and mineral food supplements only after the patient is told she is pregnant.[111] The embryo has become a fully formed human at 90 days of gestational age; the brain, spinal cord and heart form in the first 28 days of pregnancy. And so all the prenatal vitamins and minerals taken after that critical period will not correct any birth defects that already exist.[112,112a]

A 1998 survey by the March of Dimes found that only 30 percent of doctors know about the 1992 FDA recommendation for folate intake.[112b] The neural tube forms in the fourth week of pregnancy, and so folate intake must begin before pregnancy, to supply its protection during formation of limbs and organs, as well as the neural tube. Every sexually active woman of childbearing age should take at least a multivitamin containing 400 micrograms of folic acid; 800 mcg is better.[113]

Robert S. Atkins, M.D., says, "Long before you get pregnant you need to take a five-milligram [5,000 microgram] daily dose. This is a therapeutic amount, so ask your obstetrician for a prescription."[114] Insufficient folate, which is associated with high homocysteine, also increases risk of miscarriage, other placenta-mediated disorders and Down syndrome[115] (Chapter 5).

> Folate offers a critically important service that a gynecologist is unlikely to mention. Particularly with natural (but not synthetic) vitamins E and C, folate reversed cervical dysplasia — i.e., abnormal Pap smear, which really is "cancer in progress." (Rogers SA. "What your gynecologist doesn't know." Dr. Sherry Rogers' Total Wellness 1999; July: 3-5. Also, Van Niekerk W. Cervical cytological abnormalities caused by folic acid deficiency. Acta Cytol 1966; 10: 67-73. Butterworth CEJ et al. Folate deficiency and cervical dysplasia. Jour Amer Med Assoc 1992; 267: 528-533. Rogers lists four other references.
>
> (Used with permission. Dr. Sherry Rogers' Total Health. C/o Prestige Publishing, PO Box 3068, Syracuse, NY 13220. 1 (800) 846-6687, (315) 455-7862)

Expanded food fortification, which the FDA started Jan. 1, 1998, includes folate at a level estimated to provide 400 micrograms a day for persons consuming a Western processed diet. Fortification of food with folate improves people's serum folate better than consuming fresh green fruits and vegetables containing the same amount of folate. But supplemental folic acid does the best.[116] Risk of folate supplements masking B12 deficiency is very remote.[117] Fortification of processed foods with folate, B12, and B6 not only can prevent neural tube defects (NTDs) including spina bifida and anencephaly.[118] The high blood levels of the toxic sulfur amino acid homocysteine HC (called hyperhomocysteinemia) that are found with NTDs can be corrected by supplementing those same three vitamins and adding betaine (trimethyl glycine). Betaine dramatically helps many cardiac patients whose cardiac condition does not respond to vitamin B6.[119]

Supplementing the three B vitamins and betaine also lowers risk of megaloblastic anemia, SIDS-risky cervical dysplasia, occlusive vascular disease related to homocysteine, colorectal and other cancers, as well as Down syndrome. Folate deficiency, the most common vitamin deficiency, may increase SIDS risk by promoting fetal growth retardation.[120] That deficiency has now been linked to risk of leukemia,[121] it makes Down syndrome more likely (see Chapter 5) and it could increase risk of heart-attack SIDS (see Chapter 7).

Mothers who give birth to NTD babies typically have low hair levels of manganese. Most Americans are clinically deficient in the trace minerals chromium, magnesium and manganese, especially teen-age women and the elderly. Damage to the epithelium (inner lining) of arteries was 200 times greater when an animal was manganese-deficient than when it had enough manganese. (This, too, relates to heart attack SIDS, Chapter 7.) Manganese is also important in wound healing. Nuts, seeds and blueberries are good sources of manganese; a desirable daily intake is five milligrams.[122]

Pregnant women also need ample chromium for the fetus; its deficiency could lead to cardiac-risky diabetic conditions in the baby and extreme fatigue in the mother.[123]

The body requires magnesium for a multitude of functions. In Paleolithic human diets, ingested magnesium was far higher in relation to calcium than it is in most current Western diets. Magnesium needs to be supplemented to the point that magnesium intake equals calcium intake. When a pregnant woman comes in with high blood pressure and threat of preeclampsia, ob/gyns wisely inject magnesium to save the life of both mother and fetus. Magnesium deficiency promotes premature and low birthweight; magnesium supplements greatly lower incidence of SIDS-risky underweight birth and provide other important benefits.

Supplemented elemental magnesium at a few hundred milligrams daily also lowers risk of pregnancy-related seizures from too-low protein during pregnancy. Cooperating with calcium, boron, manganese and other minerals from raw organic vegetables and the minerals supplement, these also reduce risk of osteoporosis and heart attacks in later life.[124] Magnesium, a bronchial relaxant,[125] might lessen risk of disquieting pauses in babies' breathing called apnea. The number of milligrams elemental magnesium — the more important number — is lower than the total number shown on the bottle label, by varying proportions.

There is a special need for zinc during pregnancy. Pregnant women ingest only 61 percent of the zinc RDA for them of 20 mg/day.[126] Because of mildness or comparative lack of symptoms, deficiency is unlikely to be suspected until too late. The infant is already born with irreversible damage including SIDS-risky low birth weight, brain dysfunction, malformations and/or suboptimal immunocompetence (weak immune system).[127] Zinc deficiency in pregnancy promotes SIDS-risky intrauterine growth retardation and a variety of intrauterine malformations, prolonged labor, abnormal delivery and vaginal bleeding.[128,129] Zinc is particularly linked with low birth weight.

T.O. Scholl, Ph.D., evaluated 818 pregnant women. He found that those with low zinc intake had about twice the risk of having SIDS-susceptible low-birth-weight infants. Zinc deficiency contributes also to deficits in learning and mental ability.[130]

A good screening test is the zinc sulfate solution taste test, called zinc tally, which is available in many health food stores. Hold a teaspoon of 0.1 percent zinc sulfate and water in the mouth 10 seconds, then spit it out. If there's no taste or any taste is delayed, your zinc is deficient; a heavy metal taste indicates there is probably no deficiency. Insist on an rbc (red blood cell) zinc test; other tests are inaccurate.

More than 200 zinc-dependent enzymes participate in all the body's main biochemical pathways. It is a required component of both DNA and RNA polymerases. Polymerases are enzymes that promote necessary reactions of giant molecules known as polymers. Zinc participates in many hormonal activities including thymic hormone, insulin, growth hormone and sex hormones. It is essential for normal fetal brain development, especially hippocampal function. (The hippocampus is the part of the brain that handles memory and learning.) Boy babies require more zinc than girls to adequately nourish the growth and development of their testicles and prostate and, ultimately, to make viable sperm.[130]

Zinc is known for its antiviral, antibacterial, antifungal and anticancer properties.[130a,131] It actually mobilizes, i.e., it moves to the site of injury or infection such as a sore throat when one sucks a zinc lozenge and participates in the repair process.[132] Much zinc is lost in the placenta — which the mother in all other mammals *eats* immediately after giving birth.[132a]

In mice, offspring born to zinc-deficient dams had much reduced immunocompetence, especially affecting lymphoid organs, i.e., related to the body's internal garbage disposal system. This weakened immunity can persist through three generations of normally fed offspring.[133] Similarly, researchers fed rhesus monkeys a zinc-deficient diet; by the third generation, immunological function was extremely compromised. It took three generations of zinc-replete nutrition to bring the immune systems of their progeny back to normal.[133a,133b]

And so optimal dietary zinc is essential during both pregnancy and breastfeeding to ensure the baby develops an intact immune system. This maximizes ability later to tolerate a given level of toxic gases if the baby is not protected by BabeSafe® or proper mattress wrapping.

---

Mice? Over 98 percent of DNA, the stuff of inheritance, is the same in mice and in people.

---

Zinc is also required for metabolism, i.e., digestive breakdown and use of other nutrients that the body's detoxification system depends on. For example, pyridoxine kinase, which includes zinc molecules, plays a role in conversion of pyridoxine to pyridoxal 5-phosphate (PLP, the form of vitamin B6 that the body can use. See Chapter 7). Zinc is necessary in over 50 enzymes. The zinc requirements for infants, children and teen-agers are relatively high in relation to body size because of their increased requirements for physical growth and development.

Besides lowered immunocompetence, studies with pregnant rats found zinc deficiency leads to offspring born with gross congenital malformations encompassing every organ system of the body. Also seen were extreme retardation of growth, depression of plasma protein, anencephalus, abnormal estrus cycles and histological lesions in both testes and esophagus.[134] Histology concerns microscopic study of tissue structures. Zinc insufficiency also impairs absorption of folic acid, deficiency of which is now recognized as the major cause of the neural tube defect spina bifida.[135]

And so a daily supplement of 15 to 50 milligrams of zinc is appropriate. Exceeding 50 mg a day would risk lowering copper, which could in turn elevate cardiac risk [136] including likelihood of heart attack SIDS. Too low copper can weaken arterial walls by diminishing cross-linking of connective tissues, by dangerously elevating cholesterol in the 0.5 percent of patients who inherited familial hypercholesterolemia (FH),[137] and by increasing risk of anemia.[138] On the other hand, too much copper poses its own problems, particularly if the mother's blood contains a significant level of homocysteine.

---

*"Calcium requirements double during pregnancy,*
*and the majority of women, pregnant or not,*
*do not ingest enough calcium."*

---

Insufficient calcium is associated with pre-eclampsia. Calcium requirements double during pregnancy, and the majority of women, pregnant or not, do not ingest enough calcium.[141] There is an antagonistic competition between calcium and zinc, in which elemental calcium is the inhibiting factor.[142] And so it is best to take zinc separately from calcium, rather than together in a single multivitamin/mineral supplement.

Stress also plays a part.[139,140,143,144] Women working at a stressful, hectic pace had 40 percent higher risk of pre-eclampsia than women in jobs with less stress ($p < .05$).[145] ("$p < .05$" means there was less than a 5 percent probability the result would be found by chance. At $p < .05$, a reading is considered "statistically significant.") A pregnant woman standing for long hours or working in a noisy, stressful environment more than 40 hours weekly has a 70 percent increased risk of delivering a SIDS-susceptible premature baby.[146]

Stress raises catecholamine levels, and catecholamine metabolites drive up free radical levels;[147] accumulation of stress hormones has been suggested to be a factor in crib death. And so some form of stress management is appropriate; in Chapter 9 we advocate meditation, prayer and exercise as tools for managing stress.

Alcoholism, diuretic therapy, burns, surgery, diabetic acidosis and coma hinder magnesium absorption. So do cirrhosis, hepatitis, hyperaldosteronism, hyperparathyroidism (which could result from drinking fluoridated water while consuming a processed-food diet[148]), Addison's disease, epilepsy, eclampsia and kidney disease, and oral contraceptives.[149]

Estrogen replacement therapy and oral contraceptives have been found to deplete vitamins and other nutrients needed by the body to detoxify poisons inhaled, ingested or absorbed through the skin, and to manufacture hormones.[150]

Fluoride from fluoridated water, fluoridated toothpaste, fluoridated fruit juices and more, even from the air, antagonizes vitamin C.[151] It lowers SIDS-protective thyroid activity[152] and decreases rates of white blood cell migration, increasing SIDS risk by weakening immunity to infections.[153] Among many other harmful influences, fluoride also lowers magnesium and blocks absorption of other nutrients needed to resist infection.[154] Filters to remove fluoride from drinking water are expensive. (See Chapter 9.)

Because of the demands of the growing fetus, the stress of pregnancy and for other reasons, pregnant women are particularly vitamin B6 deficient.[155] The decline in serum pyridoxine is particularly rapid in the third trimester.[156] And so John Marion Ellis, M.D., gave his pregnant patients 50 to 250 milligrams of vitamin B6 a day, dosage determined by the severity of their carpal tunnel syndrome: painful wrists and hands.[157] This simple therapy eliminated not only most of the wrist and hand pain but also edema, diabetes of pregnancy, leg cramps, muscle spasms and dropping of glassware.[158] All those symptoms of B6 deficiency warn of high risk of heart attack SIDS; the supplements greatly lowered that risk. B6 supplements also help mothers to achieve other important goals, among them lowering risk of cardiac-disease promoting diabetes (Chapter 7).

Deficiency of vitamin B6 is common in depressed patients, too. In a test, B6 supplements resolved both depression during pregnancy and postpartum depression. It also lowers irritability and tiredness. See also omega-3 essential fatty acids, below.

Like L-tryptophan and unlike SSRI antidepressant drugs such as Prozac©, this vitamin raises levels of the mood-lifting neuro-transmitter serotonin. And it may reverse the effects of toxic substances associated with hyperactivity and aggressive behavior.[159] Also, a newborn baby suffered withdrawal symptoms after the mother took sertraline or Prozac© during pregnancy.[160,160a]

The common idea, "All fat is bad," is a profound error. Americans need less of some kinds of fat than are present in the SAD (Standard American Diet of largely processed foods), and more of some others. Essential fatty acids (EFAs) appear to be "essential" in diet because the body cannot synthesize them or convert one kind to another. A few scholars deny that EFAs are essential; they suggest substituting coconut oil (sidebar below) and extra-virgin olive oil.[161] Yet the results of using EFAs, cited below, cast doubt on the wisdom of that negative view. Some authorities recommend 2 percent of daily calories should be composed of omega-3 fatty acids.

Omega-3 EFAs come from cold-water fish and cold-weather plants such as flax. High-quality omega-6s come from warm-weather plants such as sunflower, sesame, pumpkin and borage. Omega-9s come from extra-virgin olive oil. The omega numbers relate to the structure of their molecules.

The omega-3 EFAs — notably DHA (docosahexaenoic acid) and EPA (eicosapentaenoic acid) — constitute an integral, substantial part of cell membranes in every system of the body, especially the brain and retina.[162,163] About 60 percent of the brain is made of fats, of which DHA is the most abundant. They are the building blocks of people's brains and central nervous systems. They also seem to be responsible for keeping arteries optimally dilated, blood platelets from clotting abnormally, and they increase flexibility of red blood cells to help them squeeze through small capillaries. Omega-3 EFAs also help protect against depression and hostility.[164]

DHA is a long chain, highly unsaturated fatty acid found in fish and shellfish, egg yolks (eggs are great nutrition for mothers, fathers and children[165,165a]) and organ meats, and in certain supplements; see below. DHA deficits have been linked to deficient brain function: mood changes, memory loss, visual impairment, depression, dementia and Alzheimer's disease.[166] They are associated with depressive symptoms in alcoholism, also with multiple sclerosis and post-partum depression.[167] DHA supplements may help against each of those.

Food manufacturers purposely remove omega-3 EFAs from processed foods to lengthen shelf life. In our highly polluted environment, a diet of processed foods does not begin to supply enough of them. And EFAs are kept out of baby formulas because, for one thing, they would add 10 cents to the cost per bottle. The U.S. Food and Drug Administration (FDA) bans use of DHA in the United States; some formulas made in Japan now contain it. It might be dangerous alone; DHA needs to be balanced with its cousin EPA, and together they need balancing with high quality omega-6 EFAs such as primrose oil.[168] Insufficiency of omega-3s promotes all kinds of degenerative diseases.[169,170] The vegetables and fruits suggested above and whole-food supplements such as Juice-Plus, Noni Juice, Lifestar's products or chlorella are excellent sources (see Sources of Information and Resources).

Omega-3 essential fatty acids are often called n3. The mother can eat cold-water fish, ideally two or three times a week. Wild fish are best. The nutritional value of fish derives from what the fish eat. Wild fish eat plankton and creatures below themselves on the nutrition scale. Farm fish eat pellets, and so their n3 is lower; and who knows what nutrients, what toxins, what drugs they contain?

For more omega-3s we also recommend natural cod liver oil (one to two tablespoons a day or, almost as beneficial, in no-taste capsules), and refrigerated flaxseed oil (one to two teaspoons). Cook with extra-virgin olive oil. And take natural anti-oxidant vitamin E (d-alpha tocopherol with mixed tocopherols), 400 IU a day or more. Seeds, nuts and beans also offer n3 EFAs.

It is omega-3's amount and balance with omega-6 (n6) that affects the immune system, inflammatory response, blood flow, blood pressure and coagulability, i.e., "thickness" of the blood. Our hunter-gatherer ancestors had a dietary ratio of n6 to n3 of five or six to one. But the current ratio is about 24 or even 40 to 1 — which is dangerous. Most of our n-6s come from polyunsaturated vegetable oils and as a result are of poor quality. They also derive from consumption of meat of animals that are fed corn and soy instead of feeding on grass in pasture.[171]

---

This imbalance of omega-3 and omega-6 EFAs probably causes much of the 20th century's epidemic of SIDS-risky ear infections among babies under 2 years of age (Chapter 8). Research recently published in Finland shows that through a complex mechanism that imbalance promotes formation of excess immunoglobulin-E (IgE).[172] Allergists accept this as the cause of true allergy, e.g., to cow milk, the gluten in wheat or one's cat.[173]

Why? It causes lack of balance among the resultant prostaglandins. Prostaglandins are powerful hormones or hormone-like substances that may be involved in control of blood pressure and other important body processes. Omega-3 fatty acids from appropriate diet and supplements actually push the omega-6 fatty acids out of cell membranes and, therefore, trigger different kinds of eicosanoids that are less inflammatory."[174,175]

These imbalances could also impair the immune system and predispose the baby to cancer and heart trouble later in life. For neural integrity and to minimize those risks, the EFA ratio should be as close as possible to 1:1, omega 3: omega 6.[176]

Barry Sears, Ph.D., popularized eicosanoids in his book "Enter the ZONE."[177] The dietary practices he advocates help some people lose weight permanently, prevent diseases and achieve the other goals emblazoned on the book's cover. For some other people, those dietary practices are not appropriate. (See Addendum at the end of this chapter.)

Omega-3 EFAs are equally crucial for integrity of the brain; see below. They are also important for signal transmission in the brain, eyes and nervous system.[178] Clinical symptoms associated with omega-3 deficiency include peripheral neuropathy, visual dysfunction, poor brain development and skin changes.[179]

Studies published in scientific and medical journals have found that breast-fed babies whose mothers take omega-3 EFA supplements such as flax oil and DHA before and after giving birth, typically:

- Have higher IQs and are less likely to develop ADHD (attention deficit/hyperactivity disorder).
- May be better able to resist infection, develop better vision and have improved chances of avoiding dyslexia and mammary tumors.
- Are likely to resist stress better as students.

ADD-like symptoms can result from an amazing range of conditions including birth trauma, predisposing genetic factors, and exposure to fetal drugs (see Chapter 5), environmental chemicals and heavy metals.

Babies fed flax oil share the benefits. One author tells, from personal experience, of children now 3 and 6 years old who were "flax babies." They are very bright and healthy and have been free from many health problems that most young children experience. He didn't say whether the flax babies had been subjected to multiple vaccinations, but it doesn't sound like it (see Chapter 6).

One also wonders whether the prevalence of infant and childhood illnesses like Epstein Barr; Candida albicans overgrowth; sinus allergies; chronic ear, nose, and throat infections; as well as so-called emotional behavior, also have their basis in infant nutritional deficiencies, particularly the lack of omega-3 essential fatty acids.

Supplemented DHA is necessary for a pregnant woman to provide an adequate supply for her baby. Seventy percent of the brain cells develop before birth. DHA content of the fetal brain should increase three to five times during the last three months of pregnancy, then triple again during the first 12 weeks after birth. The part of the brain that omega-3 affects deals with learning ability, anxiety/depression, and auditory and visual perception.

Babies fed breast milk of mothers who consume adequate DHA, or, given DHA-enriched formula, develop visual acuity faster than controls.[180]

---

*"There seems to be a growing number of children with allergies, colic and skin problems that more than likely resulted from deficiency, or even total lack, of DHA in infant formulas and later diets."*

---

The omega-3 fats also aid in balancing the autoimmune system. There seems to be a growing number of children with allergies, colic and skin problems that more than likely resulted from deficiency, or even total lack, of DHA in infant formulas and later diets. The researchers in a Mayo Clinic study confirmed all this. They suggested DHA supplementation in every pregnancy, and urged avoidance of refined and hydrogenated fats (TFAs)[181] (see below).

Martek Biosciences Corp., Columbia, Md., has released Neuromins™ offering microalgae, the (wild) fish's original source. This vegetable oil form of DHA "closely matches" that found in human breast milk. It assures the flexibility of nerve cell membranes that is essential for the transmission of these signals.

Feeding a non-nursing baby a few drops of flaxseed oil will provide needed omega-3 and high-quality omega-6 EFAs: 1/8 tsp. non-nursing, 1-6 months; 1/4 tsp. 6-12 months; 1/2 to 1 tsp. for 1- to 2-year olds; 1 tsp. for children over 2 years; 1 to 2 tsp. for adults.

Trans fatty acids (TFAs), with their abnormally shaped molecules, have no known nutritional benefit and have been implicated in the risk to coronary artery disease and a long list of other degenerative diseases of aging.[182] They appear to uncouple mitochondrial function and contribute to unfavorably changed metabolism of fatty acids.[183,184,185] The mitochondria are the energy creating "power houses" or "lungs" of every cell in the body.

TFAs are biologically inactive, easily picked up and assimilated in cellular membranes. They are found in all packaged "convenience" foods. The label or package typically carries a long list of hard-to-pronounce names of chemicals. Mothers who consume a lot of American margarines, most of which are high in TFAs, during pregnancy give birth to babies with a low birth weight[186] and increase SIDS risk. Avoid them at all times but especially during pregnancy and lactation. Recently proposed FDA labeling requirements should help do that. New government dietary guidelines issued early in 2000 unwisely ignore TFAs.

Normal thyroid secretion to stimulate the activity, i.e., the metabolism of trillions of body cells and tissues, is required for virtually every body process. The developing fetal brain needs thyroid for cell division.[187,188] And particularly during the first three months of pregnancy, the fetus requires thyroid secretion, as well as omega-3 EFAs, for neural and brain development.[189,190,191] It has been proposed, but not proved, that enough thyroid and enough iodine might lower crib-death risk.[191a] (See Chapter 8.)

Broda Barnes, M.D., Ph.D., found that 40 percent of patients, whatever their reason for consulting him, had subclinical or functional hypothyroidism — not detected by usual blood tests — particularly when taking certain drugs.[192] Mainstream medicine denies the existence of subclinical hypothyroidism. Yet when the deficiency is corrected, a lot of unwanted symptoms — some of them very serious — ameliorate or disappear. Some authorities call subclinical hypothyroidism "the common denominator for much of the Western world's illness" affecting as many as 50 percent[193] to 90 percent.[194] It is much more common among women than among men.

The need for iodine peaks during pregnancy and lactation. Thyroid or iodine deprivation in pregnancy cannot be repaired after birth; it may affect deposition of myelin, potentially elevating risk of multiple sclerosis in adult life. A baby's intelligence may depend as much on the levels of thyroid hormone reaching the brain during critical periods of development as on inheriting smart genes.[195,196] Besides hindering learning ability, thyroid deficiency may cause behavioral problems, difficulties in hearing, language comprehension, fine motor skills and extrinsic motor eye movement.[197,198]

---

If thyroid deficiency symptoms persist even while consuming recommended olive and coconut oils, a mother can easily detect and correct this deficiency. See Measures at the end of the book.

---

Contrary to widespread reports, coconut oil is safe to eat and offers nutritional advantages. The body requires some saturated fat, which coconut oil contains, to enable assimilation of other foods. Raymond Peat, Ph.D. (chemistry), regarded worldwide as an authority, and others have shown that coconut oil has wonderful antiseptic, bactericidal properties.[199,200] Like mother's milk, it is rich in lauric acid — which protects against bacteria, viruses, yeasts, fungi[201] and cancer.[202,203,204] It also stimulates thyroid function. Populations that consume a lot of coconut and coconut oil have very few heart attacks.[204a] Also, Peat and others theorize that coconut oil, like olive oil, has antioxidant properties, since it lowers our need for vitamin E.[205] But coconut milk contains too much sugar.

Sold in jars in health food stores and food co-ops, coconut oil is solid at room temperature and never oxidizes (turn rancid). Ignore a label warning not to eat it. One can use it in casseroles and spread it liberally onto hot foods where it melts.

---

What about genes and genetics? One's predisposition to disease is determined by the genes one carries. If, when and how seriously the diseases occur is up to the person's lifestyle. Genes never act alone; the environment influences them; they are modulators and not the primary determinant.[206]

Recent research likens genes to a rheostat rather than an on-off switch. A gene can be part way activated, like an auditorium lighting system.[207] And some genes relate to multiple organ systems treated by multiple medical specialties and indicate risk of diseases that may not appear on X-rays, CAT-scans and the like until decades later.

"Try to minimize use of antibiotic drugs during pregnancy, as they will allow Candida yeast overgrowth, a potential threat to mother and baby," cautions Dr. Lendon Smith.[208] They also increase risk of giving birth to a baby susceptible to sepsis, a potentially life-threatening infection[209] — i.e., it is life threatening unless the doctors are willing to liberally use vitamin C complex (see Chapter 3 and Measures). Candida infection may masquerade as almost any chronic illness, either physical or mental, and can create allergies.[210,210a]

In case of swelling from edema, avoid diuretic drugs. Besides many other benefits cited above, Dr. John Marion Ellis resolved edema of pregnancy with vitamin B6.[211] One expectant mom lost 15 pounds of water after starting use of the vitamin.[212] See Chapter 7 for ways to eliminate risk of over-publicized neurological B6 side effects.

The ideal antibiotic substitute should not only kill bacteria; it should also promote optimal immune function.[213] Candidates include Juice-Plus, Noni juices, Microhydrin and Vitamin C complex (See Sources).

No drug is safe for the unborn child. Drugs pass through the placenta and umbilical cord into the fetus, and have never been approved by the FDA as safe. So they are "experimental drugs." The PDR ("Physician's Desk Reference") is prepared by the drug companies; less biased sources are available. If any drugs have to be used, prefer ones that have been used for 10 to 20 years; any problems will probably already have surfaced.[214]

Exposure of the mother to infection during pregnancy can be a threat to her baby. Bruce Bower, writing in *Science News,* cites Robin M. Murry of the Institute of Psychiatry in London, and colleagues.[215] On average, patients who had been exposed to prenatal infections weighed less at birth and experienced more medical complications at delivery than those who had not had such infections.[216] In mothers who have had gum disease there is a sevenfold risk of giving birth to premature and underweight babies, who have high risk of SIDS. Uncorrected, infected teeth and gums also triple ultimate risk of stroke and heart attack.[217,218] See Chapter 7. Chapter 3 and Measures suggest simple home methods to minimize and cure infections.

"If a woman becomes pregnant within three months after taking ['the Great Liberator'], oral contraceptive pills," cautions Dr. Smith, "her baby may be saddled with congenital anomalies.[219] "It's time to admit there is no such thing as a 'low-dose' way of altering your entire body chemistry."[220]

These pills deplete levels of vitamins B1, B2, B4, B6 and C and the minerals zinc and manganese. They also decrease blood levels of needed amino acids, the building blocks of protein.[221]

Also, long-term use of contraceptive pills promotes development of malignant melanoma.[222] That's the kind of "skin cancer" often wrongly blamed on excessive exposure to sunlight [223] (Chapter 9). If not stopped early, melanoma metastasizes throughout the body and kills. Norplant contraceptive implants parcel out timed-release synthetic progesterone over a five-year period. Preliminary findings by Alan R. Hirsch, neurologist at Rush-Presbyterian-St. Luke's Medical Center in Chicago, suggest Norplant risks neurotoxicity and a subclinical disease. Resulting brain and nerve abnormalities that could underlie numbness in arms and legs or cognitive problems were revealed by women's memory and problem-solving tests.[224]

Routine iron supplements in pregnancy are unnecessary and unwise except in genuine iron-deficiency anemia[224a] — which can result from excessive menstrual or other bleeding. Iron deficiency is known to result in hematological (blood) and mental dysfunction. Possible contributors to such anemia include excesses of coffee, tea and blood serum copper.

The widely seen drop in iron blood levels in pregnant women signifies good expansion in blood volume, not anemia. Infectious organisms and cancer cells feed on iron and starve without it![225] And so in the first trimester this decline in iron concentration is also an innate prophylactic — that is, preventive or protective — measure to reduce the mother's vulnerability at a time when her embryo is very susceptible to harm from infection.[226] Excess iron also damages the liver and can interfere with the immune system. A striking association was seen between iron levels in the blood and SIDS-promoting pre-term delivery and low birth weight.[227] Also, pre-eclampsia is much more common in women whose iron level fails to drop in pregnancy.[228]

Leslie N. Johnson, D.V.M., of Tulsa, Okla., attributes high SIDS risk to hemochromatosis. Postmortem blood concentration of iron in 64 full-term infants dead of SIDS was about 200 times the level found in normal live infants aged 3 months. In babies born to parents, both of whom carry the hemochromatosis gene, writes Johnson, "iron overload is what literally tears these babies apart."[229]

Excess calories have been regarded as the principal aging factor, now seeming to explain why calorie restriction (without lowering minerals, vitamins and other nutrients) extends healthy life span.[230] But the iron content of diet has also been indicted as possibly the principal life-shortening factor.[231]

---

*"Why is iron so dangerous? Not only does excess iron feed hungry bacteria and cancer cells, it is also one of the most potent generators of free radicals."*

---

Why is iron so dangerous? Not only does excess iron feed hungry bacteria and cancer cells, it is also one of the most potent generators of free radicals. A free radical, as we saw in Chapter 2, is a molecule with an unpaired electron in its outer ring. As a result, free radicals are unbalanced and highly reactive. Also called oxidants, they dart about the body damaging body cells, and any cell they meet, in turn, becomes a free radical. After that happens, e.g., a molecule of beta-carotene that has become a free radical cannot be made normal by another beta-carotene molecule.[232]

Not only do free radicals severely damage any molecules they contact by "stealing" electrons. By converting those molecules into more free radicals, they can cause a chain reaction of cellular damage which, without intervention, may go on endlessly.[233] Can anyone be certain that chain reaction could not cause crib death? An antioxidant donates an electron so as to quench a free radical. Iron becomes an active oxidant and may seriously worsen any oxidative stress occurring in the body. Oxidative stress is associated with nearly all forms of degenerative disease, including ischemic heart disease (heart attacks), and also with aging.

"Perhaps the most alarming property of free radicals is their tendency to react with cellular DNA, often causing the DNA strand to actually break," says J. Warren, Ph.D. "There is also strong evidence that free radicals may not only initiate DNA mutations, but also encourage damaged cells to multiply."[234,235]

"White flour, pasta and products made from them almost all contain iron artificially added as ferrous sulfate, because of a federal law. A few years ago, someone demonstrated that they could pick up a certain iron-laden breakfast cereal with a magnet. Avoid foods with any added iron," warns Ray Peat, Ph.D.[236]

---

*"Preeclampsia, potentially fatal to both mother and fetus, is also most common in women whose iron level is not permitted to fall normally."*

---

Suppose a pregnant woman without a tested pre-pregnancy iron deficiency takes iron and ascorbic acid (Vitamin C) supplements, which facilitate iron absorption. She consumes a lot of meat, rich in the highly absorbable oxygen-carrying heme form of iron, and eats a largely processed diet polluted with poorly absorbable inorganic iron as required by the FDA. That woman may have an elevated risk of giving birth to a SIDS-susceptible baby.

Preeclampsia, potentially fatal to both mother and fetus, is also most common in women whose iron level is not permitted to fall normally. Peat cautions:

"Since the custom of giving large iron supplements to pregnant women has been established, there has been an increase in jaundice of the newborn. Women who didn't take iron supplements during pregnancy have healthy babies that don't develop jaundice. They haven't been poisoned by iron. Those supplements, along with lack of the breast milk protective factors, could also be a factor in the increased incidence of childhood cancer."[237]

Peat advises mothers to shun all processed foods that contain added iron; and "reduced" iron (a chemist's term) isn't a lower quantity but a very dangerous, reactive form of iron. Like many other food labels, this one is misleading. "We should not," Peat writes, "allow pregnant women to take iron without a blood examination to see if it is necessary." Serum ferritin or serum iron would be more reliable as guides than the hemoglobin test.[237]

On the other hand, symptoms of iron overload may be confused with those of other diseases. High levels may also be related to the genetic characteristic that concentrates iron in the body, known as hemochromatosis. "They cause the same reactions within cells that occur during exposure to high levels of radiation, and the results of these reactions are indistinguishable from those of natural aging."[238 239] (Under the proven principle of hormesis, *low* levels of radiation are healthful, not harmful.[240] See Chapter 9.)

"Coffee and tea inhibit absorption of non-heme iron by about 40 percent and 70 percent, respectively. This inhibitory effect on iron absorption," Alan Gaby, M.D., clarifies, "can be overcome by taking at the same time a relatively small amount of natural vitamin A as in cod liver oil. During the digestive process, iron and vitamin A appear to form a complex that keeps iron soluble, preventing compounds present in coffee and tea from inhibiting iron absorption."[241]

Foods that naturally contain iron are a different story. Spirulina, kale and parsley, e.g., supply ample needed iron in its naturally complexed form. Protein-bound iron, such as ferritin, transferrin and hemoglobin, is relatively stable. These forms, which are beneficial, may be compromised in persons who consume a low-protein diet or are otherwise malnourished.[242]

---

Avoid microwaving, not only during pregnancy but throughout life. Atoms, molecules and cells hit by the hard electromagnetic eradication of microwaving reverse polarity over one billion times a second. Even in the low energy range of milliwatts, no atom, molecule or cell of any organic system can withstand such destructive power. Molecules are forcefully deformed, their quality impaired.

The electrical potentials between the outer and inner side of the cell membranes — the very life of the cells — are neutralized. Natural repair mechanisms are suppressed. And, forced to adapt to a state of emergency, cells switch from normal aerobic to anaerobic (without oxygen) respiration. Instead of water and carbon dioxide, this fermentation produces hydrogen peroxide and toxic carbon monoxide.

The newly formed radiolytic compounds that result from microwaving do not exist naturally in man and nature. The impaired cells become easy prey for viruses, fungi and other microorganisms.[243,244] Warming breast milk in a microwave oven destroys 98 percent of its immunoglobulin-A antibodies and 96 percent of its liposome activity, thus reducing the milk's resistance to infectious forms of E. coli, which may be SIDS-risky.[245]

And microwaving destroys B vitamins, which are required to help avoid Down syndrome, heart attack crib deaths among a multitude of other functions.[246]

Food irradiation is far worse. It is a way to dispose of nuclear wastes, storage of which costs multi-millions of dollars yearly. Documented damage of irradiated foods has included kidney disease, testicular damage and polyploidy (an abnormal white blood cell count that can lead to leukemia). Like chlorination and fluoridation of drinking water, and like placement of toxic mercury in people's mouths, irradiation uses people as garbage cans.[247,248,249,250]

---

Smoking during pregnancy, especially if more than 10 cigarettes a day, is associated with a far higher than expected number of limb deformities. Smoking can cause SIDS-risky reduced birth weight and preterm birth, and also perinatal death.[251] (Perinatal refers to the period shortly before and shortly after birth.)

The children from a mother's smoking pregnancies had 4.35 points lower IQ at age 3 and 4 than from her nonsmoking pregnancies.[252] Chronic smoking also promotes SIDS-risky gum disease. The inhaled nicotine continually causes tiny vessels that supply tooth roots to contract, depriving the roots of their daily nutrition.[253] As Dr. Sherry Rogers expresses it, "Why would you deliberately ignite then inhale pesticides outlawed for use on foods if you loved yourself?"[254]

In Chapter 5 on Childbirth, we discuss matters that parents may want to consider so as to minimize risk of crib death and also other undesirable results such as birth defects in the baby or intolerable lifelong pain for the mother.

Chapter    Five

# CHILDBIRTH

**M**any women instinctively choose hospital birth, believing that is safer if something goes wrong. But in fact, many more things do go wrong in maternity wards than in births supervised by midwives, inside or outside a hospital. A few such mishaps could increase risk of crib death, and others can lead to outcomes that may be equally heartrending.

Home birth is the norm throughout most of the world. Childbirth can be a naturally healthy experience and need not involve medical professionals. The commonly held wisdom in the field of obstetrics is that 90 percent to 95 percent of all women can deliver normally without any help or interference.[1]

Certified nurse-midwives assisted in the delivery of 5 percent of all births in the United States in 1992; their normal procedure includes access to an obstetrician if needed. The Public Citizen Health Research Group found cesareans are at least 50 percent less likely in births with a midwife.[2]

Cesarean sections not only are more expensive than normal vaginal delivery, the mother's recovery takes longer. Also, infection and other complications can result.

Even for quite complicated deliveries, morbidity (illness) and mortality are lower in planned births using midwives than in maternity wards.[3] In 1990 births with a physician in hospital, infant mortality was 8.9 per 1,000; with midwife not in hospital, 4.3 per 1,000: 52 percent lower.[4] (The numbers given are the latest available to us at this writing.)

Explaining part of the discrepancy is the fact that doctors in hospitals handle the most difficult births. A pregnancy is regarded as high-risk if the mother has such ailments as high blood pressure, heart disease or diabetes. Yet when hospital maternity stays were shortened, mortality dropped.[5]

"Ob/gyns are strongly motivated by instinct, training and fear of malpractice suits to employ all the medical technology available to them, even when it is of dubious value in diagnosis and treatment. But everything your doctor does presents an added risk for your child. Every needle he inserts creates a new pathway into the body for infectious organisms; every drug he administers yields the possibility of harmful side effects; every X-ray he orders holds the possibility of radiation-induced damage to your child in his later years."[6] So wrote Robert Mendelsohn, M.D.[7]

Also, ob/gyns use some procedures only from habit. Fearing infection, for about 100 years ob/gyns induced labor in women whose fetal membranes had broken. Then Canadian doctors tested the procedure. Among 5,000 women with ruptured fetal membranes, they found no difference in infection rate whether labor was induced or not.[8]

Hospitals are rife with resistant-disease organisms. Such resistance develops not only from use of antibiotics with farm animals and overuse in treating patients — notably children's ear infections (Chapter 8) — but also from patients not taking all their prescribed medicine. When they feel better they stop, leaving the strongest bugs to survive and multiply.

Besides, the Centers for Disease Control and Prevention (CDC) has confirmed that over 500,000 cases of "community-acquired" pneumonia occur in America each year.[9]

"Community acquired" is a politically correct way of saying nosocomial, i.e., picked up in hospitals. Some years ago, two children died and three others suffered permanent paralysis or brain damage during an outbreak of meningitis in a Florida hospital nursery. That incident and most others like it were traced to the failure of medical personnel to wash their hands.[10] In contrast, a major part of the routine for midwives is to wash their hands frequently.

---

*"Infection with a resistant organism can make baby more SIDS-susceptible and afflict the mother for the rest of her life, which could be shortened."*

---

Hospitals exert little infection control. Cold germs, for example, are transferred from hand to hand. A sick visitor can leave germs, say, on a doorknob, and so being in the hospital even one day could expose a mother to one of them. Infection with a resistant organism can make baby more SIDS-susceptible and afflict the mother for the rest of her life, which could be shortened (see next paragraph). William Campbell Douglass, M.D., wasn't joking when he recommended wearing gloves and mask when visiting a hospital.[11]

Even potentially fatal bacteremia can result, which no medication is known to stop. Bacteria quickly spread throughout the bloodstream.[12] But if the doctors would read our Chapter 3, they could learn how. Enough vitamin C complex, generously applied to the skin in a paste with DMSO, should prevent and even cure bacteremia. Besides stopping other resistant organisms, as Drs. Klenner and Cathcart proved (see Chapter 3 and Resources). But that leaves matters in the hands of the mother and family to over-rule their skeptical doctor.

However, no statistics are known to confirm higher SIDS incidence after hospital births.

In a six-year study in Oxford, England, ultrasound scanning (fetal monitoring) picked up 55 percent of abnormal births. But about one in three prenatal diagnoses of abnormality was a "false positive."[13]

In an Australian study, women given intensive ultrasound scanning had significantly increased intrauterine growth restriction. This can lead to SIDS-susceptible low birth weight[14] (Chapter 4). Relative risk (RR) of birth weight below the 10th centile was 1.35. That means scanning was 35 percent more likely to result in important fetal growth restriction.[15]

---

**Technical Note:** The 95 percent confidence intervals were 1.09 to 1.67, p. = .006. For birth weight below the 3rd centile, RR was 1.765 (95% C.I., 1.09-2.49), p = .020.

---

In the judgment of some observers, more than 80 percent of ultrasounds performed on pregnant women are unnecessary; and, in fact, they may cause cell damage to the fetus.[16] In mice, they create changes in cells. Four and one-half hours after exposure, the rate of health-promoting cell division had dropped by 22 percent, and unwanted programmed cell death (apoptosis, Chapter 3) had approximately doubled. Researchers believe the effects in humans will be similar.

Ultrasound doubled the incidence of delayed speech, p = .0001,[17] i.e., if the test were repeated 10,000 times, the result would be the same at least 9,999 times. Even after such doubling, however, the risk was still low. But do not scan without a very important reason.[18] And do not accept "routine testing" unless there is a valid reason, cautions Dr. Lendon Smith.[19]

Prenatal testing, known as electronic fetal monitoring (EFM), is used in about three-quarters of American hospital births. It is supposed to detect cerebral palsy; but the false-positive rate in a test period was 99.8 percent. In a trial in Canada, EFM resulted in tripling the number of cesareans, putting mothers at unnecessary risk and expense.[20] The rationale for the procedure now appears to be highly doubtful. And early amniocentesis, the prenatal test for Down syndrome, is so risky that three years ago Dutch researchers abandoned their trials of it. (See also below.)

The mother's preconceptional supplementation with natural-source folate/B12/B6 can prevent neural tube defects including spina bifida[21] — as well as reversing abnormal Pap smears (Chapter 4).

Many ob/gyns think Down syndrome, which may occur in one birth in 80, is the worst possible outcome and that such births must be avoided at all cost. They need to do some reading in their own medical literature. J.C. Murdoch, M.D., and his associates found in 1977 that elderly patients who died with Down syndrome had no arterial damage.[22] And a group led by B. Chadefaux, M.D., demonstrated in 1988 that Down syndrome appears to be causally related to elevated body levels of that familiar nemesis, homocysteine[23] (Chapter 4). Consequently, with collagen folate/B12/B6 can often prevent Down syndrome. Adding betaine (again Chapter 4) can strengthen the result still further.

---

We encourage parents to visit http://www.ceri.com on the Internet to learn about successful treatment of a baby born with Down syndrome.

---

A few pioneering doctors and some caring parents have found that Down children's IQs can be raised into the normal 85-115 range, their facial appearance and physical abilities nearly normalized. Twenty-five references, nearly all from standard peer-reviewed scientific journals, support the statement.[24,25,26,27]

This throws into doubt not only the basis for the industry of prenatal testing, but, even more, the policy of routinely terminating pregnancies expected to result in Down syndrome. How do we know we are not aborting a potential musical or mechanical genius? And autism can now often be prevented or corrected through proper nutrition and detoxification.[28,29,30]

Episiotomy (episioperineorrhaphy) seeks to enlarge the birth opening; afterward it is sewn up. By lessening compression of baby's head, the medics say, it should prevent tearing of the mother's tissue. Yet such tearing occurs most often when an episiotomy is performed.[31]

Ironically, although that procedure decreases first- and second-degree lacerations it causes a fourfold increase in more severe third- and fourth-degree lacerations. And it often causes postpartum pain and discomfort, notably during intercourse.[32,33] It also promotes infection;[34] all infections are laden with blood clots.[35] And so episiotomy could increase risk of giving birth to a SIDS-prone baby.

Another potential problem is chorionic villus sampling (CVS), which can cause grotesque birth defects.[36] The chorion is the outermost of the two membranes that completely envelop a fetus. And although no figures are available, CVS can promote growth retardation, prematurity and infection, all of which are SIDS-risky.

Cesarean section is performed in one in four United States births — a higher proportion than any other country.[37] Britain considers its 11 percent rate a crisis. The U.S. rate grew from 5.5 percent in 1970 to 22.3 percent in 1992 — without a corresponding drop in infant or maternal mortality and without improved health of baby or mother.

---

*"Mothers in managed-care plans*
*are only two-thirds as likely as others*
*to be subjected to a cesarean."*

---

Rates vary among parts of the country; and cesareans are more common in hospitals with excess beds, in proprietary (for profit) hospitals, among patients with private insurance and high income. "Mothers in managed-care plans are only two-thirds as likely as others to be subjected to a cesarean.[38]"

When health maintenance organizations (HMOs) started paying doctors a fixed amount for births, regardless of the procedure used, the number of cesareans dropped rapidly.

Intervention to induce faster labor than the "leisurely" pace that may be natural can make contractions more uncomfortable, increasing likelihood of pain drugs. And strong, rapid contractions can decrease the fetus's ability to restore its supply of oxygen between contractions and makes forceps delivery or cesarean section more likely. Doctors who induce labor only for medical indications do so less often than in 10 percent of cases, some fewer than 5 percent.[39]

Obstetric drugs pass through the placenta and umbilical cord into the fetus and have never been approved by FDA as safe so they are "experimental drugs." No drug is safe for the unborn child. The PDR (Physician's Desk Reference) is prepared by the drug companies; less biased sources are available.

When epidural drugs are given, forceps are more likely to be used, with potential damage to the baby.[40,41] Examples are hemorrhage, damaged head and/or brain, nerve damage, bruising or disfigurement.[42] Newborns from epidural birth more often had acidosis, a disturbance of the body's acid-base (pH) balance that can cause breathing problems and diarrhea.[43,44] These drugs — used in disc surgery, as well as in "painless" birth — can rarely cause unbearable lifetime pain

After an epidural birth of her daughter, one woman had a medication-related headache for two weeks. She delivered her second daughter in a hot tub with the help of a midwife and needed no pain relief. "Water is such an effective painkiller that only about 10 percent of the women who select water labor request pain medication."[45]

"From time immemorial women delivered their babies in the vertical, squatting position, but in the last century science has converted this to the supine, so the obstetrician could see the process most clearly.[46]

Doulas may offer an important service. A doula (from the Greek word meaning slave) is not medically educated and does not deliver the baby. She is trained to help mothers through the physical and emotional battering of giving birth. In a comparison, doulas stayed with women for several hours after delivery, showing them how to hold their babies, breastfeed them and generally get comfortable with them. The women who enjoyed the company of a doula generally did not ask for any anesthetic.

And two months later, first-time mothers who had enjoyed the services of a doula were judged to be more affectionate to their babies than others who did not have a doula. Susan Landry, Ph.D., a University of Texas — Houston Medical Center psychologist, presented the results to the Pediatric Academic Societies of America in New Orleans.[47,48] (Accoucheurs are another class of birth-assisting professionals.)

"Mothers should be allowed to hold and bond with their newborn baby right after birth, whether at a home delivery or in the hospital. They should insist vehemently on this right."[49]

---

*"Barring an emergency, every new baby should be put to the mother's breast right away; no exceptions."*

---

Barring an emergency, every new baby should be put to the mother's breast right away; no exceptions. But a brief search is necessary for any abnormal conditions of the head, neck, heart, lungs, abdomen, genitalia and the whole skeleton.[50]

For thousands of years, the mother has tenderly lifted the tiny new human being to her breast. That's the natural, God-given way. The baby snuggles up to mother, looks adoringly into her eyes, if not blinded by toxic substances (see below), and begins to suck for colostrum. This precious initial fluid, rich in protein, is secreted by the mammary glands for several days after birth of the young. Colostrum greatly lowers risk of infection. Yet, incredibly, many ob/gyns and hospital personnel still tell mothers to discard this potentially life-saving substance. Ignore that advice.

Practically zero instruction should then be needed for successful breastfeeding, reported Earl Conroy, N.D., D.C., of New Zealand.[51] That was his testimony in an interview in Olympia, Wash. And the stimulus of the neonate's sucking on her nipples for the mother, still recovering from the pains and other sensations of giving birth, vastly improves the chance of an adequate flow developing. This way, Conroy estimates, likely two-thirds will breastfeed long enough to bring multifold rewards to mother, as well as to baby. Nursing benefits bonding, as well as nutrition (see below).

None of that happens when the newborn is whisked away for washing, wiping, testing when it's crying with everything, including the baby, neat and tidy. In fact, the messy sheen on the baby soon disappears without wiping and washing. Breastfeeding is harder to learn after such an interruption. Compared to the majority of ob/gyns' preferred way, the probability of successful breastfeeding must be at least twice as high after the traditional delivery of the baby immediately to breast,[51] as Klenner practiced 50 years ago (Chapter 3). Later, the mother can decide to substitute bottles with their many risks if she must; e.g., if she is employed long hours under high stress.

"If the mother eats sensibly along the lines suggested in Chapter 4, the fat and the proteins in her milk are precisely tailored to the needs of the baby's rapidly developing nervous system. And the low salt content of human milk is just right for the baby's immature kidneys. Breast milk provides all the calcium and phosphorus the baby needs for its rapidly growing skeleton. And breast milk is more easily absorbed in an infant's body than cow milk," writes Dr. Lendon Smith.[52]

Breast milk also contains specific antibodies that coat the newborn's intestines and respiratory tract to fight off infection. These help protect against gastroenteritis, respiratory-tract ailments, ear infections, eczema and other allergies/food sensitivities. Mothers' milk is also rich in acidophilus, inositol, immune factors, a powerful natural antibiotic[53] and protective mucin.[54]

A baby born in a difficult delivery may have hemorrhages at the base of the brain near the respiratory center. A common cause of breastfeeding failure is a TMJ (temperomandibular joint) dislocation resulting from a tumultuous delivery. A chiropractor can correct the problem with a cranial adjustment.[55]

"And unless you have a venereal disease, try to persuade your doctor not to place silver nitrate or antibiotic drops in your child's eyes at birth. The benefits do not justify the risks," wrote pediatrician Robert Mendelsohn, M.D."This treatment is predicated on the ridiculous presumption that all mothers must be suspected of having gonorrhea, which may have been transmitted to the baby during delivery."[56]

Doctors reject the argument that the mother could be tested for gonorrhea instead of inflicting silver nitrate on her baby, because the test is not 100 percent accurate. But silver nitrate is not 100 percent effective, either. And if your baby were to develop gonorrheal ophthalmia (a serious eye disease) for either reason, the problem can and will be solved by use of antibiotics.

The use of silver nitrate made some sense before antibiotics became available, but consider the price your baby pays. The eyes become seriously irritated, making it nearly impossible for the baby to see during the first week or so of life. No one knows what the long-term psychological consequences of this temporary blindness may be. The treatment may also produce blocked tear ducts, necessitating difficult surgery to correct damage done by a senseless procedure.

Silver nitrate causes chemical conjunctivitis in 30 to 50 percent of the babies who receive it.[57] That is, inflammation of the mucous membranes lining the inner surface of the eyelids and covering the front part of the eyeballs.

Mendelsohn continues: "Finally, some doctors, including me, believe that the high incidence of myopia (nearsightedness) and astigmatism in the United States may be related to the placing of this caustic agent into the delicate, tender membranes of your baby's eyes."[58]

Mendelsohn also warned against letting nurses bathe babies with hexachlorophene soap. It is absorbed through the skin and can cause neurologic (nervous system) damage in some children.59 And anything that can cause neurologic damage in a new baby can increase risk of SIDS. N.M. Kanof, M.D., chairman of the American Medical Association Committee on Cutaneous Health and Cosmetics, exposed use of this soap as folly.[60] "There appears to be no need to apply any antibacterial agent to the cutaneous surface (skin) of the normal newborn infant. Contamination of nurseries can be controlled by the use of antibacterial agents on delivery room, equipment, and personnel — the sources of infection."

Chapter    Six

# VACCINATIONS AND TOXIC GASES

Some tell us with seeming authority that "immunizations" are a good thing. For example, in Parade Magazine for Jan. 9, 2000, Isadore Rosenfeld, M.D., writes "Don't Worry About Vaccinations."[1] Yet to discerning eyes, the picture around us is worse than disquieting.[2] Why do vaccinations cause such calamitous results?

Some of the ingredients of our current vaccines (there's space in this book to detail only two) are:

(1) Formaldehyde, used in production of resins, plastics and foam insulation, and as a preservative, disinfectant and antibacterial food additive. It is a known carcinogen,[3] commonly used to embalm corpses.

(2) Thimerosal, a mercury derivative. The heavy metal mercury is toxic to the central nervous system and not easily eliminated from the body. Aluminum, formaldehyde and mercury — including the mercury in "silver" dental fillings and amalgams (see Chapter 9) — have a long history of documented hazardous effects including cancer, neurological damage such as multiple sclerosis, Lou Gehrig's disease and death.[4,5,6,7,8]

Studies report Thimerosal inhibits phagocytes, one of the body's most vital immune defenses in blood.[9,10] Then what effect will it have on healthy human cells after it is injected into the bloodstream? Jamie Murphy, a nonprofessional observer, asks, "Who would take chemicals that are carcinogenic in rats, are used in the manufacture of inks, dyes, explosives, wrinkle-proof fabrics, home insulation and embalming fluid — and inject them into the delicate body of a baby?"[11]

Among other vaccine ingredients are aluminum phosphate, aluminum adjuvants, alum and acetone; phenol is included in allergy injections.[12] Benzoic acid, a preservative whose injection into rats causes tremors, convulsions and death, is added. And then vaccine makers add decomposing animal proteins, such as pig or horse blood, cow pox pus, rabbit brain tissue, duck egg protein and dog kidney tissue.[13]

---

*"Measles virus is passed through chick embryos, polio virus through monkey kidneys and the rubella virus is passed through the dissected organs of an aborted human fetus."*

---

A glance at further steps in vaccine making is no less disturbing. To produce a "live"-virus vaccine, such as MMR (measles/mumps/rubella), the virus is passed through animal tissue several times to reduce its potency. Measles virus is passed through chick embryos, polio virus through monkey kidneys and the rubella virus is passed through the dissected organs of an aborted human fetus.[14,15,16]

Killed vaccines are "inactivated" through heat, radiation or chemicals.[17,18] The weakened germ is then strengthened with antibody boosters and stabilizers. This is done by addition of drugs, antibiotics and toxic disinfectants: neomycin, streptomycin, sodium chloride, sodium hydroxide, aluminum hydroxide, aluminum hydrochloride, sorbitol, hydrolyzed gelatin, formaldehyde (again), and Thimerosal (again).[19,20]

Injected straight into the child's bloodstream — bypassing the cellular immune system, one-half of our protective immunity mechanism, those materials destroy stores of protective nutrients in the tiny body. So it is not hard to see why epidemic vaccines worsen health throughout life.

Baby and mother are home from the hospital now. Mom already knows, from Chapter 2, how to protect her little one from crib death by toxic gases. But that is by no means the end of the story. Soon baby's pediatrician will probably suggest vaccinations, a lot of them. In fact, inoculations began right after birth in the hospital (Hepatitis B) unless the parents obtained a waiver ahead of time. This they can do before another birth by following instructions from Dr. Joseph Mercola's Internet web site. (See Resources at the end of this book.)

But what of the scores of other vaccines the pediatrician is likely to press on the parents? For babies who are protected from toxic gases using the techniques explored in Chapter 2, vaccina-

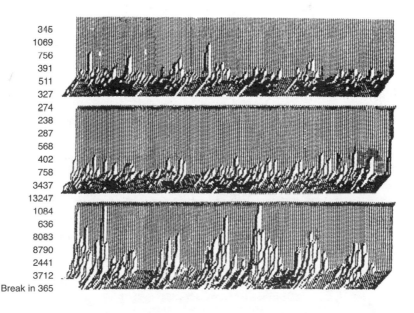

345
1069
756
391
511
327
274
238
287
568
402
758
3437
13247
1084
636
8083
8790
2441
3712
Break in 365

# DPT VACCINE: a cot death connection

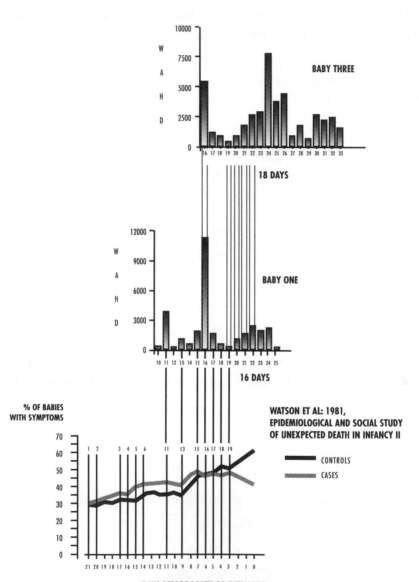

**DAYS BEFORE DEATH OR INTERVIEW**
Percentage of cases and control children with
symptoms for each of the last 21 days

tions are only an indirect factor for delayed SIDS death. Here we will explore how this new factor fits into the SIDS equation.

For babies who are exposed to those toxic gases, vaccines are a terribly serious risk. The fevers they create, promoting higher toxic gas generation, may recur immediately or at known, predictable intervals afterward, or both.[21] Either way, risk rises sharply on those days if the mattress is generating the gases. (Diagrams from Viera S. Scheibner, Ph.D., with her permission. Scheibner VS. *Vaccination: 100 Years of Orthodox Research Shows that Vaccines Represent a Medical Assault on the Immune System.* Blackheath, NSW 2785: Australian Print Group, 1993.) No one before Scheibner had ever examined all the published evidence on vaccinations. Most important, no one had studied even a considerable part of the record without prejudgment in its favor.

Researchers and physicians who are unaware of toxic gases or are not convinced by the evidence they have seen, have made a strong case indicting vaccines as the primary cause of SIDS. The rate at which American babies die in their first year of life has consistently risen since the 1950s when mass "immunization" campaigns began. Our infant mortality ranks 22nd in the world; 21 countries, most of whom vaccinate a lot less, keep their babies alive through the first year better than America. Today, infant mortality rates in some American cities match those in developing countries.[22] Also, the general health of children has worsened.

---

In Chapter 2 we showed that America's crib-death rate surged more than 400-fold after 1950 when manufacturers began to put fire-retardant chemicals into babies' mattresses. There are now around 3,000 such deaths per year. But the increase in SIDS accounts for only a small part of the total increase in infant mortality.

---

So are vaccinations the cause of crib death? In 1979 a DPT vaccination campaign in Tennessee caused eight cases of SIDS. The evidence led the U.S. Surgeon General to stop the use of the particular lot of vaccine.[23] DPT is diphtheria/pertussis (whooping cough)/tetanus. Of the three, the pertussis segment appears to be

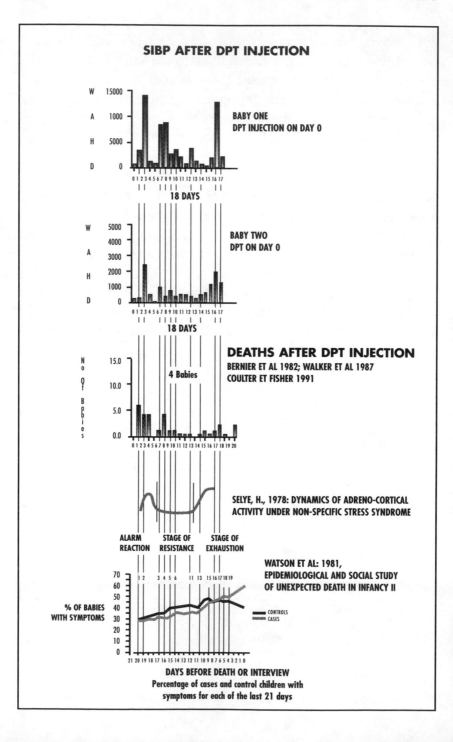

### SIBP AFTER DPT INJECTION

**BABY ONE**
**DPT INJECTION ON DAY 0**

18 DAYS

**BABY TWO**
**DPT ON DAY 0**

18 DAYS

### DEATHS AFTER DPT INJECTION
**BERNIER ET AL 1982; WALKER ET AL 1987**
**COULTER ET FISHER 1991**

4 Babies

**SELYE, H., 1978: DYNAMICS OF ADRENO-CORTICAL**
**ACTIVITY UNDER NON-SPECIFIC STRESS SYNDROME**

ALARM REACTION    STAGE OF RESISTANCE    STAGE OF EXHAUSTION

**WATSON ET AL: 1981,**
**EPIDEMIOLOGICAL AND SOCIAL STUDY**
**OF UNEXPECTED DEATH IN INFANCY II**

CONTROLS
CASES

% OF BABIES WITH SYMPTOMS

**DAYS BEFORE DEATH OR INTERVIEW**
Percentage of cases and control children with
symptoms for each of the last 21 days

the most dangerous.

In 1975, when Japanese health authorities delayed DPT vaccination from two months to two years of age, two important changes were observed. First, babies' whooping cough mortality dropped sharply. The triple-antigen shot was supposed to prevent the disease, but had shifted it into their first year, when it is life-threatening.[24,25]

Second, SIDS incidence in Japan, which had always been low,[26] declined by 85 to 95 percent.[27,28] As mentioned in Chapter 2, infant bedding used in Japan into the 1970s did not emit toxic gases. That fact explains Japan's previously low crib-death rate.

The typical chronology — the story of what happened — and pathology of SIDS babies after DPT contrasts with the paucity of symptoms in most gas crib deaths. Pathology findings included petechiae (spot-like bleeding) of lung, pleura, pericardium and thymus; vascular congestion, pulmonary and brain edema and pneumonitis.[29]

William Torch, M.D., wrote of seizures after DPT, shock, lethargy, apathy, coma, decerebrate-decorticate rigidity, spasticity and hypotonia or paralysis, among others.[30] We need not struggle to define all those scary sounding terms.

Death occurred mostly in sleep in healthy allergy-free infants after a brief period of irritability, crying, lethargy, upper respiratory tract symptoms and sleep disturbance.[31] Hundreds of American parents confirmed that series of events; many also reported long periods of high-pitched screaming after DPT.[32]

Of special importance is the second day after DPT vaccination and days 5, 6 and 8, 11, 13 to 16 and 18 to 21. In all groups, each death appeared to have been precipitated by unanimous, vaccination-caused breathing crises: apnea and hypopnea. The statistical correlation was perfect. Hypopnea is low volume, typically only 5 percent of unstressed breathing; apnea is repeated interruptions in respiration.

The children monitored after DPT were not together. Yet, reminiscent of marching soldiers, they all experienced apnea/hypopnea episodes on the identically numbered days starting from the day of vaccination.[33] Fatalities diagnosed as SIDS after DPT recounted by Marie Griffin, M.D.,[34] in New England Journal of Medicine in 1988 and by three other authors also fell on the same numbered days as those reported by Scheibner.[35,36,37]

During the 1970s in the vast, lightly populated Northern Territory of Australia, growing routine "immunization" programs more than tripled infant mortality among mostly aboriginal people, to the genocidal level of 500 per 1,000. Of these deaths, a high proportion were declared to have been SIDS.[38]

Although stated elsewhere in this book, the role of vitamin C merits repetition. Scholars attributed these Australian crib deaths to subclinical scurvy, deficiency of vitamin C not sufficient to be detected by conventional laboratory tests. It had been brought to life-threatening crisis by the immune-stressing vaccines. In American SIDS autopsies, pathologists typically reported "no evidence of vitamin C deficiency." But under their microscopes they saw inflammation, clusters of macrophages (immune system scavenger cells) and excess secretion of mucus in the larynx. Deficiency of vitamin C explains all these.[39]

Robert F. Cathcart III, M.D., probably the world's greatest authority in clinical use of vitamin C, labeled subclinical scurvy anascorbemia.[40] So low a level, he showed, can lead the heart to simply quit functioning after vaccines destroy any trace of ascorbate in the baby's body.[41] Sudden death from scurvy has been known for centuries in adults.

Present-day practitioners and up-to-date nutritionists use the entire vitamin C complex, including a variety of bioflavonoids (see Chapter 3, Resources and Measures). Ascorbic acid is only one important segment of the complex.

How did giving vitamin C prevent crib death? Dr. Jim Sprott explains that the acidity of babies' urine, dribble, sweat and vomit from consumption of ascorbic acid reverses the alkalinity required to enable fungi such as *S. brevicaulis* to generate those neurotoxic gases.[42]

Each vaccination raises the baby's temperature, multiplying gas generation in the crib if the baby is not protected against it, and hence worsening risk of death by gas poisoning. A rise in the bedding temperature close to baby's body from 98.6° F to 104° F can increase gas generation 10-fold or more.[43] In 1972, P.J. Landrigan, M.D., and J.J. Witte, M.D., reported febrile (with fever) convulsions on days 3, 7 to 10, 13, 15, 18 and 25 after measles vaccination (which is now part of MMR; see below).[44] Other researchers reported derangement of body temperature control after a variety of vaccines.[45,46]

---

*"Each vaccination raises the baby's temperature, multiplying gas generation in the crib if the baby is not protected against it, and hence worsening risk of death by gas poisoning."*

---

For babies protected by BabeSafe® or by a properly wrapped mattress, these fevers pass harmlessly with normal treatment. But for infants who are not so protected, vaccinations increase toxic gas exposure and SIDS risk directly. They also elevate crib death risk indirectly by weakening immunity and increasing incidence of fever-generating asthma and other diseases — as does pediatricians' overuse of antibiotics (see Chapter 8).[47]

Although Scheibner measured only breathing, there can be little doubt that fevers also rose on the days of apnea and hypopnea. If a baby's mattress was generating toxic gases, risk of being killed by them was high on each of those days. The infection-caused fever incited by a vaccine would generate a higher, more dangerous concentration of toxic gases. In sum, Scheibner estimates "this unscientific, useless, harmful and invasive procedure causes half of crib deaths,[48] which some have renamed Sudden Immunization Death Syndrome."[49,50]

Sprott reinterprets: "Half of all cot death babies have been recently vaccinated — an entirely different point, as any epidemiologist would know." Epidemiologists study all the elements contributing to the occurrence or non-occurrence of a disease in a population.

Contrary to repetitive claims crediting vaccinations for eliminating infectious diseases, such diseases declined almost to zero before vaccinations began. Typically, a disease was already near the end of its decline and the rate of improvement did not then accelerate. Major infectious diseases shrank away as nutrition, public health measures and sanitation built up; and they declined equally in areas where mass vaccinations were never applied. Where those conditions did not improve, vaccination programs did not affect disease incidence.

From the records of the Metropolitan Life Insurance Co., from 1911 to 1935 the four leading causes of death from infectious diseases in the United States were diphtheria, scarlet fever, whooping cough and measles. By 1945 the combined death rate from these causes had declined by 95 percent before the implementation of mass vaccination programs.[51]

The greatest factors in the decline of diphtheria, scarlet fever and whooping cough were sanitation through public health measures including, notably, clean drinking water, improved nutrition and better housing with less crowded conditions.[52]

Now for the long-term effects: vaccinations weaken our immune systems. Humans have two kinds of immunity:

(1) The humeral immune system (or Th2 function) produces antibodies, specialized defense proteins, to recognize, neutralize and actually remember antigens, i.e., unfriendly foreign particles in the body.

(2) The cell-mediated (Th1 function) immune system involves white blood cells and specialized immune cells known as macrophages ("big eaters"), which gobble up antigens and thus clear them from the body. These hungry cells function in the thymus, tonsils, adenoids, spleen, lymph nodes and the lymph sys-

tem.[53] (The lymph system throughout the body disposes of the body's garbage.) This causes skin rashes and discharges of pus and mucus from throat and lungs — typical signs of the beneficial acute inflammatory illnesses of childhood. These two poles of the immune system have a reciprocal relationship. When the humeral pole is over-stimulated, as from vaccines or allergies, the cell-mediated pole tends to be relatively inactive. Vaccines do not stimulate this pole, and so their contents never get discharged from the body. The humeral immune system needs to be tempered by the cell-mediated response, and this best happens during infectious childhood diseases.

> Louis Pasteur was a very great microbiologist. But he made one grievous error, and the results continue to bedevil us. For one thing, vaccinations are based on Pasteur's fallacious germ theory. If only health professionals had understood the cellular terrain theory of Pasteur's 19th century contemporary, Antoine Bechamp. Mosquitoes seek stagnant water, but do not cause it. Likewise, disease organisms already lurk inside the body or enter the body after exposure, as during a flu epidemic.
>
> Just as wolves seek sick deer as easy prey for dinner, disease organisms become hostile when terrain — cellular condition — shifts, i.e., when it weakens. The analytical chemist E. Douglas Hume, in the foreword to his book "Bechamp or Pasteur," expresses the concept. It explodes the germ theory and the basis of vaccinations.[54]

Mass "immunizations" cause poor lifetime health. In recent congressional testimony, a retired medical doctor who wishes to remain unidentified said:

"My final comments are drawn from my 27 years of experience as a general practitioner of medicine. Twenty-three of those years were in a rural farming community in upstate New York where as many as 50 percent of my pediatric patients were unvaccinated due to their parents' conscientious personal choice.

For 23 years, I observed my young patients grow from infancy to young adulthood and appraised their overall health and vitality. My unvaccinated children were healthier, hardier and more robust than their vaccinated peers. Allergies, asthma and pallor, and behavioral and attention disturbances were clearly more common in my young patients who had been vaccinated."

The growing incidence and severity of asthma seem to be related more to the suppression or absence of respiratory infections because of vaccinations and antibiotics than to the commonly perceived cause, air pollution. Highly polluted European cities where antibiotics and vaccines are used far less than in the United States have lower asthma rates than comparable American cities. And in Tucson, Ariz., with dry heat and lack of irritants in the air, the rate of asthma is the same as elsewhere in the country.[55,56]

More than one-third of Americans report allergies and food sensitivities.[57] But children who received a minimum of antibiotics and a minimum of early childhood vaccinations have 40 percent lower than average risk of developing allergies/food sensitivities.[58]

Explosions in asthma similar to America's developed also in Europe, Australia and Japan. The cause: lack of acute inflammatory responses and discharges in childhood, i.e., lack of childhood diseases.[59,60]

Hepatitis B vaccine causes 120 times more illnesses and deaths than the disease.[61] The recommendation to vaccinate was not based on any perceived risk of widespread hepatitis among children, but because the vaccine became available.[62] For example, measles vaccine causes adverse neurological conditions, mental retardation and more.[63]

Vaccinations, as well as antibiotics, have increased SIDS-risky otitis media (middle ear infections),[64] which can lead to autism.[65] They have increased cancer[66] and more. In Chapter 8 we discuss the topic at length.

Now a new shock. At least for genetically vulnerable children, the live-cell MMR (measles/mumps/rubella) vaccine, used since 1977, not only might promote encephalitis,[67] diabetes and Crohn's disease.[28] It also may cause autism. Natural medicine practitioner

Joseph Mercola, D.O., tells of "at least six children with autism who were 100 percent normal until they got the MMR vaccine."[69]

Here is a typical case, from recent testimony by a father to a hearing room in Washington. This was the House Committee on the Dangers of Vaccinations, chaired by Congressman Dan Burton, Republican of Indiana. The audience's reaction afterward: dead silence.

*"Russell began his life a normal, healthy, robust child, meeting all his age appropriate milestones. At 7 months old — within 72 hours after receiving his third DPT and his first Hib (Haemophilus influenzae) vaccinations — Russell developed a high fever and shrieked with a high, wailing scream for days.*

*After these vaccinations, he started losing eye contact, smiling less, losing interest in people, developed constant croup and was chronically sick. At 7 months old, Russell's life had begun to change along with the lives of all who know and love him. Within days after his first MMR vaccination at 18 months old, Russell began his final journey into the abyss of what we know as autism — losing most of his remaining skills, developing severe sleep irregularities, chronic gastrointestinal problems, and expressing constant pain by harrowing days of endless crying. He was officially diagnosed at two and a half years old with autism.[70]"*

The six- to eight-fold increase in autism in the United States and Britain from 1977 to date is not a coincidence. Before that, its incidence had been about constant for 30 years. The live cell MMR vaccine appears to create the condition by a complex web of reactions in the body including "leaky gut,"[71] which in turn makes the brain "leaky."[72] The so-called blood-brain barrier — which does not even exist in the fetus — derives from the same embryonic origin as the gut epithelium, the lining. It does not protect the brain nearly as well as was long thought, but can be modulated in an ongoing way to respond to environmental stimuli.[73]

Intestinal absorption of large particles. The following draws heavily on Ray Peat's Newsletter, January 1998, pages 1-5, by Raymond Peat, Ph.D.[74] (chemistry).

Gerhard Volkheimer rediscovered the principle called persorption in the 1960s; it had first been found a century earlier.[75]

"Even the normal intestine is able to permit passage of large molecules and particles, in many cases larger than the cells that line the intestine. Scientists demonstrated this, using particles of plastic,starch grains — which are sometimes several times larger than blood cells — and many other materials. One of those is carrageenan." None of Peat's physiology professors, when he was in college, were aware of this phenomenon. (We visit potentially mischievous carrageen again in Chapter 8.)

A seemingly low-grade, long-term immune reaction — a homeostasis, i.e., a stable condition — of ill health precedes the devastating condition autism.[76]

Andrew Wakefield, M.D., a conventional, mainline British gastroenterologist, drew heavy medical and public health reprisals by publishing the following research. The children brought to him for study of digestive system troubles had, like Russell in his father's testimony before a congressional committee, developed normally until they were given MMR. One 16-month-old baby developed autism from the measles component of MMR,[77] which is given at 12 to 15 months of age, possibly not early enough to promote crib death.

Other studies question the relationship of MMR vaccinations to autism. See Appendix at the end of this book.

Polio and Hib vaccines may be administered at the same doctor or nurse contacts where other vaccines are given.[78] When viruses are mixed together — DPT is itself a mixture — they can cause dangerous hybrid viruses. Some combined vaccines, given in months two, four and six when SIDS risk is at a peak (that would be perfect timing if the aim were to achieve the worst possible SIDS death rate), can multiply unpredictable neurotoxic viral infections.[79]

---

The difference between a virus and a bacterium. "The typical virus is a nonliving microbe made of nucleic acid DNA, or a photocopy of DNA called RNA within a protein envelope, and sometimes even a tiny membrane. These molecules are all made by human cells inside a human body. A virus reproduces by entering a living cell and commandeering the cell's resources in order to make new virus particles, a process that ends with the disintegration of the dead cell, according to Peter Duesberg, PhD.,"Inventing the AIDS Virus," Regnery, 1996.[80]

A bacterium, in contrast, reproduces by simple cell division. Some bacteria cause diseases such as pneumonia and tuberculosis. Others serve necessary functions in the body. Our trillions of "friendly" gut bacteria strengthen immunity, generate needed vitamins and serve other important functions. (See Chapter 8.)

---

Injected at different times into mice, two herpes simplex viruses were harmless. But when both were given together, 70 percent of the mice died. Their bodies contained 11 new viruses, of which eight were neurotoxic.[81] Some viruses use a "team approach." One by itself may be relatively benign but combination with other viruses "helps" the first one cause, e.g., cancer. There is no way to predict what interactions may develop among the many patent drugs that elderly Americans take. In the same way, no one can know what viral combinations result from the many vaccines injected into children and what is in the final "soup."[82]

About 98 percent of DNA sequences in mice and in people are identical. The little animals' immune systems, and probably children's as well, can also react to a memory; the immune system never forgets.[83,84] Mice given a sugary liquid mixed with poison will later sicken and die if fed the same liquid without the toxin.

In a similar manner, babies' liver function is affected for two to four weeks after DPT vaccination. If a new food such as cow milk or wheat is introduced during this period (some pediatricians now recommend "solid" food at one month old), the child's never-forgetting immune system may later react to that food as though it were DPT — that is, with an allergic or sensitivity reaction, which can cause SIDS-risky ear infections or worse.[85] See also below on risk of potentially SIDS-promoting diabetes.

When vaccines are such a disaster, why do we continue to use them and to impose ever more of them?

Today we have a system in which vaccine production by the pharmaceutical companies is largely self-regulated. Naturally, these companies are interested in profits from their products, which, in itself, is not wrong. However, arbitrary decisions in the mandating of vaccines are made by government bureaucracies, which are highly partisan to the pharmaceutical companies. With no recourse open to parents, we have all the potential ingredients for a tragedy of historical proportions.[86]

The current list of scheduled vaccinations is too long to include in this book; copies are available from local health departments. Children can get as many as 35 vaccinations before they start first grade. Two-hundred more vaccines are in the pipeline. Scenarios for the future even include consuming vaccines in nose sprays, in ointments, and in fruits and vegetables.

Vaccinations are not based on any science at all. We are vaccinating children in a vacuum of scientific knowledge; no one has ever studied long-term effects. A test would, logically, compare the results over a period of years between a group of people who got a particular vaccine and another group who did not. The FDA requires safety and efficacy tests before approving a new drug. (Many of those trials were shown to have been fraudulent. Campaign Against Fraudulent Medical Research, Australia, *"The Pharmaceutical Drug Racket,"* 1993; but at least there were tests.)

Why are there no long-term studies to assess illness and deaths related to vaccination? And why are there so few studies of what happens in the body at a cellular/molecular level afterward?

Eugene Robinson, M.D., emeritus professor of medicine from Stanford University Medical School, is a leading authority on risk/benefit analysis in medicine. He wrote the definitive book on the subject, *"Matters of Life and Death: Risks vs. Benefits of Medical Care."*[87] In it Robinson states, "The scientists who develop vaccines should be given great credit and respect for their pioneering work. But it must be recognized that once a promising vaccine is available, that should be the beginning and not the end of the process."

"Accurate assessment of the risk/benefit ratio of the vaccine by means of a controlled clinical trial should be obligatory," concurs Joseph Mercola, D.O.[88] "An educational process involving the public should be mandatory, in which the risks and uncertainties are described, as well as the potential benefits."

Here's what you can do to avoid a tragic outcome for your baby. Many American doctors refuse inoculations for their own children.[89] In a California survey reported in the *Journal of the American Medical Association,* more than 90 percent of the obstetrician/gynecologists refused to let their children be vaccinated.[90]

"If doctors themselves are afraid of a vaccine, why on earth should the law require that you and other parents allow them to administer it to your kids?" asked pediatrician and author Robert Mendelsohn, M.D.[91]

Regarding waivers, in all states but two (West Virginia and Mississippi), all parents have the right to decide if their children shall be vaccinated. And if so, when?[92] They can arrange for a waiver even when children are told, "No shots, no school." Waiver can be based on medical or religious grounds; the method and wording are different in each state, and you must know the exact procedure for your state.

Learn the methods of getting your children excused from "immunizations," including hepatitis B automatically administered in hospital maternity wards at birth. Obtain this information, state by state, from Dr. Joseph Mercola's website at http://www.mercola.com His e-mail address is mercola@pol.net

Mercola writes, "To avoid automatic hepatitis B vaccination right after birth, all that is required is to implement the consent waivers listed on my web site."[93] An excellent alternative, of course is — guided by a trusted, skilled midwife — to consider giving birth outside a hospital.

The arrangement for waivers is for the protection of the state. If vaccination were required and your child died or got terribly sick, you could sue the state for damages. With a waiver available, in defending against a lawsuit the state can reply that you should not have had the child vaccinated if you suspected danger.

If parents do elect to accept vaccines, the timing of administration is critical. Typically, children are lined up for their shots one after another, no questions asked. But to vaccinate a child who is even slightly sick (for example, sniffling — and so, vitamin C-devoid) — or who reacted badly when sensitized to the same vaccine before,[94] courts disaster. Too many deaths and total losses of lifetime health prove that statement.[95,96] Afterward, America's vaccine compensation fund, from which only about one claim out of four ever collects a dime, offers cold comfort.[97]

Lendon Smith offers his counsel: "Wise parents will consider forgoing vaccinations, or at least postponing shots until baby is a year old, when SIDS risk drops.

"The best advice I can give to parents is to forgo the shots, but make sure that the children in your care have a superior immune system. This requires a sugarless diet without processed foods, an intake of vitamin C of about 1,000 milligrams per day for each year of life up to 5,000 mgs at age 5. Plenty of fruits and vegetables are important, plus powdered dried fruits and vegetables picked when ripe and flash frozen. They have the protective antioxidants." (See Resources.)

Homeopathic remedies have been very successful in keeping childhood diseases mild. Again, see Resources.

Smith continues, "If you, as a parent, are unable to ward off the pressure from your doctor, at least give your child some fortifying nutrients the day before, the day of and the day after the shot: vitamin C, one to two grams; vitamin B6, 100 mgs; and calcium, 1,000 mgs. You are the guardian of your child's health. You have some rights."[98]

In Chapter 7 we look into infantile heart attacks as possible causes of crib death.

Chapter Seven

# INFANTILE HEART ATTACKS AS A CAUSE OF SIDS

*AND MUCH THAT PARENTS CAN DO*

*TO AVOID ADULT HEART ATTACKS*

I n this chapter we examine the evidence that infantile heart attacks cause some crib deaths. Two possible mechanisms have been proposed. The first we can dispose of rather easily. The second is plausible. Of all nutrition-related theories of crib death, to our knowledge only this one provides a credible killing mechanism. Even this theory fails, though, when placed against the toxic gas explanations in Chapter 2.

Yet we devote a chapter to it for its general interest to our readers. Information we provide here will enable parents to gain important health benefits both for the baby and for themselves. And it will help prevent serious, even tragic, outcomes other than crib death throughout childhood and in later life.

"Infant Deaths Linked to Odd Heartbeat," blared newspaper headlines in June 1998. News stories told of a study led by Peter John Schwartz, M.D., of the University of Pavia, in Italy.[1,2] From 1976 to 1994 he and members of his research team examined more than 33,000 babies, born healthy at full term in nine Italian maternity hospitals. Each was given a standard electrocardiogram (ECG) on day three or four of life. This noninvasive test measures the electrical activity that spreads over the heart muscle with every beat. Every baby was then monitored for the entire first year.

Their research indicated that a peculiarity in the ECG known as a long QT interval made SIDS risk 41 times greater than in babies with normal QT interval. Of the 33,000, 34 died. Twenty-four deaths were called SIDS; its incidence was 0.7 percent, about typical for Italy. Heart attacks that caused crib deaths in the Italian study resulted from a severely irregular heartbeat known as arrhythmia. The authors concluded that probably not fewer than 30 to 35 percent of SIDS deaths could result from arrhythmias.[3]

---

*"The authors concluded that probably not fewer than 30 to 35 percent of SIDS deaths could result from arrhythmias."*

---

But heart irregularities can have many other causes. Drinking grapefruit juice while on the pharmaceutical drug Seldane can cause the same torsade-de-pointes ventricular arrhythmias seen in the Italian study.[4]

Derrick Lonsdale, M.D., wrote, "The way to acquire the long QT syndrome is by acquiring a good case of beriberi [deficiency disease from extreme lack of thiamine, vitamin B1 or from consumption of moisture-spoiled rice and maize, i.e. corn[5]]. Beriberi is simply a major presentation of high calorie malnutrition, i.e., SAD, Standard American Diet."[6]

Certain types of arrhythmia could result from damaged heart arteries or from the pandemic, gross deficiency of magnesium, which is a bronchial and muscular relaxant.[7] Too much calcium relative to the intake of magnesium can promote arrhythmias; multiple chemical exposures, and sensitivities to food and mold can cause them as well.[8] Pandemic means virtually everyone has it.

Schwartz suggested that the long QT interval might often result from a genetic defect. But Warren G. Guntheroth, M.D., a

Seattle, Wash., authority on SIDS objected that first-degree relatives of SIDS infants have had no significant differences in QT
interval.[9,9a] Premature infants, the most susceptible to SIDS, do not
have long QT intervals[10] nor do such irregularities appear in the
near-SIDS.[11] Anyway, genes do not operate unless they are
"turned on," perhaps to varying degrees like the dimming and
brightening of lights in an auditorium. Classical Mendelian genetics as taught in schools does not immutably determine a person's
life situation. Improved diet and lifestyles can prevent activation
of nasty genes.[12] Compare comment on genes in Chapter 4.

And, writes Guntheroth,: "The age of most frequent infantile
arrhythmias, the first month, does not correspond to the age of
vulnerability to SIDS, which spares the first month and peaks at
three to four months." He adds, "Three common SIDS autopsy
findings are evidence that apnea occurs before any terminal
arrhythmia."[13] (We discussed apneas, interruptions in breathing, in
Chapter 6 on vaccines.) Moreover, he points out, the long QT
interval would not decline at six months or disappear after 12
months of age like SIDS risk.[14,15a]

That long QT, we propose, only made babies more susceptible
to poisoning by toxic mattress gases. They could not tolerate a
given concentration of gas as well; or fevers incited by or related
to the odd heart rhythm promoted higher gas generation. Like
Guntheroth, Schwartz did not mention, or appear to know of, the
negative influence of toxic gases on babies.

Also, the Italian study reported nothing about smoking exposure, or whether the mothers were using patent drugs of any kind.
All drugs are foreign to the body; the liver and kidneys must
detoxify and eliminate them.[15] Then, what about the vast area of
nutrition, what of mold in the home, electromagnetic fields, geopathic stresses? So their study is interesting, but we believe that if
the suggestions offered here are carried out, the SIDS rate can be
cut much further.

A second approach to infantile heart attacks, although little
known, is supported by research. There have been reported cases

of heart attacks occurring before birth.[26,27] Blockage of the coronary arteries can cause a fetal heart attack, just as in adults.

Heart attacks are commonly associated with arterial damage, although not always. For important exceptions, see below. Pathologist Doris Jaffe, MD, and her associates at the Research Hospital for Sick Children in Toronto, Canada, examined 176 consecutive babies who had died of any cause—usually infection or accident—in the first month of life. Ninety-six percent had at least the beginnings of arterial damage, which had presumably begun to develop in utero.[28]

On their autopsy table, using advanced techniques, they cut the extremely minute coronary arteries lengthwise, which is technically difficult. Cutting crosswise, the customary method, a pathologist could easily miss tiny arterial blockages. There was almost no lipid (cholesterol or other fats) in those arteries. None of the babies had survived long enough to begin normal nutrition, whether breast or bottle. Later, the same team of pathologists checked one thousand consecutive babies who died in their first month; one hundred percent had arterial damage.[29] So the discovery was not a fluke.

Of the 169 deaths in the 1971 Jaffe study, two were SIDS;[30] these were interpreted to have been caused by blocked coronary arteries.[29] Moses M. Suzman, MD, who was in constant touch with Jaffe by telephone from Johannesburg, South Africa, diagnosed the SIDS deaths. Dr. Suzman 'firmly believed' that most crib deaths result from infantile atherosclerosis.[31,32] (Suzman's theories of crib death launched Joseph Hattersley's 16-year study of SIDS.) In light of the large numbers of crib deaths shown to result from toxic gases, Suzman's firm belief appears to have been mistaken.

Yet, could some crib deaths result in this manner? What about the two very early SIDS deaths inside the hospital in Toronto? The Jaffe report said nothing about the presence or absence of toxic mattress gases; their existence and importance in crib death were not yet known. The mattresses probably contained fire retardants and preservatives, but it is unlikely that any fungi lived in the infants' beds where they would generate toxic gases. "In our hospitals, patients are encased in formaldehyde-based clothes and bedding smelling of Clorox, and breathing recirculated air loaded with perfumes, industrial strength cleansers, petrochemical floor waxes, and more." That description probably applied in 1971, as well — providing more toxins for the babies' livers to detoxify.[33] There is no reason to believe they would suffice to cause a crib death.

Suzman treasured sixty-seven unpublished color micrographs, prepared by Dr. Jaffe's pathology team in the 1970's. They showed arterial blockages in aborted fetuses, babies, children, teens, and adults. To him this was proof positive that arterial blockages could have caused their deaths. (The micrographs, sadly, were ultimately lost.) A thorough autopsy after a crib death includes examination of the coronary arteries. Sometimes the pathologist finds plaques there, writes Warren Guntheroth, but "severity sufficient to kill an infant is almost unheard of."[34]

---

Wolfgang J. Weninger and associates at the Departments of Anatomy and Forensic Medicine, University of Vienna, Vienna, Austria, have made a related proposal. Using a new 3-D imaging technique more accurate than computed tomography, they found a slight, not statistically significantly higher, incidence of lumen occlusion [blockage] in the parasellar carotid [neck] artery of SIDS vs. non-SIDS babies. This, they proposed, could be "a factor in the multifactorial pathogenesis of SIDS."[35,36]

We have disproved any multifactorial explanation of SIDS, but include the brief summary because it is so new.

---

Anyway, would babies with blocked coronary arteries necessarily succumb to crib death without toxic mattress gases? Among two hundred American soldiers, average age 22.1 years, autopsied in the Korean War, some had one or two totally occluded coronary arteries.[37] But they had passed induction physicals as "healthy" and presumably were fighting until killed in battle. No records exist of those two hundred men's individual health in the final weeks before their deaths.

At least thousands of people continue active, reasonably healthy lives while one or two coronary arteries are blocked. William Campbell Douglass, MD, expressed it best:[38]

"Ten years ago, the American Journal of Cardiology reported that in an advanced state of occlusion of the coronary arteries, the supply of blood to the heart muscle is fully assured through collaterals that enlarge naturally in response to blockage. The more the coronary arteries narrow [if the narrowing is gradual!], the less danger there is of heart attack."

To understand how Suzman reached his diagnosis of crib death, we need to go on a tour into nutrition. An early clue about its importance came in 1949 from the work of James F. Rinehart, MD, and Louis D. Greenberg, MD, pathologists in San Francisco. They fed young rhesus monkeys synthetic high-protein Western-style diets deficient in single vitamins. After six months to four years, each monkey given a diet somewhat lacking in — but not totally devoid of[39] — vitamin B6 (commonly known as pyridoxine) had arterial plaques similar to those seen in nearly all human adult autopsies. As in Jaffe's autopsies of new babies twenty years later, they found almost no lipids. Monkeys given extra B6 showed no arterial damage;[40] and later, the vitamin reversed such damage created by a B6-deficient diet.[41] These portentous findings were ignored in the growing, ill-founded frenzy over cholesterol.

Back in the 1940s, Suzman hypothesized that vitamin B6 deficiency is pandemic. The condition afflicts everyone consuming Western processed diets, and he blamed such deficiency as the primary cause of heart attacks. The monkey tests strongly supported the belief, and so he set out to test his hypothesis. Over a period of more than forty years starting in 1950, he instructed every non-cardiac patient referred to him to take 100 mg of vitamin B6 every day for the rest of his or her life. As an internist and cardiologist, he treated patients with a wide variety of problems.

Without any suggested change in diet, exercise, or smoking habits, this inexpensive supplement — as he expected — nearly eliminated heart attacks and other cardiac events among his thousands of non-cardiac patients. For heart patients Suzman used 200 mg of B6, other supplements, a semivegetarian diet, and heart drugs for a short time. This therapy regressed their arterial blockages; "hundreds and hundreds" of his former heart patients enjoyed improved health for decades.[42]

Suzman maintained contact with many of those recovered oldsters but didn't keep a count through the 40-plus years. No matter. The subsequent record, published in medical journals in the past five years, fully vindicates his generally ignored faith in the importance of vitamin B6 in prevention of adult heart attacks.

1) John Marion Ellis, MD, a general practitioner and pioneering researcher in Mt. Pleasant, Texas, and research pathologist Kilmer S. McCully, MD, looked back at Ellis's long-term results since 1962. Adults who took 100 to 300 mgs of B6 daily for a long time had 73 percent fewer chest pains and heart attacks than abstainers. They also lived seven to 17 years longer and felt better.[43] There is no record of whether, or how many, B6-taking patients changed their diet, took other supplements, exercised, stopped smoking, etc. The authors credited the improvement to lowering of patients' levels of the toxic amino acid homocysteine (Chapter 4); but see (2) and (3), next.

(2) Among 80,082 women followed for 20 years in the ongoing Nurses' Health Study, even after accounting for other risk factors, heart attack risk dropped 17 percent for each two-milligram increase in daily B6 consumption.[44] If we can assume that ratio, an increased supplement of eight milligrams a day might lower heart attacks by 68 percent.

(3) In the 10-year Atherosclerosis Risk in Communities (ARIC) study the people in the highest quintile of plasma vitamin B6 — that is, those ingesting the highest quantities — had 72 percent fewer heart attacks than those consuming the least B6. Notice how close that is to the finding of 73 percent among Ellis's patients. No other substance in that test correlated with lowered risk — not even homocysteine.[45]

---

What about side effects? We suggest use of only pharmaceutical grade B6. Neurological (nervous system) side effects of B6, although over-publicized, are real; and an excess of the vitamin may lower bioavailability.[46] The tablet filler can cause side effects. Yet, guided by Russell Jaffe, M.D., Ph.D., 3,500 volunteers took 200 to 2,000 mg daily for years at a time — without neuropathy because they used pharmaceutical grade pyridoxine hydrochloride.[47]

Some people cannot convert pyridoxine into pyridoxal phosphate (PLP), the form that is active in the body. This can lead to nonneurological but unpleasant symptoms. Such people can use PLP as tablet or powder. Details below; see Sources.

---

These findings also fully support proposals for fortification of processed food with vitamin B6. Ellis has suggested each six ounces of pasteurized cow milk, every half-pound of bread, every pound of processed high protein food should be fortified with three milligrams of "available" vitamin B6[48] (pyridoxine is the more heat resistant among several vitamers, i.e. forms of the vitamin[49]). Such fortification might well decimate the 20th century's plague of heart attacks, strokes and the like.

Ellis noticed that enough B6 softens fibers, and Suzman found that enough B6 removes arterial clogs. Also, this vitamin offers an anti-inflammatory benefit.[50] And so, after fortification of processed food with B6 begins — along with the epidemic of cardiac problems the industry of coronary artery bypass surgery would fade away. Even EDTA chelation therapy might not be needed as often.

Yet there is still more to explain those extraordinary successes in lowering heart attacks.[51] Ellis, we will recall, found that supplemented B6 usually prevented adult onset diabetes and diabetic retinopathy (blindness).[52] Diabetics, as a group, are two to four times more likely than others to develop stroke and heart disease.[53]

But Type II, i.e., adult onset diabetes — the class of diabetes that Ellis prevented with vitamin B6 — is now known to be a separate disease from Type I, juvenile onset diabetes. The two have different risk factors and separate outcomes.[54] Type II diabetics have elevated heart disease risk; Type I diabetics are more likely to get peripheral vascular disease (i.e., arterial clogging in the legs and arms). Some people get both.

For Type II, heart disease supplies the greatest risk of premature death, especially in women. And so the likelihood of developing stroke and heart disease is higher for Type II than for diabetics on the whole, which we cited as double or quadruple the usual risk. How much higher is not yet known.

Inflammation may play a part in Type II diabetes,[55] and vitamin B6 helps prevent inflammation.[56] Inflammation is redness, pain, heat, swelling, sometimes loss of function as a reaction to injury, infection, irritation, etc. The histamine theory of cellular biologist Bruce H. Lipton, PhD, implies a further protective mechanism for B6, as well as for vitamin C.[57,58] Histamine is not only a trigger for allergy and inflammation; it is also a potent mitogen, a stimulator of mitosis, i.e. cell division. Treatment of diabetic patients with either antihistamines[58] or vitamin B6[59] lessened vascular leakage and stemmed retinal degeneration — suggesting B6 functions as an antihistamine.[59a]

These results and these prospects concern adults and offer important information for the parents who read this book. Yet we may be able sensibly to apply the conclusions to infantile heart attacks as well.

What is so special about vitamin B6? Textbooks of nutrition list a great number of services, in the body, but they omit one of the most important. B6's protection against heart attack is utterly mysterious unless — contrary to usual biochemical theory — it is an antioxidant, i.e. removes an O2 atom. A.L. Witting, PhD, in America,[60] Fumio Kuzuya, MD (who worked with Rinehart and Greenberg after 1949),[61,62] and M. Nabu, MD,[63] in Japan, a pair of researchers in China,[64] and two in India[65,66,67] found that B6 does act as an antioxidant, at least in high enough concentration. Six separate studies confirmed it. And if antioxidant at high concentration, it must also serve antioxidant function at low concentration.

B6 may also serve an antioxidant-like function through some effect on cystathionine beta-synthase (CBS).[68] That enzyme, or facilitator, is required to enable conversion of ingested pyridoxine into pyridoxal phosphate (PLP), the vitamer of B6 that is active in the body.

And so this nutrient joins vitamins C and E, coenzyme Q10 and other well-known antioxidants. The marvels they create in improving and preserving health have been widely publicized.

The RDA (recommended dietary allowance) for vitamin B6 is only about two milligrams daily. Ingesting even that small amount in diet is not easy, and obtaining 50 or 100 mg a day is feasible only by taking a supplement. (One could derive 50 mg of B6 from sixty-seven bananas or nine pounds of raw calf liver.[69]) Pioneering Carl C. Pfeiffer, MD, PhD, believed that when properly nourished, the two and one-half to three pounds of "friendly" microorganisms in the human gut generate 200 to 300 mg of vitamin B6 a day. He reached that conclusion by considering the following facts.

When a person fasts (eats nothing), vitamin B6's functions continue, including operation of 500 enzymes that depend on the vitamin. These require about 200 milligrams a day. This suggested to Pfeiffer[70] and to the late, great researcher Karl Folkers, PhD, that 200 mg of the vitamin is created daily in the body. They suggested the RDA should be 50 mg. (Among other landmark nutritional discoveries, Folkers was the first to synthesize vitamin B6.)

Not only is deficiency of the vitamin pandemic; studies have found that people consuming Western diets are more deficient in it than in other vitamins.[71] Fats, which constitute 30 percent to 40 percent of total calories, do not contain any water-soluble B vitamins. Foods grown on soils fertilized only with three nutrients (NPK—nitrogen, phosphorus, potassium) are low in needed micronutrients including B6. And because this nutrient is fragile, most of what remains is lost in food processing, storage, transport, cooking, and so on. Typically heavy consumption of sugar depletes B6 from the body.[72,73]

Also, the air we inhale and our food and medicines are full of substances that destroy B6 inside our bodies and also increase our need for it. Stress, which acts to further deplete the vitamin,[74] is high and rising not only in the workplace and domestic life but also notably from myriad growing sources of electromagnetic radiations, wrote Robert Becker, M.D.[75] Geopathic stresses must enter, as well; see Chapter 2.[76]

---

*"In expectant moms that deficiency shows up most prominently as edema; as mentioned in Chapter 4, one pregnant patient lost fifteen pounds of water after she started to take B6."*

---

Even people taking one-size-fits-all RDA-strength vitamins as part of a multivitamin supplement — particularly elderly folks and pregnant women,[77] as mentioned earlier — have symptoms of severe B6 deficiency.[78] In expectant moms that deficiency shows up most prominently as edema; as mentioned in Chapter 4, one pregnant patient lost fifteen pounds of water after she started to take B6.[79] Other pregnancy B6 deficiency symptoms include carpal tunnel syndrome, dropping objects, leg cramps, nocturnal paralysis or "going to sleep" of arms, muscle spasms in legs and feet, and diabetes of pregnancy.[80] Failure to correct diabetes during pregnancy greatly increases risk of that disease, with its many complications including high heart attack risk, in later life. These symptoms, some of which can also result from magnesium deficiency, warn of SIDS risk through heart attack.

Ellis found that for many women, going into pregnancy with B6 deficiency can cause neurological and brain changes in the baby. The fetus and newborn must have sufficient B6 to avoid convulsive seizures, mental retardation, and sometimes autism;[81] its deficiency can alter brain biochemistry. And for the mother, it can worsen existing psychological stress including depression,[82] which is itself well known to increase cardiac risk. The B6 deficiency distorts mineral balance and hormone balance as well as fluid balance, and more.[83]

---

*"The fetus and newborn must have sufficient B6 to avoid convulsive seizures, mental retardation, and sometimes autism; its deficiency can alter brain biochemistry."*

---

What creates this extraordinary lack of B6 during pregnancy? Pyridoxal phosphate (PLP) levels decline sharply;[84] the stress of pregnancy and the demands of the growing fetus drain it from the mother's body.[85] Methionine-rich high animal protein Western diets, high dietary sugar,[86] and all the other features of Western life listed earlier, further deplete the body of it. Also, fetuses and newborns up to the traditional age of weaning are deficient or entirely lacking in cystathionine beta-synthase, which is required to enable the body to convert pyridoxine from supplements into PLP.[87]

As mentioned earlier, B6 can be used as PLP itself; about one-tenth as much suffices.[88] Since some people's bodies convert pyridoxine (PN) to PLP less efficiently than others, the precise amount needed can be better judged. Poor conversion of PN to PLP can promote development of ADHD and dyslexia. The degree of ability to make this conversion appears to be inherited;[89]

what is true of mother will be true of her baby. Adults whose bodies make that conversion poorly, too, can develop minor but disagreeable side effects. Taking PLP instead of pyridoxine hydrochloride should eliminate such problems.

Another nutritional approach powerfully strengthens resistance to cardiac disease. S.S.D. Nair, PhD, and his associates found that infusion of omega-3 essential fatty acids stopped cardiac electrical storms in laboratory animals;[90] and others prevented second heart attacks in people by supplementing omega-3 EFAs.[91] Omega-3s increase insulin sensitivity and glucose transport,[92] reducing risk of diabetes and so further lowering risk of heart attack.[93,94] Further, human populations consuming high amounts of omega-3s experience very few arrhythmias.[95] If any adult, including a mother, ingests enough omega-3 EFA's from fish and flax oil, cardiac arrhythmia may be prevented.

Briefly reviewing Chapter 4, the human body does not make omega-3 EFAs or convert omega-6 or omega-9 EFAs into omega-3's. So people must ingest them in their diet. Three generations of American babies have dined on formulas containing no DHA, the most important omega-3. To what extent is this implicated in the development of huge numbers of children wearing glasses, in burgeoning ADD/ADHD/learning disabilities and the growth of delinquent behavior?[96] Also the likelihood in old age of developing Alzheimer's and Parkinson's diseases? To these questions the true answer may be: very large indeed.

What is it that makes fetuses and newborn babies susceptible to arterial clogging? First of all, infections. Every infection, —either bacterial or viral, — is laden with blood clots,[97] and so elevates risk of scurvy SIDS (Chapter 6), as well as heart attack SIDS.

Pandemic deficiency of vitamin B6 and many other micronutrients on top of mankind's inborn deficiency of vitamin C weakens everyone's immunity. People who do not ingest enough or adequately supplement those nutrients become easy prey for infection.

GC Willis, MD, an earlier practitioner and researcher in Toronto, Canada, conducted tests with guinea pigs. Like primates including humans, guinea pigs do not generate their own ascorbate. He found that subclinical scurvy and arterial damage occur together.[98] Tiny blood clots initiate arterial damage,[99] and capillary disintegration with bleeding is typical of arterial wall thinning.[100]

But — any kind of infection? Says Guntheroth, "Most SIDS researchers believe that mild virus infections play some role, perhaps in increasing the probability of a prolonged apneic episode."[101] And among 1,372 Native Americans studied in 1997, the risk of heart attack was 2.7 times higher in individuals with periodontal, i.e. gum disease than in those with healthy gums.[102,102a] In a real sense, then, the gums are the gateway to the cardiovascular system; and without adequate oral hygiene the number of bacteria can reach a thousand billion.[103,103a] A similar rise is likely in heart attack SIDS: gum disease infections might be passed on to the baby because the parents continue harmful dietary and oral hygiene practices. Obviously, kissing a baby can pass the germs to the child.

Viral infections can be involved.[104,105] All infections, including bacterial ones and so innocent a malady as the common cold (caused by viruses), together with poor personal hygiene (notably, dirty finger nails), nutrient-poor diets and lack of exercise lower heart-protective albumin.[106] Low albumin elevates danger of heart attack including heart attack SIDS.[107,108,109] Albumin is a class of complex proteins found in milk, egg, muscle, blood, and in many vegetable tissues and fluids.[110]

Using dark-field microscopy, pioneering James Privitera, MD, found that clots cause 90 percent of strokes and heart attacks, including most spasm heart attacks and the many heart attacks with clean arteries.[111] From 1950 to 1965 while heart attacks mushroomed, arterial lesions did not increase.[112,113] The major growth was in thrombosis, i.e. catastrophic clotting. Stress, smoking, alcohol, and caffeine promote clotting; enough B6 resists clot formation.[114]

Infections also promote heart attack SIDS indirectly by raising levels of fibrinogen, a component of blood, which is the raw material for clots. Fibrinogen levels rise with high serum lipid levels, diabetes, age, stressful lives, obesity, any illness at all — and contraceptive pills.[110] High fibrinogen makes blood more viscous, i.e. sticky, and increases neuronal cell damage. Neurons are the basic cells of the brain and nervous system. Like deficiency of vitamins C and B6, high fibrinogen increases and extends formation of thrombus.

---

Cholesterol has long been mainline medicine's boogeyman. But except for about one person in two hundred who inherited unusually high levels called hypercholesterolemia,[117] all of our non-oxidized cholesterol is perfectly safe. "How could it be otherwise?" wrote Joseph Hattersley in 1991.[76] "Would God, or the process of evolution, or Whoever established life, have built a poison pill into every living animal?"

Cholesterol becomes oxidized, and therefore dangerous, from five general sources. These are (a) powdered egg yolk, powdered milk, and the like in hundreds of processed foods;[120] (b) trans fatty acids in processed "convenience" foods;[122] (c) homocysteine;[122] (d) external sources such as chlorinated water; and (e) tiny fat particles in pasteurized, homogenized cow milk carried through digestive system walls with the enzyme xanthine oxidase.[119] Compare Chapter 8. Hattersley's multi-source oxysterol injury hypothesis integrates all these.[126] That hypothesis is now relegated to a second level of importance, behind the problem of clotting.

---

Fibrinogen aggravates the starting of arterial damage by integrating with arterial lesions.[115] Consuming a diet containing adequate natural fiber lowers fibrinogen. (Sawdust is "natural" but does not qualify.) High fibrinogen levels are transmitted from the mother to her baby at birth. Smoking increases it;[114a] this could explain part of the higher SIDS risk among babies exposed to tobacco smoke. Once in the vessel wall, fibrinogen is converted to fibrin,[116] which binds LDL, the "bad" low-density lipoproteins. These carry cholesterol out to deposit on arterial walls.

Incidentally, supplemented vitamin B6 also shows potential

benefit in helping avoid cancer. Few of Ellis's smoking patients developed lung cancer; taken for decades, B6 protected them against that disease.[123] It has shown anti-cancer promise in tests with animals and in test tube trials.[124,125]

In summary: we have shown important health benefits derive from appropriate nutrition, with particular attention to vitamin B6 and omega-3 essential fatty acids. But are crib deaths caused by lack of such nutrition — or would they occur at all without toxic mattress gases?

It does not seem likely, for the following reasons. Actual proof of the above or any other any nutritional theory of SIDS must jump some high, yea insurmountable hurdles. It would require collection of tissue samples from SIDS babies and from infants who died of known causes. Then consistently lower vitamin B6 (or lower omega-3 EFA's, or iodine, etc.) would have to be found in the SIDS autopsies. After that, a mechanism would have to be proposed and supported. In this case, we have supplied a mechanism.

In light of Peter Mitchell's findings given in Chapter 2, crib death risk caused by such nutrient deficiency would have to be consistently twice as high in a mother's second baby and twice as high again for her third baby. But most families maintain about constant nutritional practices throughout their child-rearing years. And the reason for insufficiency of a nutrient to cause such upward steps in risk would have to be proposed and supported.

As a result, the MM Suzman theory of heart attacks as a cause of crib death does not stand up. But the benefit of the nutrients here discussed for future health and normal behavior of the child, and for the parents' health and well-being, cannot be doubted. We include it in our book for these many elucidated benefits.

Chapter  Eight

# Nutrition and More

F irst, let's summarize what we have said about nutrition so far. In Chapter 4, *Pregnancy and Before* and again in Chapter 7, we emphasize omega-3 essential fatty acids. Although these probably do little if anything about crib death, they certainly will help avoid ADD and ADHD. And consumed throughout life, they will probably also resist Alzheimer's, heart attacks and cancer. We suggest food-made vitamin supplements and coconut oil (see Resources), and we caution against trans fatty acids, all soy foods, Aspartame® and others. In Chapter 7 we discuss the value of vitamin B6, not only in possibly minimizing risk of crib death but also for its huge lifetime benefits in avoiding heart attacks and cancer.

---

Soy Foods: Even fermented soy, which is supposedly better than unfermented, is not recommended for anyone,[1] least of all for pregnant women, their embryos, their fetuses and their newborn babies. Soy industry publications need to be read with a critical eye. That industry has had "a team of lawyers to crush dissenters, owned television channels and newspapers, could divert medical schools and can even influence governments."[2]

Average consumption of soy foods in Japan and China is 10 grams (about two teaspoons) per day. Those people use soy foods in small amounts as a condiment — and not as a replacement for animal foods.[3]

In particular, we caution against isolated fractions of soy phytoestrogens; these can be expected to perform worse, even, than whole

---

soy food. They are powerfully denatured in manufacture[4] and are promoted with exaggerated claims, which the government appears powerless to prevent.[5]

The soy industry has done a strong sales job on American pediatricians. Twenty-five percent of American babies now drink soy-based formulas; their use has nearly doubled over the past decade. Soy formula can give an infant the equivalent of five birth control pills a day and potentially cause disastrous hormonal imbalances.[6,7,8] Birth control pills, even in normal intake, reduce body levels of vitamins B1, B2, B4, B6 and C, and the minerals zinc and manganese; they also decrease blood levels of needed amino acids.[9]

Soy proponents portrayed the extremely high phytoestrogen, or isoflavone, content of soy formula as an adaptogen, promoting normal development in both sexes. Not so. Soy formula appears to accelerate the sexual development of girls, leading to early puberty. Breast development is now seen as early as 6, 5 or even 4 years of age. And soy appears to delay or even prevent physical maturation in boys.[10] The societal consequences of this two-sided feminization might be interesting to observe. And soy formula could lead to infertility in both genders.[11]

Soy is an incomplete protein — it lacks needed cysteine and methionine — and also provides no cholesterol, which is essential for development of the baby's brain and nervous system.[12] It is not hard, then, to see why excess unsaturated oils including soy interfere with learning and behavior.[13,14]

Most soybeans grown in the United States (about 57 percent of soybean acreage,[15] and pollen can drift to other farms as much as half a mile away) are genetically engineered to allow farmers to use large amounts of herbicides. Traces of these herbicides can reach the baby and this can be bad — or good. See Chapter 9.

Soy formula is strongly suspected of promoting infantile leukemia.[16,17] Further, the aluminum content is 11 times that of other formulas. Aluminum in the brain is implicated in development of Alzheimer's disease. Research scientists in the United States, New Zealand and England agree that soy formula should be available only by prescription and should carry a warning label.[19]

With that out of the way, we can start serious discussion of nutrition. Sound scientific research demonstrates that when populations are subjected to serious, continued nutritional deficiencies, the offspring of each successive generation show an increased deterioration in physical and mental health.[20,21] In World War II fewer than 68 percent of the men could pass the induction physical, a physical that 86 percent had passed in 1918. Dietary habits have worsened since the war.[22]

Francis Pottenger foresaw such a trend in his pioneering work using 900 cats. Felines eating raw meat and raw milk were healthy and gave birth to generation after generation of healthy kittens. The first generation of those on cooked food developed our modern human ailments: heart, kidney and thyroid disease, pneumonia, paralysis, loss of teeth, difficulty in labor, diminished or perverted sexual interest, diarrhea and irritability. Liver impairment from cooked protein was progressive; their feces were so toxic that even weeds would not grow where they had been dropped.[23] Many second-generation kittens were born dead or diseased, and by the third generation the mothers were sterile.[24]

Extreme behavioral changes also occur as diets deteriorate. Price detailed again and again how previously unknown behavioral and emotional problems, as well as seriously deteriorating health, were seen in indigenous peoples with the introduction and adoption of Western food.[25] Pottenger's cats on inappropriate diets exhibited "anti-social" and perverted behavior; prison inmates' level of violence fluctuates depending on their food. Dr. T.L. Cleave corroborated those findings in his early book *Saccharine Disease: The Master Disease of Our Time*.[25a]

When we cook, we destroy the enzymes, the life force and the electromotive force. All this has been documented. Ordinary cooking precipitates proteins;[26,28] probably certain albuminoids and globulins are physiologically destroyed.[29] And it renders minerals less soluble by altering their physicochemical state.[30]

Cooking destroys the cells of fruits and veggies. Even frozen and packaged foods have been cooked. Processors blanch vegetables before freezing and packaging. The water is heated above 180° F for about three minutes — long enough to destroy the enzymes, which do not survive above 127°, some say 118° F.

"To have healthy cells, you must eat live fruits and vegetables. If you eat cooked and processed foods," wrote Charles Walters, editor of *Acres-USA,* "you are eating essentially embalmed foods. And so you are embalming yourself. When you cook, destroying the life force and enzymes, your body has to take enzymes it makes, mostly in the pancreas, and as a result they don't go to the glands in your system that need them to function properly. Ultimately, the store of pancreatic enzymes gets used up, leading to deteriorating health. And cooked food will either ferment or putrefy in your digestive system."[31]

When we overcook food, over process food, barbecue food, all past the "heat-labile" point, we change their chemical configuration. Nutritionist Nancy Appleton, Ph.D., expressed it this way: "We've evolved from early man able to eat food in a certain chemical configuration. With these new configurations, we don't have the right enzymes to digest it. The right digestive mechanism is another whole story in itself. But mostly due to processed foods and, of course, sugar in so many processed foods, we are getting degenerative diseases."[33] Burned and browned foods, highly heated fried foods, increased saturated fats, all these foods — and in particular those "convenience" foods laden with dangerous trans fatty acids — that make up a substantial part of the American diet, are greatly increasing our risk of cancer and of ill health in general.

A cooked-food diet, consumed over a period of years, "insures that your body will attempt to heal your bones and joints abnormally with resultant osteoporosis, arthritis, spurs, worn out cartilage, calcium deposits, and more."[34] Cooked food also alerts the immune system and raises the level of white blood cells. Paul Kautchkoff, M.D., demonstrated that the infection-fighting white blood cells increase in the blood 30 minutes after cooked (enzyme deficient) food is eaten. This shows the taxing effects of an enzyme-deficient diet on the immune system. The immune system is then in a constant state of readiness, lowering its reserve and its ability to resist infections and other stresses.[35] This, of course, elevates SIDS risk.

In Chapter 2 we reported that crib deaths ballooned after the early 1950s when fire-retardant and preservative chemicals were put into baby mattresses. In 1991, English researcher Peter Mitchell finally broke a seeming logjam that had been hindering thought about SIDS. He discovered that SIDS risk doubles from a mother's first to her second baby and doubles again from her second to her third. Infants of poor single parents have seven times greater risk than wealthy parents' babies.[36]

It seems reasonable to assume most families would not change their nutrition habits much during child-rearing years — at least, not enough to offset that increasing risk of toxic gases. So, how could nutrition make any significant difference in crib death? Dr. Jim Sprott concludes it does not.

In this chapter we reinforce some of that reasoning; but then we tell about practices, some of them nutritional, that could lower crib death risk. One hundred milligrams of vitamin C (as ascorbic acid) per day per month of age, used by Klenner and Kalokerinos (see Chapter 3), protected against SIDS. Vitamin C reverses the alkalinity required by those ubiquitous fungi to generate toxic gases. And so that therapy was chemical, not nutritional. For a family that does not want to go the BabeSafe® or mattress-wrapping route, that pattern of megadose ascorbate should serve the function.

Suppose a pediatrician or other doctor warns a mother who is using Kalokerinos' plan — against "too much" vitamin C. She follows the advice and the baby becomes a SIDS statistic — might the physician be held criminally liable?

Harold Foster, Ph.D., found that babies born with a low body supply of iodine frequently die of respiratory distress syndrome (RDS). And he shows high correlation of both RDS and SIDS incidence with low iodine.[40,41] But correlation doesn't prove causation. In RDS, lack of enough surfactant kills the baby. Surfactant is a one-cell-thick protective lining of alveoli, the tiny lung air sacs where exchange of carbon dioxide and oxygen is thought to occur. But that problem disappears by the end of the baby's first month, and SIDS generally occurs after one month. He does not provide any mechanism to kill a baby who is low in iodine and more than about a month old.

### SIDS MORTALITY RATE, 1984

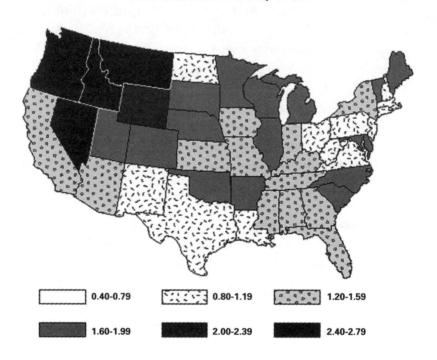

| 0.40-0.79 | 0.80-1.19 | 1.20-1.59 |
| 1.60-1.99 | 2.00-2.39 | 2.40-2.79 |

**Figure One.** A map of U.S. showing SIDS incidence, related to iodine intake.

Figure 1, a map of the United States, shows the shading is darkest where the SIDS rate was highest that year (1984). Incidence ranged from 5.0 per 1,000 in Alaska to 1.0 per 1,000 in the Southeast. SIDS risk was high where dietary intake of iodine is low; and low SIDS risk accompanied high iodine intake. All those SIDS rates are lower now, but the relationships among them probably have not changed. Also, the crib death rate today is about two times higher in states where goiter, associated with low iodine and other factors, was endemic before iodination of salt — than in the other states.[42] There still is no specific killing mechanism.

Similarly, Derrick Lonsdale, M.D., found that SIDS rates are high in areas where beriberi is common and low where intake of thiamine, its primary preventive, is ample.[43,44] He halted baby apnea and prevented what he judged to be inevitable SIDS deaths by supplementing thiamine.[45] But he, too, does not supply a mechanism. In a letter he told of a baby who nearly became a SIDS casualty from a slow carbon monoxide leak.[46] Even if there were a mechanism of killing, proof of any nutritional theory of SIDS would have to leap the five insurmountable hurdles we outlined at the end of Chapter 7 on *Infantile Heart Attacks as a Cause of Crib Death.*

Poor nutrition tends to accompany low-income status, and that leads to re-use of fungus-infected bedding. This explanation can lead to seeming absurdities, as well as perfectly sensible findings. In California, SIDS incidence in 1972 ranged from 0.51 per 1,000 among Chinese and Japanese Americans who consume iodine-rich seaweed, to 5.93 per 1,000 among Native Americans, who ingest little iodine.[47,48] One could reason that the incomes of the Oriental Americans were much higher than the Native Americans' and that they therefore did not resort as much to used baby mattresses.

But Figure 1[49] shows SIDS incidence at least twice as high in the Pacific Northwest as in California and the Pacific Southwest. That difference would be hard to explain by considerations of family income. Foster tells of a second SIDS risk factor compounding the risk from lack of iodine: low soil selenium. Selenium is low in the soils of the Pacific Northwest and other areas of high rainfall, but there still isn't any killing mechanism. So Sprott's, Peter Mitchell's and our theory of SIDS does not clarify everything. But it may well account for more than 95 percent of crib deaths. That is our estimate.

What about ear infections? What if baby screams with pain from one of them? William Campbell Douglass, M.D., tells mothers what to do about an ear infection.

Egyptian doctors knew, thousands of years ago, that an infection of tissues had to have the pus drained away or it would not heal. And doctors learned this principle in medical school: drain trapped pus.

Pediatricians, instead, assume that their antibiotic will kill all the bugs and that's that. The infection goes away temporarily and the doctor is a hero to the concerned mother. When the infection returns, which it often does, the mother doesn't realize that it's connected to the first infection and that the child has the same bacterium, which will become steadily more resistant with each infection to the only antibiotic the pediatricians seem to know — amoxycillin.

This recrudescence of the infection leads to "glue ear," deafness, and plenty of business for the ear, nose and throat (ENT) doctor who puts a little plastic tube through the ear drum to allow it to drain and thus prevent further middle-ear infection. So, as you can see, an incision was eventually made anyway — after the damage was done. If, with the first attack, the child had had an incision of the ear drum, or if the drum had been allowed to rupture, the journey to the ENT doctor (with hearing loss) would never have occurred.

Ear infections are the most common cause of children's hearing loss. Even worse, thanks to being overloaded with antibiotics, some of these children can now develop antibiotic-resistant pneumonia or meningitis and die.

Action to take:

(1) Do nothing but pain relief (children's Advil seems to work the best) and hot compresses; wait for the ear drum to rupture. The usual pain relievers must be used with caution in young children. Also, warm mineral oil dripped into the ear may be very helpful. I've heard a couple of drops of tea tree oil and lavender oil in each ear will work wonders.

2) At the first sign of an ear infection, drip 3 percent hydrogen peroxide into the ear. This may allay an infection of the middle ear. Try to keep the child lying with the infected ear down against the hot compress or heating pad to facilitate drainage.

3) If there is no improvement by the next morning, call an ENT specialist to see if the infected ear drum needs piercing.

Pediatricians can unthinkingly, and certainly unintentionally, promote crib death. Ear infections afflict two out of three American children before the age of two. American pediatricians write millions of prescriptions every year for antibiotics, hoping usually to cure these middle-ear infections, otitis media. In 1980, 876,000 prescriptions for cephalosporins were recorded for its treatment; by 1992, nearly 7 million. In 1999 approximately 30 million such prescriptions were written to treat an estimated 10 million cases.[49a]

These infections cause fevers, which promote higher toxic gas generation in beds of babies not protected by BabeSafe® or by proper mattress wrapping. And so, for unprotected babies, avoiding such infections can be expected to reduce SIDS risk; doing so also offers significant long-term health benefits. Below, we discuss several ways to prevent ear infections, and detail some of the ultimate rewards.

Antibiotics correct only the infectious symptoms caused by any germs, and not the cause. And they can cause diarrhea, leading to loss of valuable magnesium, zinc and other nutrients; this can weaken immune function.[50]

Antibiotic drugs also hinder phagocyte function.[51] Phagocytes are specialized white blood cells that ingest and destroy inappropriate cells, microorganisms and other foreign matter in the blood and tissues. (Chapter 6)

Antibiotics also destroy the immunity-building "friendly" bacteria in the gut along with the target disease germs, allowing harmful gut bacteria to proliferate. The gut endothelium, i.e., the lining, is the home of about 60 percent of humans' immune cells. And since bacteria in the gut — the alimentary canal and especially the intestines — generate needed vitamin K, antibiotics can deplete it along with calcium, magnesium, folic acid, potassium and vitamins B6 and B12.[52] Vitamin K offers immunity strengthening and other benefits, as well as preventing excess bleeding. It benefits long-term bone strength, calcium metabolism and more,[53,54,55] and it lowers risk of infantile as well as adult atherosclerosis.[56] Blood thinners including aspirin, other common medicines and excessive caffeine deplete body vitamin K stores, along with many other important micronutrients.[57]

Antibiotics abuse promotes development of resistant organisms.[58] Exposure to antibiotics enables bacteria to mutate, making themselves immune to those antibiotics. And these resistant bacteria can then spread their resistance to other bacteria. Moreover, long-term use of antibiotic drugs is the worst single cause of development in young adulthood of devestating yeast infections.[59]

Many, if not most, ear infections are viral rather than bacterial,[60,60a] and viruses do not respond to antibiotics. Moreover, 75 percent to 80 percent of these infections may result from allergies and food sensitivities typically caused by consumption of pasteurized, homogenized cow milk.[61] We saw in Chapter 4 that allergies are promoted by low body temperature and the presence of parasites, which prosper at lower temperatures. And so allergies are a bit quixotic.[61a]

Vaccinations can promote development of ear infections. Babies' liver function is affected for two to four weeks after DPT vaccination. If a new food such as cow milk or wheat is introduced during this period, the child's never-forgetting immune system may later react to that food as though it were DPT — that is, with an allergic or sensitivity reaction, which can cause SIDS-risky ear infections or worse.[62]

"Because pasteurized, homogenized cow milk is such a problematic food — not only often causing allergies, which can lead to chronic ear infections and colds, but also increasing the risk of diabetes and potentially affecting iron absorption — we recommend that children drink pasteurized cow milk rarely, if at all,"

> Switching early from breast to pasteurized cow milk increases risk of childhood diabetes, the most dangerous variety of America's fourth-leading killer (after heart attacks, cancer and prescription drug errors). This it accomplishes via a cellular and humeral immune response (see Chapter 6 on vaccinations), which may cross-react with a beta-cell antigen Children with this type I (insulin-dependent) diabetes typically drank pasteurized cow milk at an earlier age than others.[63]

advises Steve Austin, N.D.[64]

That advice, however, does not apply to certified raw milk. Natural milk products have a long history of conferring good health on residents in many parts of the globe. For example, three areas noted for the great longevity of local populations — the Caucacus Mountains in Russia, the village of Vilcabamba in Ecuador and the land of the Hunza in northern India — all use whole milk products. And Weston Price, studying isolated population groups in the 1930s, found many very healthy populations using cow milk as their principal food.[65] Milk products form the backbone of the Hindu diet.

J.E. Crewe at the Mayo Clinic in 1929 cured patients of anemia, hypertension, tuberculosis and many other diseases and conditions using large quantities of raw milk. In his work, pasteurized milk accomplished little against disease because, he wrote, the heat of pasteurizing destroys the enzymes in milk, needed for its complete utilization and to enable it to do its healing work.[66]

How does this natural, healing food get transformed into a liquid with such great health problems including allergens and carcinogens?

Sally Fallon, MA, and Mary E. Enig, PhD, explain:[67]

> Processing is the problem. The path that transforms healthy milk products into allergens and carcinogens begins with modern feeding methods that substitute high-protein, soy-based feeds for fresh green grass; and breeding methods to produce cows with abnormally large pituitary glands so that they produce three times more milk than the old fashioned scrub cow. These cows need antibiotics to keep them well.

> Their milk is then pasteurized so that all valuable enzymes are destroyed—lactase for the assimilation of lactose, galactase for the assimilation of galactose, phosphatase for the assimilation of calcium. Literally dozens of precious enzymes are destroyed in the pasteurization process; without them milk is very difficult to digest. The human pancreas is not always able to produce these enzymes; overstress of the pancreas can lead to diabetes and other diseases.

> The butterfat of commercial milk is homogenized, subjecting it to rancidity or, even worse, removed altogether. Skim milk is sold as a health food but the truth is that butterfat is in milk for a reason. Without it the body cannot absorb and utilize the vitamins and minerals in the water fraction of the milk.

Public health officials and the National Dairy Council have worked together in this country to make it very difficult to obtain wholesome fresh raw dairy products. However, they can be found with a little effort. In some states you can buy raw milk directly from farmers. Whole-pasteurized non-homogenized milk from cows raised on organic feed is now available in many gourmet shops and health food stores. It can be cultured to restore enzyme content, at least partially, as noted above. Cultured buttermilk is often more easily digested than regular milk; it is an excellent product to use in baking. (Quotation used with the authors' permission.)

Still other factors:

1) Researchers in Edinburgh, Scotland, found that infants less than 6 months old who lived in homes with air fresheners experienced 30 percent more ear infections (and also 22 percent more episodes of diarrhea) than babies not so exposed. From the air freshener they inhaled volatile organic compounds such as aldehydes, xylene and ketones.[68]

2) Smoking increases risk of respiratory infections, especially during the first two years of life. It also increases the number of new episodes and duration of otitis media with effusion. Particularly infants with lower birth weights had a high risk of recurrent otitis media during the first year of life with a heavily smoking mother.[69,70,70a] See also Chapter 2. Healthy newborns weighing less than 3.5 kg (7.7 lb.) at birth, when mother smoked 20 or more cigarettes per day, had threefold elevated risk for recurrent otitis media. Of course, all those infections bring risk of fevers, which promote SIDS through faster toxic gas generation if the baby is not protected from these gases.

The antibodies that the baby's body creates against allergens can attack and damage its nervous system. When gluten (in wheat, for example) was removed from diet in a test group, incurable neurological conditions got better over time—including Alzheimer's.[75]

Allergies, which can cause so many ear infections, can have other causes. Among these are traumatic emotional episodes[70] and habitual overbreathing, which can also cause asthma. Learned slight underbreathing using what is called the Buteyko Method can cure hyperventilation-caused asthma and often dispatches accompanying allergies (see Chapter 9).[71] Chlorinated water is allergenic to some; this can take many forms from skin rash to intestinal symptoms to arthritis, headaches and more.[72,73] Allergy and food sensitivity can also result from residues of farm antibiotics in common foods.[74]

Concerned mothers can minimize risk of allergies and also colic by rotating the formula the baby drinks. Use a four-day rotation; that is, change the type of formula daily for four days. A child may be able to safely and comfortably drink even a cow-milk formula if he or she does not drink it every day. Other options include rice-based beverages, goat milk or one of the hypoallergenic formulas. Rotating and not giving the infant the same food every day, she is less likely to develop a sensitivity or allergy to any one of them.

Detecting and correcting allergies and food sensitivities isn't terribly difficult. First, learn if a child is eating a food to which he or she reacts. "Compare the resting pulse-rate to that count a few minutes after eating a meal. If the pulse rate rises by more than five percent [e.g., heartbeat has risen from 80 to 84 per minute], the presence of an allergen in that meal is virtually confirmed."[75a] See also The Pulse Test (Barricade; revised 1994).

But which foods? Many children react with faster pulse to white sugar and white flour, confirming the wisdom of steering clear of them.

Parents can often detect causes of allergies and food sensitivities by keeping a 30-day food diary and using an elimination diet; eliminate one food at a time. In addition to true allergies, this detects non-allergy mediated food intolerances, which are responsible for a significant proportion of children's symptoms.[76,77] Or start a true fast under a physician's supervision; begin with pure water and add one food at a time.[78] One's favorite food could cause allergic or reactive symptoms. Some people can eliminate a severe allergy by consuming a very large quantity of the suspect food; this technique must be monitored by a health professional.[79]

---

*"If an antibiotic drug must be used, follow immediately with a healthy dose of probiotics containing lactobacillus acidophilus to prevent diarrhea and Candida overgrowth."*

---

If an antibiotic drug must be used, at the same time take a healthy dose of probiotics containing *lactobacillus* acidophilus to prevent diarrhea and *Candida* overgrowth. "Continue this about two weeks, after the antibiotic capsules or pills are gone. It is more health promoting to restore good bugs as competition for the bad. Remember that good bugs kill bad bugs and nourish the gut in the process."[80] To be effective the mixture must be guaranteed to contain some billions of organisms.[81]

Bacteria form the largest segment in the flora of the GI tract. Their number in the large bowel, about 60 trillion, exceeds the number of cells in the human body 10-fold,[82,83] even though in an adult they probably weigh only two and one-half to three pounds. "These bacteria synthesize half a dozen vitamins [notably B6, Chapter 7], adding to those obtained from food and supplements. They convert dietary fibers into small fatty acids that nourish the cells of the large intestine. They degrade dietary toxins and render them less harmful. And by crowding out pathogenic bacteria, the beneficial ones decrease the risk of food poisoning. They stimulate the development of a vigorous immune response; three-fifths of the body's immune system cells are located in the endothelium, the lining, of the small intestine."[84]

Getting a child off a food to which he shows an allergic or sensitivity reaction can improve behavior and learning. During a five-month test, one pupil doubled her school performance: from 4th to 8th grade level.[85]

Like the National Institutes of Health, we wholeheartedly advocate consumption of vegetables and fruits. But in quantity, only for those whose blood type makes these foods appropriate, via Peter d'Adamo (Sources of Information). The vegetables are best eaten raw, or lightly steamed. However, a diet excessively high in fruits, fruit juices and vegetables can be too alkaline; and a chronically alkaline diet can nudge the body into allergies. Since bacteria — like those mattress fungi discussed in Chapter 2 — love an alkaline environment, such a diet can also promote severe tooth decay. "If this applies to your baby, back off the carbohydrates and sugars (fruits, vegetables, fruit juices) for a while. Add some meat, whole grains and whole grain cereals," advises Bruce West, D.C.[86,86a] As to the claimed virtues of organic food, we refer readers to Chapter 9.

---

The antioxidant effect of green tea extracts was greater than that of ascorbic acid and equivalent to natural vitamin E in an in vitro (test tube) LDL-oxidation study. If completely absorbed, one cup of green tea per day may provide an adequate intake of protective polyphenols. Green tea, lacking any known adverse side effects, also has antibacterial properties, including help against bacteria that cause dental plaque.[87] Black tea, which is simply oxidized green tea, lacks most of those health benefits.[88]

---

Garlic supplies multiple antibiotic and antiviral (and a lot of other) benefits. And like vitamin C and other nutrient infection fighters, it doesn't discriminate against resistant organisms. Also, taking about 300 milligrams a day (not a large quantity) makes people's aortas a lot more flexible and delays progression of adults' arterial disease.[89] Millions of Greeks and Italians enjoy garlic's strong benefits along with a healthful Mediterranean-type diet.

But on a mostly processed food diet, garlic must be used

with caution, if at all.[90] Robert C. Beck, D.Sc., found that for people eating that way, garlic "triples the reaction time and desynchronizes the brain." He reported that military and airline pilots had long been warned not to touch garlic within 72 hours of starting a flight.[91]

Chlorophyll has proved to be a very valuable remedy for treating head colds, rhinitis, inner-ear infections and inflammations;[92,93,94] it might in that way help avoid heart attack SIDS. Homeopathic remedies such as arsenicum album, chamomilla, mercurius vivus, podophyllum and sulfur allowed children in a test group to recover much more quickly than those taking a placebo.[95] Consult a homeopathic practitioner or a nutritionist informed on the subject; see also Resources.

Pantothenic acid, sometimes called vitamin B5, can cure some allergies, and at 500 mg a day it is very effective at prevention.[96] Start low and increase the quantity. In "*Let's Get Well*," published in the 1960s, nutritionist Adelle Davis repeated the discovery of the great Roger Williams, PhD, and suggested pantothenic acid for allergy. One of the authors of this book found confirmation of Davis' advice. Coenzyme Q10 is also potent against allergies.[97] Eeither one might work for a baby; consult a knowledgeable practitioner on the quantities to use.

"Others routinely perform a 'liver detox.' Almost immediately, the foods they are presently allergic to, they become no longer allergic to. The detoxification works quickly, because the liver is filthy from just eating poor food and living in this contaminated environment."[98] For details see medical doctor Sherry A. Rogers' "*Wellness Against All Odds*" in Resources.

Miscellaneous. Taken before meals, professionally prepared enzyme supplements can largely replace the enzymes destroyed in cooking and other preparation. They can in that way promote digestion and assimilation.[99]

Taken between meals they attack disease organisms.[100] (See Resources.) For a baby, open the capsule and put a little of the powder into baby's food. For breastfeeding, make it into a paste with water and put on the nipples, as Dr. Lendon Smith long instructed mothers to do with ascorbic acid.

Snacking or, when to eat. Lower animals such as rats nibble or graze. Force-fed their same fodder in three meals daily, they become obese, cholesterol rises and sugar metabolism is deranged. Limited research suggests that dividing an unchanged human diet among six to 17 meals a day, on average lowers obesity, corrects carbohydrate metabolism, lipid metabolism and all other forms of metabolism as compared to matched controls on three meals a day.[101]

Seventeen meals a day are hardly practical, but five or six can be: three major meals and two or three snacks. Needless to say, snacks should be vegetable- and fruit-oriented like the meals, not doughnuts and chemicals-tainted "snacks." And food eaten early in the day is used better for energy than that eaten late in the day. The French, accordingly, eat their biggest meal at mid-day instead of at our dinnertime.[102]

In Chapter 9 we discuss a mélange of matters that will, we think, interest our readers.

## Chapter Nine

# LOOSE ENDS

T wo U.S. government agencies pursue policies that are harmful because they result from officials' failure, for whatever reason, to keep up with scientific research. We offer correct information that young parents can use instead of following those agencies' wrong advice. After that we take up other interesting and important odds and ends, some of them positive, to be encouraged, and others negative.

The Environmental Protection Agency (EPA) has a phobia about ultraviolet (UV) light. It warns, "Protect yourself from UV any time you can see your shadow." But in fact, moderate UV exposure promotes good health. A healthy baby, with fewer infections, will be less likely to suffer fevers that could promote toxic gas generation unless protected against toxic gases. The trace amounts of UV radiation in natural daylight are required for lifetime physical and mental health, civilized behavior, muscle strength, energy and learning.[1,2,3] Full-spectrum light is also helpful against seasonal and nonseasonal depression.[4]

To help minimize SIDS risk and promote maximum longterm health, mother and baby should seek moderate sustained outdoor exercise including some direct sun exposure. By sustained we mean all in one session. A mother might walk around the house 20 minutes or more during the day. But to exert healing effects the 20 minutes (or whatever time is used) need to be 20 consecutive minutes.

Start with about five minutes and vary the length of time in the sun to individual need. The huge benefits of full-spectrum light reach both mother and baby (and all of us) through the eyes and skin. If possible, while outdoors the mother should not wear any lenses and, in particular, no sunglasses. Even clear lenses filter out much of the needed UV.

---

*"A pregnant woman who stays indoors or who, following EPA advice, habitually wears sunglasses and sunscreens while outdoors increases her risk of having a SIDS-susceptible baby."*

---

People who deprive themselves of any UV exposure gradually ruin their disposition and their health. They increase their risk of multiple sclerosis,[5,6,7] heart attack,[8] schizophrenia,[9] Alzheimer's and Parkinson's diseases.[10] A pregnant woman who stays indoors or who, following EPA advice, habitually wears sunglasses and sunscreens while outdoors increases her risk of having a SIDS-susceptible baby. The pineal gland needs stimulus from daytime full-spectrum light through the eyes, to secrete needed melatonin at night. (Compare Chapter 2.)

Ordinary skin cancers, which can result from repeated moderate sun exposure, are harmless when promptly removed. Malignant melanoma, often wrongly blamed on sunshine, shows up on parts of the body that are seldom exposed to sunlight.[11] It afflicts mostly people who work primarily indoors,[12] typically exposed to fluorescent lighting.[13,14,15] Malignant melanoma can also result from taking contraceptive pills.[16] Excess exposure to the shortest-wave part of UV, as in tanning salons[17] or from extremely bright halogen lamps, can increase risk of neural tube birth defects by destroying folate in the body.[18]

Further caution: The chemicals in commercial sunscreens penetrate the skin, enter the circulation and add to the burden of poisons to be detoxified.[19] Natural, as well as commercial, sunscreens block needed skin synthesis of essential vitamin D3, which is not the same as the vitamin D that is added to milk. This lack hinders calcium absorption and can increase risk of the bone thinning of osteoporosis and hip fractures in later life.[20]

The word hormesis may be new to our readers. What does it mean? Just this: Increasing exposure to substances that are considered dangerous may reduce rather than raise risk.

First, we state the extreme position against any toxins. "There is no such thing as an 'acceptable risk' from carcinogenic or toxic pesticides known to harm the people who produce pesticide-treated food and those who eat it," says Michael Colby, executive director of Food and Water Inc., the national organization spearheading a movement for food safety. The EPA estimates that the average American child exceeds acceptable lifetime cancer risk (one-in-a-million) by the first birthday.

Many scientists, worldwide, agree that farm chemicals have no safe tolerance level. Since 1945 American farm use of insecticides has grown more than 10-fold; peeling fruits and vegetables discards bioflavonoids and valuable minerals and is futile anyway because many farm poisons are systemic - they penetrate the produce. Pesticide residues also lower the content of vitamin C, carotenes, naturally occurring sugars and starch, proteins, calcium and iron. The commercial farmer does not care about the health of consumers but only about his maximum financial bottom-line. The organic farmer does care. See also "Organic Foods," below.

The EPA admits that no toxicological data are available for more than three-quarters of the 1,700 chemicals that are officially known to be added to pesticides as so-called "inerts."[21] Even chemicals that have been banned for use as "active" ingredients can be added to a pesticide as long as they are classified as "inert" and are therefore unlabeled and kept secret from the public.[22] One of these is DDT.[23]

Meanwhile, under World Trade Organization rules, increased levels of DDT and other pesticides are allowed on imported produce — seemingly threatening further increases in breast cancer (but see *"A New Controversy Over Cancer"* below). "Much of the produce found in your local supermarket is imported from countries that have no regulatory agencies. Much is grown in unsanitary conditions using DDT — a pesticide banned for many years in this country."[24] But restricting food imports to maintain high nutrient quality or low toxicity is regarded as a trade barrier and is outlawed.

---

A study found the levels of intelligence-lowering, violence-promoting[25] lead in homes are highest at the entrances to houses, where people wipe their shoes. Small children crawl around and repeatedly put their hands into their mouths. Some discerning people remove their shoes on entering and ask guests to do likewise.

"Fluoridation increases lead exposure especially to children: (a) the fluoride (F) mixture added to drinking water often contains up to 400 mg of lead per liter; (b) The corrosive action of F extracts lead from pipes and solder joints. (c) Cheaper silicofluorides, used in 90 percent of American water fluoridation, cause people to absorb more of the lead to which they are exposed."[26,27,28]

---

Silicofluorides are waste products from phosphate fertilizer manufacture in Florida; they are banned from ocean dumping but approved for addition to drinking water! When fertilizer-plant waste was introduced into fluoridation of drinking water, the EPA and Public Health Service waived all testing procedures.[29] They cause people to absorb more lead; this blocks the action of calcium atoms in fostering production of neurotransmitters in the brain. Among these are dopamine and serotonin, which appear to suppress violent behavior. The finding came from statistical analyses of 25 communities in Massachusetts and 129 mostly rural communities in Georgia. People living there have higher blood levels of lead than people elsewhere. Cocaine addiction appears to be tied to low levels of dopamine in the brain; lead in the brain depresses dopamine levels.[30]

A frightening picture indeed.

So, does hormesis seem to deny almost all that? In truth, it denies a lot of it. The following examples will clarify its meaning.

(1) Researchers were surprised to find an inverse correlation of lung cancer to second-hand smoking, inhaling smoke of others. More smoke, less lung cancer.[31]

(2) Health is better rather than poorer as a result of low exposures to radiation and toxic chemicals. Giving Beagle dogs 10 parts per million of DDT in their diet improved their health.[32] "The natural intrinsic mutation rate is so high that we need extensive biochemical machinery to cope with it," wrote Arthur B. Robinson, Ph.D., president and research professor at Oregon Institute of Science and Medicine. "That machinery works better in the presence of low-level damage from extrinsic factors, and that damage improves our health. This discovery [unless it is simply ignored] is going to cause a virtual revolution in environmental politics."[33] See technical note below.

Early in 2000, U.S. government agencies finally admitted what close observers have known all along. People who have long worked at the Hanford Nuclear Reservation in Washington state and at 13 other sites around the country have been seriously over-exposed, have developed cancer and have died as a result.[34] They handled materials in great bulk and with limited understanding of the risks.[35] The handling methods have long since been corrected.

But people who worked in factories generating radioactive substances who followed appropriate safe-handling practices have had less cancer, enjoyed better immunity and lived longer lives than people who worked elsewhere.[36] Workers at Los Alamos received, on average, a three-fold higher exposure to plutonium than the maximum currently recommended by the National Council on Radiation Protection (0.01 Sv times age). The number of exposed workers who have died has been 57 percent lower than in the general population and 43 percent lower than among Los Alamos workers who were not exposed.[37]

Those who went into Hiroshima the first day after dropping of the A-bomb had less cancer, better immunity and longer lives than people who visited Hiroshima two or more days after the bomb. The same is true of low-level exposure to medical and dental X-rays. And fruit flies exposed to high levels of radiation experience many mutations. But fruit flies exposed first to low-level radiation experience far fewer mutations when then hit by the high radiation. Some animal data indicate that pre-exposure to low fluorine concentrations may provide some resistance to the lethal effects of fluorine in fluoridated drinking water.[38]

"The most sensible use of low-level radioactive waste," added Dr. Robinson, "is as an additive to concrete and insulation in residential homes - especially in areas where there is insufficient natural radiation for optimum health."[39]

(3) A chart relating risk of cancer to the level of radon gas in the home is J-shaped, we propose, rather than U-shaped as others suggest. Radon rises into houses from underground. At "very low" concentrations of radon the cancer risk is worse than at higher concentrations up to approximately 230 Bq per cubic meter of air, which is as far as the data extend.[40] Bq per cubic meter is the standard unit of measure.

In other words, the correlation between lung cancer and radon exposure is negative; and "p" is less than .001.[41,42] Somewhat higher levels of radon in homes yield lower incidence of lung cancer and other cancers, better immune systems and longer life. At very high radon concentrations such as in deep underground mines - the steeply rising arm of the "J"—the risk rises into the danger zone.[43,44,45]

Except for the statement in the preceding sentence, all this contradicts the "solidly established concept in environmental health that the effects of toxic agents fall on a continuum of biological change, ranging from undetectable effects at the lowest levels of exposure to severe health damage at very high doses."[46]

That concept is based on straight-line assumption; no tests have confirmed its accuracy around the lower end. It is nothing but an assumption.

---

**Technical Note:** "That linear, no-threshold theory is a logical consequence of the view that a single particle of radiation interacting with a single-cell nucleus can initiate a cancer; the number of initiating events is proportional to the number of particles of radiation, and hence to the dose. However, there is nothing in this line of reasoning about the role of biological defense mechanisms that prevent the billions of potential initiating events we all experience from each developing into a fatal cancer.

"A substantial body of evidence now indicates that low level radiation does indeed stimulate such biological defense mechanisms.[47,48] For example, human lymphocyte cells previously exposed to low level radiation suffer fewer chromatid breaks when later exposed to large radiation doses,[49] and this effect has been traced to stimulated production of repair enzymes by the low level radiation."[50,51] (Cohen BL. Test of the linear no-threshold theory of radiation carcinogenesis for inhaled radon decay products. Health Physics 1991; 68: 157-174.) In this article Cohen demonstrates many further examples of the strong healing response stimulated by low-dose radiation. The concept is revolutionizing health physics.

---

Well, how does all this relate to crib death? The National Institutes of Health and the EPA — flouting the past 50 years' health physics research — are conducting a scare-mongering campaign to lower household radon. This we hear incessantly on radio.

The EPA and NIH are thus promoting illness and increasing risk of fevers.[52] These can promote faster toxic gas production leading to crib death among babies who are not protected as described in Chapter 2. Now, it seems, they want to mandate "safety standards" for radon in drinking water, as well.[53] (No pun is intended).

The weakened immune systems of young mothers resulting from purposely lowering radon exposure in the air they breathe and the water they drink, and excessively lowering toxin exposure in the food will increase the risk of giving birth to a SIDS-susceptible baby. The baby itself may be more susceptible through neurotoxic gas-promoting fevers (Chapter 2) - and the father more likely to produce sick sperm.

Our recommendation: Paying a qualified contractor to measure radon to see if the level in the house is high enough to protect you is OK. As for mandated lower radon in drinking water, share the truth here presented with others. Such a mandate would not, however, be but a small fraction as harmful as a proposed federal mandate of fluoridated drinking water. See later.

The value of organic food can be considerably deflated, though not debunked. First, what is organic food? Food must have been produced on soils managed without spraying or artificial fertilization for at least three years, and preferably longer. There must be a proactive farm plan for improving soils and increasing biodiversity; and third-party independent certification is required.

Certified organic food is nutritionally superior. Bob Smith of Doctor's Data, West Chicago, Ill., found organic fruits and vegetables offered up to four times more trace elements, 13 times more selenium, 20 times more calcium and manganese than supermarket foods.[54,55] Virginia Worthington, Ph.D., a clinical nutritionist, found much higher levels of vitamins as well as desirable minerals.[56] Organic food often tastes better, too, because of the greater content of wanted minerals. And so it is probably well worth its extra cost.

---

*"If one extracted all the toxic compounds in a commercially grown vegetable and divided them into two piles — natural and synthetic — the natural pile would weigh, on average, several thousand times as much as the synthetic one."*

---

But the claimed lower toxicity of organic food is a chimera. Both Smith and Worthington reported they had found lower levels of toxic materials in organic produce. But they missed the big picture; they counted only a tiny fraction of the whole. "Amounts of synthetic pesticide residues on fruits or vegetables in a typical U.S.

supermarket are minuscule compared to the amounts of natural toxins these plant foods contain. If one extracted all the toxic compounds in a commercially grown vegetable and divided them into two piles — natural and synthetic — the natural pile would weigh, on average, several thousand times as much as the synthetic one. And some organic vegetables contain much higher levels of natural toxins than their ordinary supermarket counterparts."[57]

Toxins evolved in plants through natural selection, to protect them from hungry animals. To defend themselves, animals develop new abilities to detoxify the chemicals in the plants they eat. So the "arms races" between plants and animals continue indefinitely, leading to a huge development of toxins in plants and of resistant enzymes in animals.

"Many of these plant toxins seek to disrupt animal fertility by making chemicals that mimic the animals' reproductive hormone estrogen. The chemical structure of these phytoestrogens, as they are called, may not resemble estrogen; yet they can bind to the receptors in animal tissues that are designed to bind estrogen, leaving fewer receptors free to bind estrogen itself."[58] In the case of soy, phytoestrogens are so abundant they become dangerous. (See Chapter 8.)

A long-running controversy over cancer appears to have been resolved. Although widely blamed on toxic chemicals, cancer cannot exist in humans without intestinal parasites. Hulda Clark, Ph.D., N.D., proved this.[59] (See also Sources of Information). Thieu L. Nghiem, M.D., Ph.D., of Olympia Wash., confirmed that Clark is absolutely right. Nghiem is a medical scientist qualified in parasitology, who stands head and shoulders above the crowd of "scientists" who must "find" what the source of their grant wants — or be fired. Dietrich Klinghardt, M.D., Ph.D. and Louisa L. Williams, M.S., D.C., N.D., corroborated D. Clark's finding too. And they confirm her important discovery that isopropyl alcohol and other solvents destroy the tough shell surrounding the eggs of the human intestinal fluke, increasing the risk of cancer and more.[60] Isopropyl alcohol is widely used in hospitals, doctors' offices and at home in a variety of personal care products. The statement appears to be true of all cancers. Parasites enter the human body through dirty food and through broken areas of skin contacting polluted materials.

"The environment is of no importance in the etiology [development] of cancer. The notion of chemical and environmental agents causing cancer is derived from observations in laboratory animals. Parasites are the decisive etiologic factor in human malignancy."[61]

The following information, although technical, is so very important that we must ask our readers to try to understand this bombshell. Hartwig Schuldt, Dr. Med., Dipl. Ing, in Hamburg, Germany, uses bio-energetic therapy against cancer. It employs an electric current in the micro-amperage (millionths of an ampere) range for both diagnosis and treatment.

His technique diagnoses parasites much more accurately than conventional laboratory methods. In Western cultures, the most common are *Enterobius vermicularis* and *Taenia saginata*. In other parts of the world, other parasites can be involved. He uses various vermifuges to defeat parasites; vermifuges are substances whose function is to do exactly that. Diagnosis is accomplished in minutes; and it typically uncovers in a patient a variety of adverse health conditions.

The technique correctly diagnoses cancerous and other conditions that are not detected by conventional means, often at an early enough stage for preventive measures to start. All the cancer patients he has treated the past 22 years recovered completely from cancer and their other adverse conditions, and now enjoy normal health. He finds no evidence to support a genetic origin of cancer. The therapy appears also to resolve infection with HIV ("human immunodeficiency virus.") He uses homeopathic remedies to resolve a patient's conditions other than cancer.[62,63]

Luckily, Schuldt practices in Germany. If he tried to use those techniques in the United States, specifically California, he would be languishing in prison. Physicians are permitted to treat cancer only with chemotherapy, drugs and radiation.

Are the National Institutes of Health, the National Cancer

Institute and the rest of the cancer industry listening?

Yet Israel reduced breast cancer mortality by 50 percent from 1976 to 1986 while the disease was spreading everywhere else, even though risk factors associated with it, such as the use of excessive dietary animal fats rose. The reason for the decline: DDT and other pesticides in milk and other dairy products were banned there in 1978.[64,65] Their level had been excessive. As noted above, all people getting cancer also had to have parasites.[66] There again we see the "J." At low levels of toxins intake by Beagle dogs, the curve measuring risk slants down. But approaching some minimum (a level not yet known), the curve levels out, forming the bottom of the J. And to the right it rises gradually, then steeper and steeper, to much higher levels of risk than at very low concentrations.

---

*"The ecological disaster in the former Soviet Union provides a window on the future of America if environmental degradation is not taken seriously. "*

---

The ecological disaster in the former Soviet Union provides a window on the future of America if environmental degradation is not taken seriously. It illustrates the steep right-hand rising arm of the J. The following information is taken from Feshback M, Friendly A. Jr. *"Ecocide in the USSR."* NY: Basic Books Division of Harper Collins Publishers, 1992, and from *The Economist* magazine.

In the area around what is left of the Aral Sea in Uzbekistan of the former USSR (now a more or less independent state), two-thirds of babies were born with severe birth defects caused by mothers' ingestion of pesticide residues.[68] Drinking water was taken from "a brew of pesticides, defoliants, fertilizers and raw sewage, purified only partially in the towns by Soviet-era equipment."[69]

So much chemical waste has been dumped into the water supply that mothers in the Aral region cannot breastfeed their babies without running the risk of poisoning them. And "every pregnant woman examined by Dr. Andrei Vervikhvost, head of a maternity unit in Nukus, in the Oxus delta, was found to be anemic. He attributes the anemia to poor nutrition, bad water and the generally unhealthful environment."[70]

Concentrations of DDT measured in fish in the USSR ranged from 0.09 percent to 4.24 percent.[71] That is 4.24 parts per hundred, not parts per billion, or ppb, the usual unit of measurement for toxins. Since one billion is 1,000 million, 4.24 percent would be 4.24 x 10 million parts per billion or 42,400,000 parts per billion. Concentrations in people who had been poisoned by DDT must then have been many, many times higher than in the United States and Europe.[72]

Brilliant confirmation of our theme on hormesis appears in *Paracelsus to Parascience: The Environmental Cancer Distraction,* by Bruce N. Ames and Lois Swinsky Gold. The treatise was submitted to Mutation Research Frontiers and is available

---

The area of Cleveland, Ohio, peeked into the "window on the future" and pulled back in the 1950s-1960s. Ms. Chris Carson of Olympia, Wash., told vividly, the Cuyahoga River burned time after time when she was growing up, and so the fire department bought a fireboat. She told of people who had migrated from the South catching fish from that chemical slime that were obviously cancer-ridden - to eat![73]

---

from the Division of Biochemistry and Molecular Biology, University of California at Berkeley, Berkeley, CA 94720.

Ames and Gold discuss the facts that: 1. Toxicity is dose-dependent; 2. Natural chemical exposures far exceed synthetic; 3. Insufficiency of micronutrients is carcinogenic; and 4. Large expenditures of resources on imagined dangers from trace chemical exposures harm cancer victims by diversion of attention from real risks.[74]

Yet cancer is by no means the whole story. When American children's blood pesticide levels were lowered by as little as one-tenth of a part per billion, their IQ improved by five to all of 15 points. Such findings about effects on intelligence appear to contradict the proven principle of hormesis. How they will ultimately be reconciled with it remains to be seen. And although pesticide residues are not known to cause SIDS, neither have they been proven not to cause it.

For every molecule of pesticide and other toxin to be detoxified, a molecule of the major antioxidant superoxide dismutase (SOD) is sacrificed. SOD supplements are useless because stomach acids destroy them, but enough dietary and supplemented selenium encourages the body to generate its own SOD.[75] The selenium must be one member of a broad supplements program accompanying a sensible diet. (See Chapter 4.)

Minimizing exposure to all these exotoxins, we are told, is crucially important for the pregnant mother. Prenatal exposure to any of seven heavy metals including cadmium, lead, mercury and nickel lowers a child's cognitive skills at 3 years of age and increases the number of childhood illnesses reported. Such sicknesses can cause fevers, which would promote toxic gas generation and SIDS in babies not protected against the gases. These statements, too, appear to conflict with hormesis. Exotoxins are poisons that enter the body from the environment (broadly defined to include diet); endotoxins originate inside us.

Sherry A. Rogers, M.D., points out that the typical American baby's mattress outgases carcinogenic formaldehyde from the foam stuffing, also pesticides and carcinogenic dyes used to produce the colors. The crib headboard or bed frame is usually constructed of particleboard, pressed wood shavings glued together with a urea-formaldehyde resin.

Disposable diapers are made of a bleached paper that emits a slow, steady dose of carcinogenic dioxins. The newborn baby gets his nutrition from a plastic bottle lined with a plastic baggie that outgases phthalates (plasticizers), which can be measured in his bloodstream. As for baby food, one jar of meat mixture (all brands) contains 100 times the EPA daily limit for dioxins.[76] All these might make a baby more susceptible to SIDS caused by a given level of gas.

But might some or all of them be on the gently downward sloping left side of our "J"? One can't do a controlled trial using babies. A group would be exposed as Rogers outlines, another group not so exposed. But of course such comparisons are out of the question, so we'll probably never know.

The formula he drinks, continues Rogers, is deficient in the essential fatty acids needed to promote optimum brain development, prevent later learning and behavior difficulties and more,[77] as well as further to strengthen immunity. That confirms the evidence we presented in Chapter 4.

Habitual Deep Breathing: Do not do it, except during strenuous physical exertion and at high altitudes. We have all heard advice to inhale more oxygen; some nurses even instruct a mother to lift her baby's arms up and down rhythmically to inculcate the habit of deep breathing. But this advice is based on no objective evidence at all. Ancient Eastern cultures do teach deep breathing, but the breath is exhaled very slowly, keeping the CO2/oxygen ratio amply high.

Konstantin Buteyko, M.D., Ph.D., of Siberia found that over-breathing creates literally a multitude of problems including high blood pressure and angina in adult life, asthma and allergies.[78] Asthma and allergies could potentially cause fevers and so promote toxic gas generation in unprotected babies' beds.

Learned underbreathing can often ameliorate or even eliminate these problems.[79] In Russia the Buteyko Method, here sketched, is considered applicable in treatment of 150 diseases,[80] after conventional medical practice failed. This may seem surprising until one looks at the scope of physiological effects connected with carbon dioxide. Buteyko breathing yields the same health benefits claimed by practitioners of Qi Gong in China and

Pranayama in India. The physiological changes that result are similar, although Qi Gong and yoga are associated with deep slow breathing.

The Buteyko Method, using breath holding while in training and the controlled reduction of ventilation, is thought to be quicker and more direct. One who has learned this system has the advantage that the breathing control center in the brain wants less air than before. And so from then on, using the Method requires little if any conscious attention. Buteyko's therapies are officially recognized and widely practiced in Russia and several other former Soviet republics. They are practiced in England and Australia,[81] and attempts are being made to organize training classes in America.[82]

In 1979, formula manufacturers reduced fluoride (F) in their products to a "low" level. But years later, P.J. Riordan, Ph.D., reported a 2.8-fold increase in risk of fluorosis associated with early cessation of breast-feeding.[83] The mother's body appears to filter some F out before nourishing her baby. D.G Pendrys, M.D., and colleagues reported a 3.3-fold increase in risk of fluorosis associated with infant formula based on pasteurized, homogenized cow milk. They also noted a seven-fold increase in risk of fluorosis with soy-based infant formula.[84]

Fluorosis results from excessive ingestion of fluoride, and is hugely worsened by processed-food diets. It starts as discoloring and softening of teeth and spreads to the skeleton causing a multitude of health problems.

Twenty-five percent of American children take fluoride (F) supplements;[85] some prescribing physicians fail to consider total intake without the supplements.[86] If the water, too, is fluoridated, a child's exposure can be eight times greater than established U.S. safety levels.[87] F at much lower levels suffices to reduce intelligence in children as, shown in IQ tests,[88,89] and in adults as revealed in clinical and laboratory observation.[90,91] Other ill effects of fluoride are legion.[92]

Drinking-water fluoridation may increase risk of Down syn-

drome and crib death;[93,94] perinatal deaths were 15 percent higher
in fluoridated parts of Britain than in unfluoridated areas.[95] A possible mechanism: F atoms appear to carry viral particles and
increase their ability to penetrate tissues;[96] this would increase risk
of fevers leading to higher toxic gas generation.

Most water filters do not remove fluoride. A reverse-osmosis
water purifier that removes 87 to 93 percent of fluoride and comparable percentages of other toxins, is known as The Duchess. It
retailed for $650 but was available at discount. Current availabil-
ity is not known

Mercury fillings or dentist-installed root canals in the mother's mouth potentially create infections anywhere in her body[97]
and can promote fever-generating, toxic-gas promoting infections
in the baby.[98,99] Placing or removing mercury fillings during pregnancy can worsen SIDS risk. Unless proper protective measures
are used, during the procedure the mother inhales and swallows
mercury.

Other assorted helpful practices: Get outdoors into parks, near
beaches and waterfalls, and in mountains. The air there is filled
with negative ions, which build health and good feeling.

Abundant houseplants. The Russians discovered and NASA
confirmed, houseplants relieve indoor air of trichloroethylene
(dry cleaning fluid), formaldehyde and benzene, the most common household pollutants. What is poison to mothers, fetuses and
babies, and to the rest of us, is food to the plants. Each species
specializes in consuming a particular chemical; and so a variety of
indoor plants strongly promotes health.[100] If the level of toxins is
not lowered enough to increase risk through hormesis, that would
include fewer toxic gas-promoting fevers.

Music: Peter Tompkins and Christopher Bird showed in "The
Secret Life of Plants" that plants exposed to classical music
thrived, those inflicted with rock music withered or died. It is the
same with people. Prayer and various techniques of meditation
have been proved to succeed. Also see Sources of Information.

# Appendix

There is another side to autism. Stephen B. Edelson, M.D., of Atlanta, Ga., specializes in environmental medicine. Among 100 autistic children he treated in the past five years, all had fetal overloads of heavy metals, usually mercury, tin and lead. And many had fetal brain concentrations of fatty poisons (the brain is 65-70 percent fat) 1,000 to 26,000 percent higher than in the blood among a sample of 500 healthy adults! All the 100 have defective liver detoxification; nearly all have allergies/food sensitivities and were eating deficient diets.

By detoxifying these children, Edelson brings many up 65 percent to 75 percent, in one case to 96 percent of normal. The detoxification uses medically supervised sauna at 160°F (20 minutes, four times a day), individualized nutritional supplementation of a wide variety, EDTA chelation and many other methods. At a conference he showed movies of children before and after treatment; audience impact, even only hearing the audiocassette, was enormous.

So it seems the MMR vaccine may only precipitate a symptom complex that is already developing. (EDTA is ethylene diamine tetraacetic acid.)

Developmental pediatrician Mary Megson, M.D., greatly strengthens autistic children's condition using a variety of treatments including, most importantly, the RDA level of natural source vitamin A in cod liver oil. (Natural cod liver oil also supplies important omega-3 essential fatty acids and vitamin D.) After starting this single supplement, many aphasic children start talking, begin to exhibit more socially appropriate behavior and experience other health benefits.

- Edelson SB, Cantor DS. Autism: Xenobiotic influences. *Toxicology & Industrial Health* 1998; 14; 4: 553-563.
- Edelson SB. Speech and workshop Neurotoxic etiology of the autistic spectrum disorders. ACAM (American College of Advancement in Medicine) Spring conference, Orlando, FL, Mar 1999.
- Edelson SB. Speech and workshop. Neurotoxic etiology of the autistic spectrum disorders. Op. cit.
- Megson M. Interview on Bland JS, *Funct Med Update* 1999; Sept.

# Measures

## 1. How to Wrap a Baby's Mattress to Prevent Cot Death

The advice to wrap mattresses applies to every mattress on which a baby sleeps (except a BabeSafe® mattress) and includes mattresses of other children; adults' mattresses; and all mattresses made of or containing natural products such as sheepskins, goatskins, kapok, tree bark, coconut fibre.

The most convenient way to wrap a baby's mattress for cot-death prevention is by means of a BabeSafe® mattress cover. These covers are manufactured in six sizes and are available at baby-care retail outlets throughout New Zealand and by mail order in some other countries. As an alternative, parents can make mattress wraps using specified polythene sheeting. If this option is selected, the following instructions apply:

1. Use thick, clear (not colored) polythene [same as polyethylene] sheeting. The thickness of the polythene must be at least 125 microns. Do not use PVC (polyvinyl chloride) for mattress wrapping.

2. Place the polythene over the top of the mattress and down the ends and sides, and secure it firmly on the underside of the mattress with strong adhesive tape.

3. The polythene on the underside of the mattress should not be airtight. It must be airtight on the top and sides, however. It is imperative to use the correct bedding on top of a BabeSafe® mattress, BabeSafe® mattress cover or polythene-wrapped mattress. Use a fleecy pure cotton underblanket and tuck this in securely. Then make the bed using sheets and pure woolen or pure cotton overblanket/s. Do not use any type of moisture-resistant mattress protector, sheepskin, sheep fleece underlay, acrylic blanket, sleeping bag or duvet. BabeSafe® mattresses, BabeSafe® mattress covers and polythene-wrapped mattresses should be cleaned by wiping with pure soap and water. Do not use chemical bleaches or sterilants.

*Used by permission of Dr. T.J. Sprott.*

The manufacturers of BabeSafe® mattress covers solicit further expressions of interest from overseas distributors, who are invited to contact Dr. Sprott at:

>T.J. Sprott, OBE, MSc, PhD FNZIC
>10 Combes Rd.,
>Remuera, Auckland 5, New Zealand.
>www.cotlife2000.com
>sprott@iconz.co.nz
>Phone and fax: 011-64-9-5231150

Neither he nor the authors of this book have any financial relationship with the manufacturers.

**U.S. sources of BabeSafe® mattress-covers:**

>Denton Davis, M.D.,
>8381 El Paseo Grande
>La Jolla, Calif. 92037
>(619) 456-5897
>drd@criblife2000.com

>Health Freedom Nutrition, LLC
>(800) 976-2783
>(707) 284-3129 (fax)
>www.hfn-usa.com

**2. To defeat an infection and to minimize the after-effects of any kind of stress — and to stop an incipient infection "at the pass."**

See Chapter 3. The quickest approach is to grind up "vitamin C" tablets from Lifestar Millennium, San Rafael, Calif. (415) 457-1400. Those tablets include the entire vitamin C complex, including bioflavonoids. Add the contents of grape-seed extract capsules, which also contain the entire C-complex.

Begin to do this at the first tickle in the throat, the first unusual sneeze or after any unusual event that makes one feel unusually stressed and tired. There will be false alarms — but who cares?

Make a paste of all that with a little water, adding the contents of a vitamin A or cod-liver oil capsule. Add ground-up magnesium tablets and ground-up zinc lozenges to the mixture. Also add contents of Juice-Plus or Noni tablets. Then spread the paste liberally on any convenient part of the skin. This paste will store very well, so do not discard any but keep for later use.

Short of that, grind up "vitamin C" (ascorbic acid) tablets to make the same paste. Add quercetin, echinacea and any other parts of the C-complex from a health food store or mail order. Again, add vitamin A, magnesium and zinc. If fighting an infection, also take enzymes and extra Juice-Plus or Noni capsules between meals.

### 3. To restore low body supply of iodine.

If thyroid deficiency symptoms persist even while consuming olive and coconut oils, a mother can easily detect and correct this deficiency. Get a small bottle of inexpensive, dark-red iodine tincture from a drug store. Carefully "paint" about a one-by-two-inch swath of leg skin (the red liquid stains clothes, so let it dry).

Unless a trace is visible 24 hours later, the body needs more iodine. Do this daily until the trace remains 24 hours later; repeat occasionally to maintain the "visible 24 hours later" status.

This perfectly safe self-treatment, (references 173,174 from chapter four) usable by anyone except the few who are allergic to iodine, can mitigate many hypothyroid conditions. Unbeknownst to many pediatricians and gynecologists, doing so is extremely important for the health of both mother and baby.

In some cases, a natural thyroid glandular supplement containing prescribed ratios of T4 and T3 serves better; it can be used only under supervision of a health professional.(reference175 from chapter four) T3 is the active form of thyroid; the body converts T4 into T3.

- PPNF Health Journal, 1998; Apr.
- Douglass WC. Second Opinion 1998; June.
- Lita Lee, PhD with Lisa Turner and Burton Goldberg. The Enzyme Cure. Future Medicine Publishing, Tiburon, Calif., 1998.

# SOURCES

## Nutritional Supplements
Health Freedom Nutrition, LLC
(800) 976-2783
(707) 284-3129 (fax)
www.hfn-usa.com

## Juice-Plus
- (503) 526-8728.
- www.juiceplus.com/usos/1628800.asp
- www.juiceplus.allaire.net

## Noni Juices
- Life Balances International. (503) 244-4777.
- www.lifebalancesintl.com
- www.healthwiz.com

## Vitamin C complex
- Lifestar Millennium. San Rafael, CA (415) 457-1400.
  Vitamin and mineral products genuinely made from food;
  more expensive as a result.

**Also N-zymes,** a combination of professionally prepared plant
enzymes.
- A variety of professionally prepared enzymes:
  Lita Lee, Ph.D., P.O. Box 516, Lowell, Ore. 97452.
  (541) 937-1123.
  litaleephd@aol.com

## Grape seed extract
- Two good brands are Country Life and Enzymatic
  Therapies; both are available in health food stores.

## Microhydrin
- Philpott Medical Services 17171 SE 29th St., Choctaw,
  OK 73020 (405) 390-3009
- James A. Bonnell (517) 773-9716
- Also katfiedler@aol.com or (860) 434-9249.
  Also (800) 266-6801.

# Sources of Information

For a directory of physicians who use alternative techniques call:

1.   **Life Extension Foundation,** (800) 841-5433
2.   **Murdock Pharmaceuticals/NuPro, Inc.** (800) 962-8873
3.   **New Age Journal Publications** (800) 782-7006.

(Other directories may be or become available.)

---

How to find a nutritionally oriented physician for a reliable nutritional checkup. Call or write for the name of a physician in your area. If you write, send long, self-addressed stamped envelope.

1.   **American Preventive Medical Association**
     PO Box 458
     Great Falls, VA 22066
     (703) 759-0662

2.   **Journal of Orthomolecular Medicine**
     16 Florence Ave.
     Toronto, Ontario, Canada M2N 1E9
     (416) 733-2117

3.   **American Association for Naturopathic Physicians**
     601 Valley St., Suite 105
     Seattle, WA 98109
     (206) 298-0126

4.   **American College for Advancement in Medicine**
     23121 Verdugo Dr., Suite 204
     Laguna Hills, CA 92653
     (Send self-addressed, long envelope with postage for two ounces.)
     Web:http://www.acam.org

# Alternative Physicians

**Check the yellow pages for naturopaths.** In some states, they offer limited prescription writing; they will refer a patient to an M.D. if necessary. All these doctors hope so to improve your well-being that you will seldom need prescriptions and will want to refer your health-seeking friends.

- Alternative Medicine Yellow Pages, Future Medicine Publishing. 21 Tiburon Blvd., Tiburon, CA 94920.

- Alternatives for the Health Conscious Individual. C/o Mountain Home Publishing. PO Box 829, Ingram, TX 78025. Publishes monthly. Dr. David Williams.

- American Academy of Environmental Medicine, PO Box 16106, Denver, CO 80216; 303/622-9755. Treats people with allergies, sensitivities, adverse reactions to chemicals and pollutants.

- American Association of Naturopathic Physicians, 2366 Eastlake Ave., Suite 322, Seattle, WA 98102; (206) 323-7610. Provides names and addresses of naturopaths (NDs).

- American Chiropractic Association, 1701 Clarendon Blvd., Arlington, VA 22209; (703) 276-8800.

- American Preventive Medical Association, 459 Walker Rd., Great Falls, VA 22066;1 (800) 230-2762.

- Dr. Robert Atkins' Health Revelations is published monthly. 819 N. Charles St., Baltimore, MD 21201. (410) 895-7900.

- Health Alert c/o Dr. Bruce West, 5 Harris Ct., #N6. Monterey, CA 93940. Publishes monthly.

- National Center for Homeopathy, 801 No. Fairfax, Ste. 306, Alexandria, VA 22314. (703) 548-7790.

- Organic Network, 12100 Lima Center Rd., Clinton, MI 49236-9618; (517) 456-4288. Provides information on suppliers of organic foods.

- Raymond Peat, Ph.D. Ray Peat's Newsletter. PO Box 5764, Eugene, OR 97405; www.efn.org/~raypeat. (Very technical.)
- Dr. Sherry Rogers' Total Health. C/o Prestige Publishing, PO Box 3068, Syracuse, NY 13220. 1 (800) 846-6687, (315) 455-7862. Published monthly.

- Second Opinion is published monthly by William Campbell Douglass, MD, PO Box 467939, Atlanta, GA 31146-7939. (404) 668-0432.

- Townsend Letter for Doctors and Patients, 911 Tyler St., Port Townsend, WA 98368-6541; (360) 385-6021. Eleven issues a year.

- What Doctors Don't Tell You is published monthly by the organization of that name, at 819 North Charles St., Baltimore, MD 21201.

---

## Chapter Two

Dr. Jim Sprott. *Cot Death Cover-up?* Auckland: Penguin-NZ, 1996. Available from Sprott for $20 U.S. 10 Combes Rd., Remuera, Auckland 5, New Zealand.

http://www.cotlife2000.com
emailto: sprott@iconz.co.nz
Phone and fax: 011-64-9-523115

- Robert O. Becker, MD. Cross Currents, The Perils of Electropollution. *The Promise of Electromedicine*. Jeremy P. Tarcher Inc., 1990.

---

## Chapter Three

- Archie Kalokerinos, M.D. *Every Second Child*. New Canaan, CT: Keats Publishing, 1982.

## Chapter Four

- K. Morales, Charles B. Inlander. *So You're Going to Be a Mother.* Allentown, PA; People's Medical Society, 1995.

- Preconception Care Foundation Inc., 5724 Clymer Rd., Quakertown, PA 18951.

- Aspartame Consumer Safety Network, PO Box 780634, Dallas, TX 75378; (214) 352-4268.

- John R. Lee, MD. Natural Progesterone, What Your Doctor May Not Tell You About Menopause, and What your Doctor May Not Tell You About Premenopause. Available from bookstores.

## Chapter Five

- American College of Nurse-Midwives, 1522 K St., NW, Washington, DC 20005; (202) 347-5445.

- Informed Birth & Parenting, PO Box 3675, Ann Arbor, MI 48106; (313) 662-6857.

- International Childbirth Education Assoc., PO Box 20048, Minneapolis, MN 55420; (612) 854/8660.

- Midwives Alliance of North America (MANA), PO Box 1121, Bristol, VA 24203; (615) 764-5561.

- National Association of Childbirth Assistants, 219 Meridian Ave., San Jose, CA 905126. (409) 225-9167.

- International Lactation Consultants Association (ILCA), 200 N. Michigan Ave., Chicago, IL 60601.

- La Leche League International (ILLLI), 1400 North Meacham Rd., Schaumburg, IL 60173-4840.

- In 1993, Australia's Campaign Against Fraudulent Medical

Research published carefully documented evidence of fraud in many American drug trials. The Pharmaceutical Drug Racket, Parts 1 and 2. CAFMR, John Lesso Coordinator. PO Box 234, Lawson, NSW 2783, Australia.

---

## Chapter Six

- Neil Z. Miller. Immunization: Theory vs. Reality. Expose on Vaccinations. Santa Fe, NM: New Atlantean Press, 1996.

- New Atlantean Press, PO Box 9638-925, Santa Fe, NM 87504. The world's largest selection of vaccine information. Free catalog.

- National Vaccine Information Center/Dissatisfied Parents Together (NVIC/DPT). 512 W. Maple Ave., #206. Vienna, VA 22180; 1 (800) 909 SHOT (7468) or (703) 983-DPT3. Publishes The Vaccine Reaction, a national, bimonthly subscription newsletter.

- Health Alternatives & Vaccine Awareness Committee. (HAVAC). PO Box 881-A, Trabuco Canyon, CA 92678. (714) 589-0932.

- National Health Federation (NHF). PO Box 688-R, Monrovia, CA 91017. (818) 357-2181. Nonprofit consumer rights and health freedom organization, publishes Health Freedom News bimonthly.

- The International Vaccination Newsletter. C/o Kris Gaubloumme, M.D., Krekenstrasat 4, Genk N-3600, BELGIUM. Phone 011-32-11-227869. Quarterly networking publication to provide accurate, critical information about vaccinations; linking people and organizations throughout the world who are in this field.

# Reliable Laboratories

- Doctor's Data, PO Box 111, West Chicago, IL 60185;1 (800) 323-2784. Doctor-referred testing for hair minerals and urine and blood amino acids.

- Great Smokies Diagnostic Laboratory. 18-A Regent Park Blvd., Asheville, NC. 1 (800) 522-4762. Specializes in testing for parasites in stool, bacterial overgrowth of the small intestine; comprehensive digestive and stool analysis, liver detoxification profile, intestinal permeability, lactose intolerance and oxidative stress.

- Lendon H. Smith, M.D., *Feed Your Body Right*. M Evans & Co., Inc., NY: 1994. I have worked with John Kitkoski, who put the Life Balances Program together (1 (800) 488-2840). With his help I wrote the book. The program removes the guesswork from supplementation. By a combination of the standard blood test (24-chemical screen, complete blood count), and a complete history of diseases and lifestyle, the methodology can produce for the participant a comprehensive, scientifically oriented program of what supplements would be most appropriate for an individual's health. The blood analysis is run through a computer and the results are charted according to the deviation from the mean.

The main ingredients of the program are (1) electrolytes to be taken with milk or juice, (2) 20 bottles of vitamins and minerals that one takes depending upon the subjective response from smelling the contents, and (3) six dropper bottles of minerals that may be needed for those with nutrient deficiencies. The program is compatible with other modalities of therapy including chiropractic, naturopathy, homeopathy, psychology and massage. It will allow those other methods to produce results more surely and more rapidly.

# Books

Most of these books can be ordered through bookstores; in a few cases, access phone numbers are shown.

- Peter d'Adamo, MD. *4 Blood Types, 4 Diets Eat Right 4 Your Type*.

- Nancy Appleton, Ph.D. *Licking the Sugar Habit; A Life Saving Guide*, 1996.

- Russell L. Blaylock. *Excitotoxins: The Taste that Kills*. Santa Fe, NM: Health Press, 1994.

- Hulda Clark, Ph.D., N.D. The Cure for All Cancers. www.naturalearthdirection.ow/markets/product/itm00255.htm.

- Mary G. Enig. *Trans Fatty Acids in the Food Supply:* A Comprehensive Report Covering 60 Years of Research, 1993. Enig is a leading authority on fats, oils and related matters. She is widely published over the past 35+ years.

- Sally Fallon, M.A., and Mary G. Enig, Ph.D. *The Ploy of Soy*. $10; 1 (888) 593-8333.

- SS. Hendler. *The Doctors' Vitamin and Mineral Encyclopedia*. NY: Simon & Schuster, 1990.

- Hal A. Huggins, D.D.S., M.S. and Thomas E. Levy, M.D., J.D. *Uninformed Consent. The Hidden Dangers in Dental Care*. Charlottesville, VA: Hampton Roads Publ., 1999. 1 (800) 766-8009)

- Archie Kalokerinos, M.D. *Every Second Child*. New Canaan, CT: Keats Publ, 1982.

- John R. Lee, M.D. *Natural Progesterone: The Multiple Roles of a Remarkable Hormone*. BLL Publ, Sebastapol, CA:, BLL Publ, 1993; See also above for Lee's other books.

- Lita Lee, Ph.D. (chemistry). *Radiation Protection Manual*, 3rd edition, 1990. PO Box 516, Lowell, OR 97452.

- Lita Lee, Ph.D., with Lisa Turner and Burton Goldberg. *The Enzyme Cure*. Future Medicine Publishing, Tiburon, Calif., 1998.

- Joseph Mercola, D.O. *Healthy Natural News You Can Use*. http://www.mercola.com

- Waivers to excuse a child from vaccinations, state by state. www.mercola.com Inquiries: Mercola@pol.net

- Linus J. Pauling, Ph.D. *How to Live Longer and Feel Better.* NY: Avon Books, 1987.

- Weston Price, D.D.S. *Nutrition and Physical Degeneration.* 6th ed. New Canaan, CT: Keats Publ, 1997.

- James S. Privitera, M.D., and Alan Stang. *Silent Clots: Life's Biggest Killers.* Covina, CA: The Catacombs Press. (818) 966-1618.

- Sherry A. Rogers, M.D. *Tired or Toxic?* Syracuse, NY: Prestige Publishing, 19901.

- *The E.I. Syndrome*

- *You Are What You Ate*

- *The Cure Is in the Kitchen*

- *Wellness Against All Odds.* Syracuse, NY: Prestige Publ, 1994.

- *Depression: Cured at Last.* Sarasota, FL: SK Publishing, 1996.

- William Sears, *M.D.D. S I D S: A Parent's Guide to Understanding Sudden Infant Death Syndrome.* Boston: Little, Brown, 1995.

- Lendon Smith, M.D. *How to Raise a Healthy Child.* NY: M. Evans, 1996.

- *Sounds of Healing:* A Physician Reveals the Therapeutic Power of Sound, Voice, and Music. By Mitchell Gaynor, M.D. Broadway Books, 1999.

- Dr. Bruce West. The cholesterol folly, in *Total Health and Wellness for the 1990s.* Carmel, CA: West Publ, 1990.

- Dr. David G. Williams. *Miracle Healer: D.M.S.O.* Sixth Ed, 1997. Ingram, TX: Mountain Home Publishing, 1997.

- *Wolf's Digest of Alternative Medicine: A Plain English Resource on the Science of Health,* PO Box 2049, Sequim, WA 98382-2049. 1 (800) 683-7014.

- *World Research News.* World Research Foundation. 41 Bell Rock Plaza, Sedona, AZ 86351.

# REFERENCES

## CHAPTER TWO

1. Sprott TJ. Interview in Vancouver, BC, June 10, 1999.
2. Cullen WR, Reimer KJ. Arsenic speciation in the environment. *Chem Rev* 1989;89:713-764.
3. Greenwald MJ. SBS and SIDS. *Annals of Emergency Medicine* 1984; 13;22:1.
4. Decreased kainate receptor binding in the arcuate nucleus of the sudden infant death syndrome. *Jour Neuropathology & Experimental Neurology* 1997;56;11:1253-1261.
5. Rajs J, Hammarquist F. Sudden infant death in Stockholm. A forensic pathology study covering ten years. *Acta Paediatr Scand* 1988;77:812-820.
6. Bergman AB, Pomeroy MA, Beckwith JB. The psychiatric toll of sudden infant death syndrome. *Gen Practice* 1969;40:6.
7. French JW, Beckwith JB, Graham CB, Guntheroth W. Lack of postmortem radiographic evidence of nasopharyngeal obstruction in the sudden infant death syndrome. *Jour Pediatrics* 1972;81:1145-1147.
8. Scheibner VS. Shaken baby syndrome. *Nexus* 1998;Aug/Sept:31-34, 75.
9. Viera Scheibner, PhD, *VACCINATION*. 100 Years of Orthodox Research Shows that Vaccines Represent a Medical Assault on the Immune System. Blackheath, NSW 2785, Australia: Australian Print Group, 1993.
10. Scheibner VS. Shaken baby syndrome.
11. New Zealand Ministry of Health, Dec. 24, 1999.
12. Sprott TJ. Personal communication, 2000.
13. Sprott TJ. Personal communication, 2000.
14. Gosio B. Azione di alcune muffe sui composti fissi d'arsenico. *Rivisto d'Igiene e Sanita Publica.* 1892;3:201-230,261-273.
15. Gosio B. Action de quelques moisissures sur les composes fixes d'arsenic. *Arch Ital Biol* 1893;18:253.
16. Sprott TJ. The Cot Death Cover-up? Auckland: Penguin Environmental-NZ, 1996 (available from Dr. Sprott for US$20.00).
17. Richardson BA. Cot mattress biodeterioration and SIDS. *Lancet* 1990;335:670.
18. Richardson BA. Sudden infant death syndrome: A possible primary cause. *Jour Forensic Science Society* 1994;34:199-204.
19. Sprott TJ. *The Cot Death Cover-up?* Op. cit.
20. Sprott TJ. *The Cot Death Cover-up?*
21. Knobel HH, Yang WS, Cjen CJ. Risk factors of sudden infant death in Chinese babies. *Amer Jour Epidemiology* 1996 Dec. 1;144; 11:1070-1073.
22. Denton Davis. A simple explanation for SIDS (crib deaths). *Healthy Natural News You Can Use* #132, 1999;Dec. 19. www.mercola.com.
23. Skadberg BT, Morild I, Markestad T. Abandoning prone sleeping: Effect on the risk of sudden infant death syndrome. *Jour Pediatrics* 1998;132;2:240-243.
24. Mitchell EA, Tuohy PG, Brunt JM et al. Risk factors for sudden infant death syndrome following the prevention campaign in New Zealand: A prospective study. *Pediatrics* 1997;100;5:835-839.

25.  Gibson AAM. Current epidemiology of SIDS. *Jour Clinical Pathology* 1992;45(suppl):7-10.
26.  Sudden Infant Death Syndrome (SIDS). Report of the expert working group into the hypotheseis that toxic gases evolved from chemicals in cot mattress covers and cot mattresses are a cause of SIDS. London: HMSO; May,1991.
27.  Fitzpatrick M. SIDS and the toxic gas theory (ltr). *New Zealand Med Jour* 1998;Dec. 11:482-483.
28.  Sprott TJ. *Cot Life* 2000. 1999;May.
29.  Fitzpatrick MG. *New Zealand Med Jour,* 1998.
30.  Sprott TJ. *Cot Life* 2000 1998;July:1-3.
31.  Rognum TO, Sanstad OD, Ovasater S, Olarsen B. Elevated levels of hypoxanthine in vitreous humor indicate prolonged cerebral hypoxia in victims of sudden infant death syndrome. *Pediatrics* 1988;82:615-617.
32.  Ray M. Fountain of health. Lecture tape, 1996.
33.  Harman D. Role of free radicals in the aging process. Speech to conference on Aging Healthfully: *Nutrition Perspective,* New York.
34.  Myers R. FHES: Flanagan Hydrogen Enhanced Silica. Ranson Hill Press, 1998.
35.  Tyler J. *Sudden Infant Death (S.I.D.S): Probable Cause and Simple Prevention.* NY: Sterling Publ., 1986.
36.  Poets CF, Samuels MP, Noyes JP et al. Home event recordings of oxygenation, breathing movements, and heart rate and rhythm in infants with recurrent life-threatening events. *J Pediatrics* 1993;123:63-701.
37.  *Nurses Dictionary,* 15th ed. Roper N, Ed. Churchill, Livingstone, 1978.
38.  Bunn HF, Poyton RO. Oxygen sensing and molecular adaptation to hypoxia. *Physiological Rev* 1996;76:839-885.
39.  Halliwell B, Gutteridge JMC. *Free Radicals in Biology and Medicine* (3rd ed). Oxford: Oxford Univ., Press, 1998.
40.  Halliwell B, Gutteridge JMC. *Free Radicals in Biology and Medicine.* Op. cit.
41.  Rogers SA. IP6: The taming of the cancer cell. *Dr. Sherry Rogers' Total Wellness* 1999;June:2-4.
42.  Gunn AJ, Gluckman PD, Gunn TR. Selective head cooling in neonatal infants after perinatal asphyxia: A safety study. *Pediatrics* 1998;102:885-892.
43.  Biagas K. Hypoxic-ischemic brain injury: Advancements in the understanding of mechanisms and potential avenues for therapy. *Curr Opin Pediatr* 1999;11:223-228.
44.  Waters KA, Meehan B, Huang JQ, Gravel RA et al. Neuronal apoptosis in sudden infant death syndrome. *Pediatric Research* 1999; 45;2:166-172.
45.  Meyn ER. Programmed cell death in normal development and disease. *Cancer Bull* 1994;46:120-124.
46.  Filiano JJ, Kinney HC. Arcuate nucleus hypoplasia in the sudden infant death syndrome. *J Neuropathol Exp Neurol* 1992;51:394-403.
47.  Waters KA, et al. Neuronal apoptosis in sudden infant death syndrome. Op. cit.
48.  Tyler J. *Sudden Infant Death (S.I.D.S).* Op. cit.
49.  Leist M, Nicotera P. Apoptosis, excitotoxicity, and neuropathology. Exp Cell Res 1998;239:183-201.
50.  *Applied Organometallic Chemistry* 1997;11:471-483.
51.  Sprott TJ. *The Cot Death Cover-up?* P.45.
52.  Sprott TJ. Personal communication, 1999. Readers will note quite a number of such entries. They represent research that Dr. Jim Sprott has completed but has not yet published.

53.    Sprott TJ. *Idem*. P 45.
54.    Sprott TJ. *Cot Life 2000*. 1998;March:2.
55.    Rogers SA. *Dr. Sherry Rogers' Total Wellness* 1999;Feb:p. 3.
56.    Eustace Mullins. *Murder by Injection: The Medical Conspiracy Against America*. Staunton, VA: National Council for Medical Research, 1988.
57.    *Health Naturally,* July 1993.
58.    Suzman MM. Personal communications, 1984-1992.
59.    Cross T et al. Gas phase cigarette smoke (CS) induces lipid peroxidation in human plasma. *Free Rad Biol Med* 1990;9(suppl):69 (Abstr.)
60.    Klonoff-Cohen S et al. The effect of passive smoking and tobacco exposure through breast milk on sudden infant death syndrome. *JAMA* 1995;273;10:795-798.
61.    Holborow P. Cot deaths linked to diet. *Soil & Health* (New Zealand) 1994;Oct/Nov:8.
62.    Klonoff-Cohen S et al. *The effect of passive smoking and tobacco exposure.* Op. cit.
63.    Ponsonby A-L, Dwyer T, Kasl SV, Cochrane JA. The Tasmanian SIDS case-control study: Univariable and multivariable risk factor analysis. *Paediatric & Perinatal Epidemiology* 1995;9:256-272.
64.    Fleming PJ, Blair PS, Bacon C et al. Environment of infants during sleep and risk of the sudden infant death syndrome: Results of 1993-5 case-control study for confidential inquiry into stillbirths and deaths in infancy. *BMJ* 1996;313:191-198.
65.    Carpenter R, Shaddick CW. Role of infection, suffocation and bottle-feeding in cot death. From *Proc. of the Conference on Sudden Death in Infancy*. Seattle, Sept. 1963.
66.    Avery M, Frantz I. To breathe or not to breathe; What we learned about apneic spells and SIDS. *New Eng J Med* 1983;309:107-108.
67.    US Dept. Health & Human Services. *The Health Consequences of Involuntary Smoking: A Report of the Surgeon General*. Washington, DC: US Govt Printing Office, 1986:38-59.
68.    Naeye R. When mom smokes, umbilical cells shrivel. *Med World News* 1981;Jan 5:37-38.
69.    Smoke gets in your cervix and fetus. *Sci News* 1996(May 4);149: 282.
70.    Sprott TJ. Personal communication, 1999.
71.    Sprott TJ. *The Cot Death Cover-up?*
72.    Sprott TJ. *The Cot Death Cover-up?*
73.    Sprott TJ. Telephone interview, 1999; Oct. 6.
74.    Sprott TJ. Personal communication, 1999.
75.    Sprott TJ. Personal communication, 1998.
76.    Carpenter FG. *Role of infection, suffocation and bottle feeding in cot-deaths.*
77.    Carpenter R, Shaddick CW. Role of infection, suffocation and bottle-feeding in cot death. *Br J Prev Soc Med* 1965;19:1-7.
78.    *Los Angeles Times* 1999;Apr. 7.
79.    Sprott TJ. Personal communication, 1999.
80.    Guntheroth W. *Seattle Post-Intelligencer* 1991;ltr.
81.    West B. *Health Alert* 1997(May);14;5:6.
82.    *Pediatrics* 1996;June.
83.    *Pediatrics* 1996;June.
84.    Idem.

85. Rajs J, Hammarquist F. *Sudden infant death in Stockholm.* Op. cit.
86. Ponsonby A-L, Dwyer T, Couper D, Cochrane J. Associations between use of a quilt and sudden infant death syndrome: Case-control study. *BMJ* 1998;316:196-197.
87. Report: U.S. slips in fight to cut infant mortality. *Los Angeles Times/Press & Sun Bulletin* 1999;March 1; p. 1A.
88. Constantin E, Waters KA, Morielli A, Brouillette RT. Head turning and face-down positioning in prone-sleeping premature infants. *Jour Pediatrics* 1999;134:558-562.
89. Sprott TJ. *Cot Life 2000,* 1999;Spring.
90. Sprott TD. Medical and physiological theories for the cause of cot death: All refuted by epidemiology. *Cot Life 2000,* 2000;Feb:1-3
91. Willard HN. *Life Situations, Emotions and Dyspnea in Lifestress and Bodily Disease.* Baltimore: Williams and Wilkins, 1950, p. 583.
92. Brown EB. Physiological effects of hyperventilation. *Physiological Rev* 1953;33: 445-471.
93. Tyler J. *Sudden Infant Death (S.I.D.S).* Op. cit.
94. Kohlenderfer K, Kiechl S, Speri W. Living at high altitude and risk of SIDS. *Arch Dis Child* 1998;79:506-509.
95. Rajs J, Hammarquist F. Sudden infant death in Sweden. *Acta Paediatr Scand* 1988;77: 812-820.
96. Sprott TJ. Personal communication, 1999.
97. Rajs J, Hammarquist F. *Sudden infant death in Stockholm.* Op. cit.
98. Pall ML. Personal communication, 1999.
99. Sprott TJ. Personal communication, 1999.
100. Sears W. *S I D S. A Parent's Guide to Understanding and Preventing Sudden Infant Death Syndrome.* Boston: Little, Brown, 1995.
101. Mosco S, Richard C, McKenna J. Infant arousals during mother-infant bed sharing: Implications for infant sleep and sudden infant death syndrome. *Pediatrics* 1997;100;5: 841-849.
102. Mosko S, Richard C, McKenna J et al. Maternal proximity and infant CO2 environment during bedsharing and possible implications for SIDS research. *Am J Physical Anthropology.* 1997;103;3:315-328.
103. Doyle LW, Charpak N. Kangaroo mother care (KMC). *Lancet* 1997; 350:1721-1722.
104. Ruiz-Pelaez JG et al. Kangaroo mother versus traditional care for newborn infants </= 2000 grams: A randomized, controlled trial. *Pediatrics* 1997;100: 682-688.
105. Sears W. *S I D S.* Op. cit.
106. Rajs J, Hammarquist F. *Sudden infant death in Stockholm.* Op. cit.
107. Paul Brodeur, Currents of Death. NY: Simon & Schuster, 1989.
108. Lita Lee, PhD (chemistry). *Radiation Protection Manual,* 3rd edition, 1990. PO Box 516, Lowell, OR 97452.
109. Hileman B. Health effects of electromagnetic fields remain unresolved. *Chem Eng News* 1993;Nov:15-29.
110. Ott JN. Lecture tape, 1991.
111. Selye H. Forty years of stress research: Principal remaining problems and misconceptions. Can Med Assoc J 1976;155;1:53-56.
112. Selye H. *The Stress of Life.*
113. Maes W. Baubiologie. *Lecture to World Research Foundation,* 1991.

114.  Maes W. Baubiologie. *PPNF Health Jour* 1990. 14:1-12.
115.  Portier CJ, Wolfe MS, eds. *Assessment of health effects from exposure to power-line frequency electric and magnetic fields.* Quality paperback, gratis. Natl Institutes of Environmental Health Sciences, PO Box 12233, MD A3006, Research Triangle Park, NC 27709 USA. 508 pages.
116.  Maes W. Baubiologie. *PPNF Health Jour* 1990. Op. cit.
117.  Belanger K, Leaderer B et al. Spontaneous abortion and exposure to electric blankets and heated water beds. *Epidemiology* 1998 (Jan.);9:36-42.
118.  Savitz D. *Amer Jour Epidemiology* 1990.
119.  Murphy PJ, Myers BL, Badia P. Nonsteroidal anti-inflammatory drugs alter body temperature and suppress melatonin in humans. *Physiol Behav* 1996;59:133-139.
120.  Science News 1992(Aug 8);144:109.
121.  Life Extension Foundation. *Life Extension Update* 1993;June.
122.  Oxidation strongly linked to aging. *Sci News* 1993;Aug 14:109.
123.  Sandyk Reuven. Interview on Bland JS, *Prev Med Update* 1996;Dec.
124.  Grimes DS. Sunlight, cholesterol and coronary heart disease. *Quarterly J Medicine* 1996;89:579-5891
125.  Grimes D. Interview by Kirk Hamilton, PA-C, "The Experts Speak," *Clinical Pearls News* 1997(Sept.);7;9:99,109-111.
126.  Coogan PF et al. Occupational exposure to 60-Hertz magnetic fields and risk of breast cancer in women. *Epidemiology* 1996; 7:459-464.
127.  Carpenter D. *Biological Effects of Electric and Magnetic Fields* (2 vol). Academic Press Inc., 1994.
128.  Magnetic field therapy. Chapter in *Alternative Medicine: The Definitive Guide.* Tiburon, CA: Future Medicine Publ., 1995.
129.  Philpott W. *Philpott Medical Services,* 1998.
130.  Jones R. EMFs. (Australasian) *Health & Healing 1999;18;3(May-July):18-20.*
131.  Lita Lee, PhD. *Radiation Protection Manual,* 3rd edition, 1990. PO Box 516, Lowell, OR 97452.
132.  Paul Brodeur, *Currents of Death.* NY: Simon & Schuster, 1989.
133.  Carpenter D. *Biological Effects of Electric and Magnetic Fields* Op. cit.
134.  Ponsonby A-L et al. Free-flow waterbeds are potentially deadly to infants. *Med J Australia* 1995;162:391-392.
135.  Brodeur P. *Currents of Death.* Op. cit.
136.  Lee L. *Radiation Protection Manual.* Op. cit.
137.  Scott-Morley AJ. *Geopathic Stress and its Significance.* Institute of Bioenergetic Medicine, Dorset, England, 1985.
138.  Thunell-Read J. Geopathic stress. *Int Jour Alt & Complementary Med* 1994;Apr:17-19.
139.  *Deadly Zones, Degeneration from Geopathic Interference.* Available from The Royal Rife Research Society, 7040 Avenida Encinas #104-291, Carlsbad, CA 92009.
140.  Gordon R. *Are you sleeping in a safe place?* Dulwich Health Society, 130 Gipsy Hill, London SE19 1PL, England, 1993.
141.  Cowan D, Girdlestone R. Safe as Houses? *Ill Health and Electro-Stress in the Home.* Bath, UK: Gateway Books, 1995.
142.  Antonova AE, Fligel DS, Dovbnja BV. Some properties of geomagnetic field pulsations in the 0.1-1.0 Hz frequency range: A quantitative description and comparison with the satellite and ground-based observations. *Planetary Space*

*Sci* 1981;29:793-801.
143.  O'Connor RP, Persinger MA. Geophysical variables and behavior: LXXXV. Sudden infant death, bands of geomagnetic activity, and PC1 (0.2 to 5 Hz) geomagnetic micropulsations. *Perceptual & Motors Skills* 1998;88;391-397.
144.  Pozo D, Reiter RJ, Calvo JR et al. Inhibition of cerebellar nitric oxide synthase and cyclic GMP production by melatonin via complex formation with calmodulin. *Jour Cellular Biochemistry* 1997;65:430-442.
145.  O'Connor RP, Persinger MA. Op. cit.
146.  O'Connor RP, Persinger MA. Op. cit.
147.  Fraser-Smith AC. Some statistics on pcl geomagnetic micropulsation occurrence at middle latitudes: Inverse relationship with sunspot cycle and semi-annual period. Jour Geophysical Research, *Space Physics* 1970;75:4735-4745.
148.  Mitchell EA, Stewart AW. Deaths from sudden infant death syndrome on public holidays and weekends. *Aust NZ Jour Med* 1988;18: 861-863.
149.  Ponsonby A-L et al. Op. cit, 1995.
150.  Gordon R. *Are you sleeping in a safe place?* Op. cit.
151.  Cowan D, *Girdlestone R. Safe as Houses?* Op. cit.

## CHAPTER THREE

1.  Dettman G, Kalokerinos A, Dettman I. *Vitamin C: Nature's Miraculous Health Missile*. Melbourne: Frederick Todd, 1993.
2.  Sprott TJ. *Cot Death Cover-Up?* Penguin Health Environmental-NZ, 1996.
3.  Sprott TJ. Personal communication, 1999.
4.  Lewin S. *Vitamin C. Its Molecular Biology and Medical Potential*. NY: Academic Press, 1976: p. 231.
5.  Stone I. *The Healing Factor: "Vitamin C" Against disease*. NY: Grosset & Dunlap, 1972.
6.  Douglass WC. *The Milk Book*. Atlanta: Second Opinion Publ, 1994.
7.  Stone I. *The Healing Factor: "Vitamin C" Against Disease. Op. cit.*
8.  Ely JTA. Ascorbic acid and other modern analogs of the germ theory. *Jour Orthomolecular Med* 1999; 14; 3:143-156.
9.  Cheraskin E. *Vitamin C: Who Needs It?* Birmingham, AL: Arlington Press & Co., 1993.
10.  Klenner FR. Observations on the dose and administration of ascorbic acid when employed beyond the range of a vitamin in human pathology. *Jour Applied Nutr* 1971;23:61-88.
11.  Morishige F, Murata A. Vitamin C for prophylaxis of viral hepatitis B in transfused patients. *J Intl Acad Prev Med* 1979; 5: 54-58.
12.  Javert C, Stander HJ. Plasma vitamin C and prothrombin concentration in pregnancy. *Surgery, Gynecol & Obstet* 1943; 76: 115-122.
13.  Klenner FR. The treatment of poliomyelitis and other viral diseases with vitamin C. *Southern Med Surg* 1949; 101: 209-214.
14.  Klenner FR. Massive doses of vitamin C and the virus diseases. *Southern Med and Surg* 1951; 103: 101-107.
15.  Klenner FR. Significance of high daily intake of ascorbic acid in preventive medicine. *J Prev Med* 1974; Spring: 45-69.

16. Cathcart RF III. The method of determining proper doses of vitamin C for the treatment of disease by titrating to bowel tolerance. *J Orthomolecular Psych* 1980; 10(2): 125-132.
17. Ely JTA. Ascorbic acid and other modern analogs of the germ theory. *Op. cit.*
18. Smith LH. *Clinical Guide to the Use of Vitamin C. The Clinical Experiences of Frederick R. Klenner, MD.* Portland, OR: Life Sciences Press, 1988.    P. 26.
19. Pauling LJ. *How to Live Longer and Feel Better.* NY: Avon Books, 1987:p. 413.
20. Ely JTA. Ascorbic acid and other modern analogs of the germ theory. *Op. cit.*
21. Klenner FR. Observations on the dose and administration of ascorbic acid when employed beyond the range of a vitamin in human pathology. *Op. cit.*
22. Javert C, Stander HJ. Plasma vitamin C and prothrombin concentration in pregnancy. *Op. cit.*
23. Williams DG. *Miracle Healer: DMSO.* Sixth Ed, 1997. Ingram, TX: Mountain Home Publishing, 1997.
24. Wright JV. Unpublished memo, 1993
25. Hoffer A, Osmond H, Callbeck MK, Kahan I. Treatment of schizophrenia with nicotinic acid and nicotinamide. *Jour clin Exp Psychopathol* 1957;18;2:131-158.
26. Bland JS. *Funct Med Update* 1998;June.
27. Semba RD. Vitamin A as "anti-infective" therapy, 1920-1940. *Jour Nutrition* 1999;129: 783-791.
28. Golden I. *Vaccination? A Review of Risks and Alternatives.* 1995.
29. Bellavite P, Signorini A. *Homeopathy: A Frontier in Medical Science.* Berkeley, CA: North Atlantic Books, 1995.
30. Podmore ID, Griffith HR et al. Vitamin C exhibits pro-oxidant properties. *Nature* 1998; 392: 559.
31. Bland JS. *Funct Med Update* 1998;June.
32. Noroozi M, Angerson WJ, Lean ME. Effect of flavonoids and vitamin C on oxidative DNA damage to human lymphocytes *Am J Clin Nutr 1998;* 67: 1210-1218.
33. Cathcart RF III. Interview on Bland JS. *Prev Med Update* 1994; Sept.
34. Rogers SA. Reader's question of the month. *Sherry Rogers' Total Wellness* 1998; Dec: 5.
35. *Cancer Research* 1999; Sept. 15.
36. Valdes-Dapena M. The pathologist and the sudden infant death syndrome. *Amer Jour Pathology* 1982; 106: 118-131.
37. Rognum TO, Sanstad OD, Ovasaeter S, Olarsen B. Elevated levels of hypoxanthine in vitreous humor indicate prolonged cerebral hypoxia in victims of sudden infant death syndrome. *Pediatrics* 1988; 82: 615-617.
38. Pauling LJ. *Vitamin C, the Common Cold and the Flu.* SF: 1976.
39. Selye H. *The Stress of Life.* NY: McGraw-Hill, 1978.
40. Klenner FR. The clinical evaluation and treatment of a deadly syndrome caused by an insidious virus. *Tri-State Med Jour* 1957; June.
41. Klenner FR. Significance of high daily intake of ascorbic acid in preventive medicine. *Jour Preventive Med* 1974; Spring: 45-69.
42. Ely JTA. Ascorbic acid and other modern analogs of the germ theory. *Op. cit.*
43. Thieu L. Nghiem, MD, PhD. Interview, 1999.
44. Tainsh AR. Second thoughts on beri-beri. *Townsend Ltr Doc/Patients* 1998; Nov: 78-82.
45. Pauling LJ. *How to Live Longer and Feel Better. Op. cit.*

46.  Levine M, Conry-Cantilena C, Wang Y et al. Vitamin C pharmacokinetics in healthy volunteers: Evidence for a recommended dietary allowance. *Proc Nat Acad Sci* USA 1996; 93: 3704-3709.

47.  Cathcart RF III. Lecture, 1982.

48.  Miller NZ. *Immunization: Theory vs. Reality. Expose on Vaccinations.* Santa Fe, NM: New Atlantean Press, 1996.

49.  Phillips A. Vaccination: Dispelling the Myths. *Nexus New Times Magazine* 1997; 4; 76(Oct/Nov): 17-22,74.

50.  Dettman GC, Kalokerinos A. Ascorbate intake of Fijians. *Med Jour Australia* 1977; 26: 2-5.

51.  Kalokerinos A. *Every Second Child.* New Canaan, CT: Keats Publ, 1982.

52.  Cathcart RF III. The method of determining proper doses of vitamin C for the treatment of disease by titrating to bowel tolerance. *J Orthomolecular Psych* 1980; 10; 2:125-132.

53.  Kalokerinos A. *Every Second Child. Op. cit.*

54.  Every Second Child. *Op. cit.*

55.  Dettman G, Kalokerinos A, Dettman I. *Vitamin C: Nature's Miraculous Health Missile. Op. cit.*

56.  Dettman G, Kalokerinos A, Dettman I. *Op. cit.*

57.  Kalokerinos A, Dettman G. The spark of life. *Health and Healing, Journal of Alternative Medicine* 1981; 1: 15-19.

58.  Scheibner VS. Personal communication, 1995.

---

# CHAPTER FOUR

1.   Weston Price, DDS. *Nutrition and Physical Degeneration. A Comparison of Primitive and Modern Diets and Their Effects.* Sixth ed. Price-Pottenger Nutrition Foundation, 1989. Introduction, p. 3.

2.   Abrams, *Food and Evolution.* 1987.

3.   William Rea, MD. Lecture, 1999.

4.   Lendon Smith, MD. *How to Raise a Healthy Child.* NY: M. Evans, 1996.

5.   Shull F. *Townsend Ltr Doc* 1989; Mar (ltr).

6.   Lendon Smith, op. cit.

7.   U.S. General Accounting Office, *Special Supplemental Food Program for Women, Infants and Children,* 1995. Reported by Physicians Committee on Childhood Hunger, Tufts University, School of Medicine.

8.   Belanger K, Leaderer B et al. Spontaneous abortion and exposure to electric blankets and heated water beds. *Epidemiology* 1998 (Jan.); 9: 36-42.

8a.  Smith LH 1996, p.12.

9.   Savitz D. *Amer Jour Epidemiology* 1990.

10.  Adams MM. *The continuing challenge of preterm delivery.*

10a. Health vectors. *Health & Healing Wisdom of Price-Pottenger Nutrition Foundation* 1998; 22; 1: 6-7. From Reddy S, Sanders TAB, Obeid O. The influence of maternal vegetarian diet on essential fatty acid status of the newborn. *Eur J Clin Nutr* 1994; May: 48; 5: 358-368.

11.  Bergman AB, Ray G, Pomeroy MA, Wahl PW, Beckwith JB. Studies of the sudden infant death syndrome in King County, Washington. III. Epidemiology.

*Pediatrics* 1972; 49; 6: 860-870.

12. Lendon Smith. Op. cit.
13. Robert Zimmerman, University of Michigan psychology department.
14. Billions can be saved with vitamin regimen. *Health Notes* 1997; Dec: 3.
15. Schmidt M. Interview on Bland JS. *Prev Med Update* 1995;Nov.
15a. *JAMA* 1995; 273; 9: 739-740.
16. Nelson KB, Grether JK. Can magnesium sulfate reduce the risk of cerebral palsy in very low birthweight infants? *Pediatrics* 1995; 95: 263-269.
17. Shanahan K. Three months pregnant, no weight gain. *Villager AllHealth.com.* 1999; Sept.17.
18. Smith LH. Op. cit. p. 11.
19. Hunter A. Food allergies and hereditary illness — Is this the solution? *Int Jour Alt Comp Med* 1999; Oct: 13-18.
20. Hughes DA. The influence of the diet on the maturation of the immune system. *Allergy* 1998; 53 (suppl 46): 26-28.
21. Hamilton K. *Clin Pearls News* 1999; Aug: 150-151.
22. Lendon Smith, op. cit.
23. Campbell JD. Minerals and disease. *J Orthomolecular Med* 1995; 10: 177-188.
24. Price W. *Nutrition and Physical Degeneration.* Op. cit.
25. Pottenger F. *Pottenger's Cats.* La Mesa, CA: Price-Pottenger Nutrition Foundation, 1983.
26. Underwood EJ. *Trace Elements in Human and Animal Nutrition,* Manganese. NY: Academy Press, 1977: 170-195.
27. Hidiroglou M, Williams CJ, Siddiqui IR, Khan SU. Effects of manganese deficit feeding to ewes on certain amino acids and sugars in cartilage of their newborn lambs. *Am J Vet Res* 1979; 40: 1375-1377.
28. Ashton B. Manganese and man. *J Orthomolecular Psychiatry* 1980; 9: 237-249.
29. Passwater RA, Cranton EM. *Trace Elements, Hair Analysis and Nutrition.* New Canaan, CT: Keats Publ., 1983: 161-169.
30. Profet M. *Protecting Your Baby-to-Be. Preventing Birth Defects in the First Trimester.* Reading, MA: Addison-Wesley Publ, 1995.
31. Brandes JM. First trimester nausea and vomiting as related to outcomes of pregnancy. *Obstet Gynecol* 1967; 30: 427-431.
32. Weigel RM, Weigel MM. Nausea and vomiting of early pregnancy and pregnancy outcomes: A meta-analytical review. *Br J Obstet Gynecol* 1989; 96: 1312-1318.
33. Smith LH. Op. cit.
33a. Smith LH 1996 p. 9.
34. DiAdamo P. *4 Blood Types, 4 Diets.*
35. Lindenbaum J, Healton EB, Savage DG et al. Neuropsychiatric disorders caused by cobalamin deficiency in the absence of anemia or macrocytosis. *New Eng J Med* 1988: 318: 1720-1728.
36. ShultzTD, Leklem JE. Vitamin B6 status and bio-availability in vegetarian women. *Amer Jour Clin Nutr* 1987; 46: 647-664.
37. Norbert Freinkel, MD, Northwestern Medical School.
38. Malnutrition accounts for over half of child deaths worldwide, says UNICEF. *Nutrition Week* 1998(Jan 2); 27; 1: 1-2.
39. Bland JS. Prev Med Update 1996;May — from *JAMA.*
40. Crayhon R. The manganese story: An interview with Dorothy Klimis-Tavantzis,

PhD. *Townsend Ltr Doc/Patients* 1998; June: 84-86.

41.  Chappell LC et al. Effect of antioxidants on the occurrence of pre-eclampsia in women at increased risk: A randomised trial. *Lancet* 1999; 354: 810-816.

42.  Norbert Freinkel, MD, Northwestern Medical School.

43.  Smith LH. *How to Raise a Healthy Child.*

44.  Smith LH. *How to Raise a Healthy Child.* p. 12.

45.  Lipton BH. Maternal emotions and human development. *The Golden Thread.*

46.  Smith LH. Personal communication, 1998.

47.  Privitera J. Fighting for your life begins with clear arteries. *Jour Longevity* 1999;5; 12: 6-9.

48.  Knox EG. Anencephalus and dietary intakes. *Brit J Prevent Soc Med* 1972; 26: 219-223.

49.  Raloff J. Dioxin's fowl deed: Misshapen brains. *Sci News* 1997;152: 133.

50.  *Sci News* 1996; Sept. 14.

51.  Pogoda JM, Preston-Martin S. *Environmental Health Perspectives* 1997; Nov.

52.  Steinman D. Getting ready for baby. *Health Freedom News* 1993; June: 24-30.

53.  Pediatric Research 1998; Jan; 43: 1-7.

54.  Smith DB, Roddick JH, Jones JL. Potato glycoalkaloids: Some unanswered questions. Trends Food Sci & Tech 1996; 126: 31; also Bland JS. *Prev Med Update* 1996; Sept.

55.  Tucker ME. Talk toxicity to patients using herbal drugs. *Skin & Allergy News* 1997; Mar:31.

56.  Tieraona Low Dog, MD (Albuquerque, NM). Interview on Bland JS, *Funct Med Update* 1999; Dec.

57.  *New Eng Jour Med* 1999(Nov 25); 341: 1639-1644, 1688-1689.

58.  Rodgers A. Effect of cola consumption on urinary biochemical and physico-chemical risk factors associated with calcium oxalate urolithiasis. Urol Res 1999; 27: 77-81.

59.  Blaylock RL. *Excitotoxins: The Taste that Kills.* Santa Fe, NM: Health Press, 1994.

60.  Klebanoff MA, Levine RJ, DerSimonian R, et al. Maternal serum para-xanthine, a caffeine metabolite, and the risk of spontaneous abortion. *New Eng J Med* 1999; 341: 1639-1944.

61.  Caffeine, quilts linked to sudden infant death. Medical Tribune 1998; Feb 19. Citing study by Rodney Ford et al. Heavy caffeine intake in pregnancy and sudden infant death syndrome. *Arch of Dis Childhood* 1998; 78: 9-13.

63.  Fenster L et al. Caffeinated beverages, decaffeinated coffee, and spontaneous abortion. *Epidemiology* 1997; 8: 515-523.

64.  *New Eng J Med* 1999 (Nov 25); 341: 1639-1644, 1688-1689.

65.  Mercola J. *Healthy news you can use.* #130; 1999; Dec. 5.3-5.

66.  Rogers SA. *Tired or Toxic?* Syracuse, NY: Prestige Publ., 1990.

67.  Sahley BJ. *The Anxiety Epidemic.* San Antonio, TX: Pain & Stress Publications, 1999.

68.  Keon J. The Truth About Breast Cancer: A 7-Step Prevention Plan. Mill Valley CA: Parissound Publ., 1999.

69.  Keon J. *The Truth About Breast Cancer.* Op. cit.

70.  Sahley BJ. *The Anxiety Epidemic.* San Antonio, TX: Pain & Stress Publications, 1999.

71.  Roberts HJ. Aspartame (NutraSweet®) addiction. *Townsend Ltr Doc/-Patients* 2000; Jan: 52-57.

72.   Hattersley JG, Treacy K. Overbreathing and its harm to health. *Townsend Letter Doctors and Patients*. 1998; Jan: 92-95. An update: http://www.angelfire.com/wa/jhattersley/content.html
73.   Blaylock R. *Excitotoxins: The Taste that Kills*. Santa Fe, NM: Health Press, 1995.
86.   Whitaker JM. *The great vitamin hoax*. MD's Wellness Journal. 2000; Jan: 2-5.
87.   Williams RJ. *Biochemical Individuality*. Wiley, 1954, 1992.
88.   Williams RJ. *Nutrition Against Disease: Environmental Prevention*. NY: Bantam, 1973.
89.   Boone CS, Kelloff G. *Cancer Chemopreventive with Antioxidants Derived from Food*. Association of Cancer Prevention and Symposium on Cancer Prevention.
90.   The Alpha-Tocopherol, Beta Carotene Cancer Prevention Study Group. The effect of vitamin E and beta-carotene on the incidence of lung cancer and other cancers in male smokers. *New Eng J Med* 1994; 330: 1029-1035.
91.   Robinson AB. Nutrition and cancer. *Access to Energy* 1998; 25; 9 (May): 1-3.
92.   Hoffer A. Editorial: The public reaction to double-blind controlled clinical trials. *Jour Orthomolecular Med* 1999; 14; 4: 179-184.
93.   Rothman KJ, Moore LL, Singer MR et al. Teratogenicity of high vitamin A intake. New Eng J Med 1995 (Nov 23); 333: 1369-1373.
94.   *Sci News* 1995 (Oct 14); 148: 244.
94a.  Oakley GP, Erickson JD. Vitamin A and birth defects: Continued caution needed (ltr). *New Eng J Med* 1995 (Nov 23); 333: 1414-1415.
95.   West B. *Health Alert* 1996; Feb: 6-7.
96.   Semba RD. Vitamin A as "anti-infective" therapy, 1920-1940. *Jour Nutrition* 1999; 129: 783-791.
97.   Howell E. *Enzyme Nutrition: The Food Enzyme Concept*. Wayne, NJ: Avery Publ Group Inc., 1985.
98.   Lita Lee, PhD. *The Enzyme Cure: How Plant Enzymes Can Help You Relieve 36 Health Problems*. Tiburon, CA: Future Medicine Publ., 1998. PO Box 516, Lowell OR 97452. (541) 937-1123.
99.   *Health Naturally*, 1998; Feb/Mar.
100.  Rogers SA. Alcohol, the double-edged sword. *Dr. Sherry Rogers' Total Health* 1998; Dec: 6-7.
101.  Bellantani S et al. Drinking habits as cofactors of risk of alcohol induced liver damage. *Gut* 1997; 41: 845-850. Day CP. Commentary. 857-858.
102.  Smith LH 1996 p. 8.
103.  Lee L. Polyunsaturated fats (PUFA's). Unpublished manuscript, 1998.
104.  Statement by a representative of Protein Technologies, Inc., 1999.
105.  Myths and truths about nutrition. Wise Traditions. Weston A. Price Foundation (SM) 1999.
106.  Sally Fallon and Mary G. Enig. *The Ploy of Soy*. $10; 1(888) 593-8333.
107.  West B. Get ready for soy. *Health Alert* 2000; 17; 1: 7-8.
108.  Porterfield SP, Hendrich EC. The role of thyroid hormones in prenatal and neonatal neurological development — current perspectives. *Endocr Rev* 1993; 14(1): 94-106. Cited in Foster HD. Cretinism: The iodine-selenium connection. *J Orthomolecular Med* 1995; 10:1 39-144.
109.  Jovanovic-Peterson L, Peterson CM. Vitamin and mineral deficiencies which may predispose to glucose intolerance of pregnancy. *J Amer Coll Nutr* 1996; 15(1): 14-20.
110.  Hoffer A. Megavitamin therapy. *Townsend Ltr Doc/Patients* 1996; June: 56-60.

112.  Hawkins D. The prevention of tardive dyskinesia with high dosage vitamins: A study of 58,000 patients. *Jour Orthomolecular Med* 1986; 1: 24-26.

112a.  Dyall D. Letter in Health Freedom News June/July 1998, summarizing *Rare Earths, Forbidden Cures* by Joel Wallach and Ma Lan.

112b.  Roan S. Women's folic acid mandate: 400 micrograms of prevention. *Los Angeles Times; Seattle Times* 1999; Nov. 14: L4.

113.  Amer Jour Clinical Nutrition 1999; Sept. 28.

114.  Atkins RC. *Dr. Robert Atkins' Health Revelations* 1998; 6; 3:7.

115.  Ray JG, Laskin CA. Folic acid and homocyst(e)ine metabolic defects and the risk of placental abruption, preeclampsia and spontaneous pregnancy loss: A systematic review. *Placenta* 1999; 20: 519-529.

116.  Cuskelly GJ et al. Effect of increasing dietary folate on red-cell folate: Implications for prevention of neural tube defects. *Lancet* 1996; 347: 657-659.

117.  Metz J. Folate, B12 and neural tube defects: The benefits of food fortification outweigh the possibility of adverse effects. *Med J Australia* 1995 (Sept 4); 163: 232-233.

118.  Regine M et al. Maternal hyperhomocysteinemia: A risk factor for neural-tube defect? *Metabolism* 1994; 43: 1475-1480.

119.  Wilcken DEL, Dudman NPB. Homocystinuria. The effects of betaine in the treatment of patients not responsive to pyridoxine. *New Eng Jour Med* 1983; 30: 448-453.

120.  Goldenberg RL et al. Serum folate and fetal growth retardation. *J Obstetrics & Gynecology* 1992; 79: 719-722.

121.  *Proc Natl Acad Sci* USA 1999; Nov.

122.  Crayhon R. The manganese story: An interview with Dorothy Klimis-Tavantzis, PhD. *Townsend Ltr Doc/Patients* 1998; June: 84-86.

123.  Rosenbaum M. G T F chromium. *The Vitamin Supplement*. 1989 (Aug): 61-62.

124.  *Magnesium Research* 1994; 7; 1: 49-57.

125.  Pavka E. Book reviews: Firshein RN. *Reversing Asthma: Reduce Your Medications with this Revolutionary New Program*. NY: Warner Books, Inc., 1997.

126.  Simmer K, James C, Thompson RPH. Are iron-folate supplements harmful? *Am J Clin Nutr* 1987; 45: 122-125.

127.  Campbell JD. *Minerals and disease*. Op. cit.

128.  Jameson S. Effects of zinc deficiency on human reproduction. *Acta Medica Scandinavica* 1976; 197A, Suppl 539: 3-82.

129.  Jameson S. Zinc status and human reproduction, in *Zinc in Human Medicine*, pp. 61-80. Toronto: Til Publications Ltd., 1984.

130.  Scholl TO et al. Low zinc intake during pregnancy. *Amer J Epidem* 1993; 137; 10: 1115-1124.

130a.  Campbell JD. Minerals and disease. *J Orthomolecular Med* 1995; 10: 177-188.

131.  Tuormaa TE. Adverse effects of zinc deficiency: A review from the literature. *J Orthomolecular Med* 1995; 10: 149-164.

132.  Lindeman R et al. *Trace Elements in Human Health and Disease*. NY: Academic Press, 1976.

132a.  Association for the Promotion of Preconceptual Care (n.d.), *A layperson's notes on the interpretation of mineral analysis*, n.p.

133.  Golub M, Gershwin M, Hurley L et al. Studies of marginal zinc deprivation in rhesus monkeys: II. Pregnancy outcome. *Amer Jour Clin Nutr* 1984; 39: 879-887.

133a. Beach RS, Gershwin ME, Hurley LS. Gestational zinc deprivation in mice: Persistence of immunodeficiency for three generations. *Science* 1982; 218: 469.
133b. Hurley LS. Zinc deficiency in the developing rat. *Am J Clin Nutr* 1969; 22; 10: 1332-1339.
134. Starkebaum G, Harlan JM. Endothelial cell injury due to copper-catalyzed hydrogen peroxide generation from homocysteine. *Jour Clin Investig* 1986; 77: 1370-1376.
135. Bryce-Smith D. Prenatal zinc deficiency. *Nursing Times* 1986 (March 5): 44-46.
136. Bland JS. Prev Med Update 1995 Nov.
137. De Villiers LS, Serfontein WJ. *Your Heart: The Unrefined Facts*. Pretoria:HAUM Educational Publishers, 1989.
138. Bland JS. *Prev Med Update* 1993.
139. Selye H. Forty years of stress research: Principal remaining problems and misconceptions. *Can Med Assoc J* 1976; 115; 1:53-56.
140. Sapolsky R. *Why Zebras Don't Get Ulcers*. NY: WH Freeman & Co., 1998.
140a. Truswell AS. Nutrition for pregnancy. *British Med Jour* 1985; 291: 263-266.
141. *Jour Amer Coll Nutr* 1987; 46: 324-328.
142. Argiratos V, Samman S. The effect of calcium carbonate and calcium citrate on the absorption of zinc in healthy female subjects. *Eur J Clin Nutr* 1994; 48: 198-204.
145. Wergehad E, Strand K. Workplace conditions and prevalence of pre-eclampsia in Norway, 1989. *Int J Gynecol Ob* 1997; 58; 2: 189-196.
146. *Jour Obstetrics & Gynecology* 1995; Sept.
147 Demopoulos HB. The development of secondary pathology with free radicals reactions as a threshold mechanism. *J Am Coll Toxicology* 1983; 2; 3: 173-184.
148. Teotia SPS, Teotia M. Fluoride and calcium interactions: Syndromes of bone disease and deformities [human studies]. In: Frame B, Potts JT Jr (Eds). Clinical Disorders of Bone and Mineral Metabolism. Amsterdam: *Excerpta Medica,* 1983.
149. Rosenbaum M: *G T F chromium.*
150. Pelton R. *Drug-Induced Nutrient Depletion Handbook*. Lexi-Comp, 1999.
151. Fluoride a known vitamin C antagonist. *Prevention* 1965; June.
152. Yiamouiannis J. *Fluoride: The Aging Factor.*
153. Nieper H. Lecture, 1992.
154. McCully KS. Homocysteine theory: Development and current status. *Atherosclerosis Rev.* 1983; 11: 157-246.
155. Ellis JM. *Free of Pain*. Rev. ed. Dallas: Southwest Publ, 1985.
156. Ueland PM, Refsum H. Plasma homocysteine, a risk factor for vascular disease: Plasma levels in health, disease and drug therapy. *Jour Lab Clin Med* 1989; 114: 473
157. Ellis JM. *Free of Pain*. Rev. ed. Dallas: Southwest Publ, 1985.
158. Doll H et al. Pyridoxine (vitamin B6) and the premenstrual syndrome: A randomized crossover trial. *J R Coll Gen Pract* 1999 (Sept); 39: 364-368.
159. Bernstein AL. Vitamin B6 in clinical neurology. *Ann NY Acad Sci* 1990; 585: 250-260.
160. Szaloadi E. Fluvoxamine withdrawal syndrome (ltr). *Brit J Psychiatry* 1992; 160: 283-284.
160a. Kent LSW, Laidlaw JDD. Suspected congenital sertraline dependence. *British J Psychiatry* 1995; 167: 412-413.
161. Peat R. *Ray Peat's Newsletter* 1997; Apr: 3-4.

162. Howell E. Enzyme Nutrition: The Food Enzyme *Concept. Op. cit.*
163. Bercz JP. Toxicology of drinking water disinfection byproducts from nutrients. Rate studies of destruction of polyunsaturated fatty acids in vitro by chlorine-based disinfectants. *Chem Research in Toxicology,* 1992; 5: 418-425.
164. Hibbeln JR et al. Do plasma polyunsaturates predict hostility and depression? Nutrition and Fitness: Metabolic and Behavioral Aspects in Health and Disease. *World Rev Nutr Diet* 1997; 82: 175-186.
165. Hattersley JG. Eggs are great food! *Townsend Ltr Doctors and Patients* 1996;Jan:46-49.
165a. Hattersley JG. *The sunny side of eggs. What Doctors Don't Tell You.* 1999;10;2:12.
166. Terano T et al. Docosahexaenoic aid supplementation improves the moderately severe dementia from thrombotic cerebrovascular diseases. *Lipids* 1999; 34 (Suppl): S345-S346.
167. Hibbeln JR, Salem N Jr. Dietary polyunsaturated fatty acids and depression: When cholesterol does not satisfy. *Am J Clin Nutr* 1995; 62: 1-9.
168. Mercola JM. Current health news you can use. *Townsend Ltr Doc/Patients* 1999; Nov:50-53.
169. Kromhout D et al. The inverse relation between fish consumption and 20-year mortality from coronary heart disease. *New Eng Jour Med* 1985; 312: 1205-1209.
170. Leaf A, Weber PC. Cardiovascular effects of n-3 fatty acids. *New Eng Jour Med* 1988; 318: 549-557.
171. Eaton SB, Konner M. Paleolithic nutrition. *New Eng Jour Med* 1985; 312; 5: 283-289.
172. Kankaanpaa P. Dietary fatty acids and allergy. *Ann Med* 1999; 31: 282-287.
173. Marinkovich V. Interview on Bland JS. *Funct Med Update* 1999: Oct.
174. Kankaanpaa P. *Dietary fatty acids and allergy.* Op. cit..
175. Hamilton K. *Clinical Pearls News* 2000; Jan:6-7.
176. Crawford D, Marsh D. *The Driving Force: Food, Evolution and the Future.* NY: Harper & Row, 1989.
177. Barry Sears, PhD, with Bill Lawren. *Enter the ZONE. A Dietary Road Map.* NY: Regan Books imprint of Harper Collins Publishers, 1995.
178. Natural Pharmacy: DHA — New brain nutrient from algae helps depression and infant nutrition. *Alternative Med Digest* 1997; #18: 78-80.
179. Jones JW. DHA in perinatal nutrition. *Townsend Ltr Doc/Patients* 1997; July: 82-83.
180. Gibson RA et al. Effect of dietary docosahexaenoic acid on brain composition and neural function in term infants. *Lipids* 1996; 1: 99-105.
181. Holman R, Johnson S, Ogburn P. Deficiency of essential fatty acids and membrane fluidity during pregnancy and lactation. Biochemistry. *Proc Nat Acad Sci USA* 1991; 88: 4835-4839.
182. Enig MG. *Trans Fatty Acids in the Food Supply: A Comprehensive Report Covering 60 Years of Research,* 1993.
183. Ascherio A, Willett WC. Health effects of trans fatty acids. *Am J Clin Nutr* 1997; 66 (suppl): 1006S-1010S.
184. Shapiro S. Do trans fatty acids increase the risk of coronary artery disease? A critique of the epidemiologic evidence. Am J Clin Nutr 1997; 66 (suppl): 1011S-1017S.
185. Are trans fatty acids a serious risk for disease? Discussion. *Am J Clin Nutr*

1997; 66 (suppl): 1018S-1019S.

186. Well Mind Association Bulletin 1994; Jan.

187. Chappell JE, Clandinin MT, Kearney-Volpe C. Trace fatty acid in human milk lipids: Influence of maternal diet and weight loss. *Am J Clin Nutr* 1985; 42: 49-56.

188. Smith 1996 p. 89.

189. Gaitan E. In vitro measurement of antithyroid compounds and environmental goitrogens. *J Clin Endocrinol Metab* 1983; 56: 767-773.

190. Williams GR et al. Thyroid hormone receptor expression in the "sick euthyroid" syndrome. *Lancet* 1989 (Dec. 24): 1477-1481.

191. Essential trace elements and thyroid hormones. *Lancet* 1992; 339: 1575-1576.

191a. Foster H. Sudden infant death syndrome: The Bradford Hill criteria and the evaluation of the thyroxine deficiency hypothesis. *J Orthomolecular Med* 1993; 8: 201-226.

192. Berkowsky B. Hypothyroidism: A pandemic symptom. *Health Freedom News* 1992; Sept: 8-13.

193. West B. The cholesterol folly, in *Total Health and Wellness for the 1990s*. Carmel, CA: West Publ, 1990.

194. Lee L. Personal communication, 1993.

195. Zang Y, Wang M, Wang G et al. Primary study of the cause of goiter and low intelligence among the children in endemic goiter areas, in *Abstracts, International Symposium on Environmental Life Elements and Health*. Chinese Academy of Sciences: Beijing, 1988: p. 86.

196. Colborn T, Dumanoski D, Myers JP. *Our Stolen Future. Are We Threatening our Fertility, Intelligence and Survival? A scientific Detective Story*. NY: Dutton, 1996.

197. Rosman NP, Malone MJ. Brain myelination in experimental hypothyroidism: Morphological and biochemical observations. In *Graves GD (ed.), Thyroid Hormones and Brain Development*. NY: Raven Press, 1977. pp. 169-198.

198. Porterfield SF, Hendrich CE. The role of thyroid hormones in prenatal and neonatal neurological development — Current perspectives. *Endocrine Reviews* 1993; 14: 94-106 (157 ref).

199. Peat R. *Ray Peat's Newsletter* 1997; Apr:3,4.

200. Wang LL, Johnson EA. Inhibition of Listeria monocytogenes by fatty acids and monoglycerides. *Applied and Environmental Microbiol* 1992; 58; 2; 624-629.

201. Enig M. Lauric acid-rich coconut oil: Saturated yet outstanding. *Search for Health* 1996 (Mar/Apr): 11-18.

202. Price W. *Nutrition and Physical Degeneration: A Comparison of Primitive and Modern Diets and Their Effects*. La Mesa, CA: Price-Pottenger Nutrition Foundation, 1970.

203. Ip C, Sinha DK. Enhancement of mammary tumorigenesis by dietary selenium deficiency in rats with a high polyunsaturated fat intake. *Cancer Research* 1981; 41; 1: 31-34.

204. Peat R. Coconut oil. *Ray Peat's Newsletter* 1994; July. Raymond Peat, PhD, PO Box 5764, Eugene, OR 97405; website: www.efn.org/~raypeat.

204a. McNamara DJ. Dietary cholesterol: Effect on lipid metabolism. Curr Opin *Lipidology* 1990;1; 18-22. Also Werbach MR. Personal communication, 1995.

205. Atkins R. A nutritional paradise in "forbidden oils." *Dr. Robert Atkins' Health Revelations* 1997; 5; 12: 6-7.

206. Shull F. *Townsend Ltr Doc* 1989; Mar. (ltr).

207.  Bland JS. *Funct. Med Update*, 2000;Jan.
208.  Smith LH. Op. cit.
209.  *Amer Jour Obstetrics Gynecology* 1999; Oct; 181: 816-821.
210.  Jackson JA, Riordan HD, Hunninghake R, Revard C. Case from the Center:
      Candida albicans: The hidden infection. *Jour Orthomolecular Med* 1999; 14; 4:
      198-200.
210a. Peter S. Hidden dangers: An overview of food allergies. *Advance for Physicians
      Assistants* 1997; 5; 12: 46-47.
211.  Ellis JM. *Free of Pain,* rev. ed. Dallas: Southwestern Publ., 1985.
212.  Ellis JM. Personal communication, 1994.
213.  Superbugs. *Vitamin Research News* 1999; Sept: 1-2,4-5,16.
214.  Steinman D. Getting ready for baby. *Health Freedom News* 1993; June: 24-30.
215.  Robin M. Murry, Institute of Psychiatry, London, and colleagues. December
      1995 *American Journal of Psychiatry*.
216.  Bower B. Schizophrenia: Data point to early roots. *Sci News* 1995 (Dec 16);
      148: 406.
217.  Sunday Telegraph Sept. 21, 1997, page 23. From a recent issue of *Stroke*.
218.  Hal A. Huggins, DDS, MS and Thomas E. Levy, MD, JD. *Uninformed Consent.
      The Hidden Dangers in Dental Care*. Charlottesville, VA: Hampton Roads
      Publ., 1999. (1-800-766-8009)
219.  Smith op. cit. p. 2.
220.  McTaggart L. The pill on trial. *What Doctors Don't Tell You* 1995; Dec: 6.
221.  Pelton R, Lavalle J, Hawkins E et al. *Drug-Induced Nutrient Depletion
      Handbook*. (Lexi-Comp, 1999.)
222.  Beral V, Ramchara S, Faris R. Malignant melanoma and oral contraceptive use
      among women in California. The Walnut Creek Contraceptive Drug Study. *U.S.
      National Institutes of Health, vol. III*, 1986, pp. 247-252.
223.  Garland FC et al. Occupational sunlight exposure and melanoma in the U.S.
      Navy. *Arch Environmental Health* 1990; 45: 261-267.
224.  U.S. General Accounting Office. Special Supplemental Food Program for
      Women, Infants and Children, 1995. Reported by Physicians Committee on
      Childhood Hunger, Tufts University School of Medicine.
224a. Halliwell B, Gutteridge JMC. Oxygen free radicals and iron in relation to biolo-
      gy and medicine: Some problems and concepts. *Jour Biochem & Biophys* 1986;
      246: 501-514.
225.  Weinberg ED. Iron withholding: A defense against infection and neoplasia.
      *Physiological Rev* 1984; 64: 65-95.
226.  Patricia Stuart-Macadam, University of Toronto.
227.  Smith LH. Op. cit.
228.  *What Doctors Don't Tell You* 1995; Jan; 6;1.
229.  Raha-Chowdhury R., Moore CA, Fagan DG, Worwood M. From *Abstracts, 4th
      Int Conf of Hemochromatosis and Clinical Problems in Iron Metabolism*.
230.  Lee C-K, Klopp RG, Windruch R, Prolla TA. Gene expression profile of aging
      and its retardation by calorie restriction. *Science* 1999; 285: 1390-1393.
231.  Peat R. Iron — Cumulative danger. *Ray Peat's Newsletter* 1996; Dec: 1-5.
      Citing Choi JH, Yu PB. Modulation of age-related alterations of iron, ferritin
      and lipid peroxidation in rat serum. *Age* 1994; 17; 3: 93-97.
232.  Ray M. Fountain of health. Lecture tape, 1996.
233.  Warner J. Deadly chain reaction: Prime cause of aging. *Jour Longevity* 1998; 4;
      3: 18-20.

234. Warner J. Deadly chain reaction: Prime cause of aging. Op. cit.
235. Barber DA et al. Oxygen-free radicals and antioxidants. A review. *Amer Pharmacy* 1994; NS34; 9: 26-35.
236. Peat R. Iron — Cumulative danger. *Ray Peat's Newsletter* 1996; Dec: 1-5.
237. Peat R. Iron — Cumulative danger. Idem.
238. Riley PA. Free radicals in biology: Oxidative stress and the effects of ionizing radiation. *Int J Radiat Biol* 1994; 65; 1: 27-33.
239. Warner J. Deadly chain reaction: Prime cause of aging. *Jour Longevity* 1998; 4; 3: 18-20.
240. Cohen BL. Test of the linear no-threshold theory of radiation carcinogenesis for inhaled radon decay products. *Health Physics* 1991; 68: 157-174.
241. Gaby AR. Literature review & commentary. On Layrisse M et al. The role of vitamin A on the inhibitors of nonheme iron absorption: Preliminary results. *J Nutr Biochem* 1997; 8: 61-67.
242. McCord JM. Free radicals and pro-oxidants in health and nutrition. *Food Technol* 1994; May: 107-109.
243. Lee L. *Radiation Protection Manual* 3rd ed., 1990. Lita Lee, PhD. PO Box 516, Lowell OR 97452. (541) 937-1123.
244. Microwave tragedy. PPNF *Nutr J* 1994; 18; 1&2; June: 1-5.
245. Quan, R. et al (1992), Effects of microwave radiation on anti-infective factors in human milk, *Pediatrics* 89: 667-669.
246. Microwaves bedevil a B vitamin. *Sci News* 1998; 153: 105. Drnjevic P. Note, 2000 Jan. 23. Emailto: pauldrn@silverlink.net
247. Shaw M. Effect of irradiated sucrose on the chromosomes of human lymphocytes. *Nature* 1966; 211: 1254.
248. Lee L. *Radiation Protection Manual*. 3rd ed., 1990.
249. Domisse JV. The experts speak interviews. In *Hamilton K. Clin Pearls News* 1998; Mar: 51-52.
250. *Organic View,* an e-mail publication of the Organic Consumers Association. 2000; 2; 1 (Jan 23). http://www.purefood.org/irradlink.html
251. Kallen K. Maternal smoking during pregnancy and limb reduction and malformation in Sweden. *Am J Pub Health* 1997; 87: 29-32.
252. Olds DL. Intellectual impairment in children of women who smoke cigarettes during pregnancy. *Pediatrics* 1994; 93: 221-227.
253. Rogers SA. Reader's question of the month. Got a bad tooth brewing? *Total Wellness* 1998; Dec: 5.
254. Rogers SA. Toxic alerts at a glance. *Dr. Sherry Rogers' Total Health in Today's World* 1998; 2; 8: 1-2.

--------

# CHAPTER FIVE

1.   Morales K, Inlander CB. *So You're Going to Be a Mother.* Allentown, PA; People's Medical Society, 1995.
2.   Montale JKI. Case study. *What Doctors Don't Tell You. (WDDTY)* 1996; Feb: 10.
3.   Robbins J. *Reclaiming Our Health: Exploding the Medical Myth and Embracing the Source of True Healing.* HJ Kramer, Publisher, 1997.

4.    National Center for Health Statistics, National Linked Birth and Infant Death File, 1990.
5.    *JAMA* 1990; 264: 1984-1988.
6.    Mendelsohn, RS. *How to Raise a Healthy Child: In Spite of Your Doctor.* NY: Ballantine Books, 1984.
7.    Health care in America: Your money or your life. *The Economist* 1998; Mar 7: 23-26.
8.    Hannah ME et al. Induction of labor compared with expectant management for prelabor rupture of the membranes at term. *New Eng J Med* 1996 (Apr 18); 334; 16: 1005-1010.
9.    *Idem,* special supplement.
10.   Hand-washing patterns in medical intensive care units. *New Eng J Med* 1981; June
11.   Smith WC, *Second Opinion,* 1995 Apr.
12.   Williams DG. *Alternatives for the Health-Conscious Individual,* 1997; June.
13.   *Lancet* 1998; 352: 1568-8, 1577-81.
14.   Keise MJNC. Frequent perinatal ultra-sounding: Time to think again. *Lancet* 1993; 342 (Oct. 9) 878-879.
15.   Newnham JP et al. Effects of frequent ultrasound during pregnancy. A randomly controlled trial. *Lancet* 1993 (Oct 9); 342: 887-891.
16.   Willix RD Jr. Confessions of a Former Heart Surgeon. Baltimore, MD: *Health & Longevity,* 1995.
17.   Campbell JD, Elford RW, Brant RF. Case-control study of prenatal ultrasonography exposure with delayed speech. *Canad Med Assoc J* 1993; 149; 10: 1435-1440.
18.   *New Scientist* issue 1476, 1999; Thurs June 10.
19.   Smith LH. *How to Raise a Healthy Child.* NY: M. Evans, 1996, p. 5.
20.   *New Eng J Med* 1996: Mar: 7.
21.   Fowkes S. Interview, 1999.
22.   Murdoch JC et al. Down's syndrome: An atheroma-free model? *British Med J* 1977; 6081: 226-228.
23.   Chadefaux B et al. Is absence of atheroma in Down syndrome due to decreased homocysteine levels? *Lancet* 1988; 2: 741 (Ltr).
24.   McTaggart L. Down: Doing the Impossible. *WDDTY* 1997(May); 8;1: 2-5.
25.   Kane P. Reversing autism with nutrition. *Alt Med Digest* 1997; #19: 36-44.
26.   Whitaker J. *Health & Healing* 1997; July.
27.   Several references in a recent issue, *Journal of Applied Nutrition.* 1999.
28.   Edelson SB. Speech and workshop Neurotoxic Etiology of the Autistic Spectrum Disorders. *ACAM* (Amer College of Advancement in Medicine) Spring conference, Orlando, FL, Mar 1999.
29.   McTaggart L. *Down: Doing the Impossible.* Op. cit.
30.   Autism: Another "treatable" condition. *WDDTY* 1997 (May); 8: 1;5.
31.   Morales/Inlander, Op. cit., page 156.
32.   Thorp JM Jr., Watson AB Jr. Episiotomy: Can its routine use be defended? *Am J Obstet and Gynecology* 1989; 160; 5: 1027-1030.
33.   Serota RA. *NY Times* 1995; June 29; ltr.
34.   Grimes D. Letter to Bland JS. *Prev Med Update* 1996; Dec.
35.   Privitera JS, Stang A. *Silent Clots: Life's Biggest Killers.* Covina, CA: The Catacombs Press. (818) 966-1618.
36.   *McCall's.* 1995; Jan.

37.  *National Center for Health Statistics.*
38.  Robbins J. *Reclaiming Our Health.* Op. cit.
39.  *Statistical Bulletin* 1989; Oct-Dec.
40.  Morales/Inlander. Op. cit.
41.  *BMJ* Nov 18, 1995.
42.  *WDDTY* Feb 1996:7.
43.  Morales/Inlander. Op. cit.
44.  *JAMA* 1998; Dec. 23.
45.  Crandall MA. Alternative birth: Returning full circle to women helping women. *Alt Comp Therapies* 1997; 3; 3: 212-216.
46.  Smith 1986 Op. cit., p. 22.
47.  McConnaughey J. Study: TLC during labor makes moms more loving. *Pasadena Star-News* 1998; May 3.
48.  Helwick C. Presence of "doulas" during difficult labors may reduce rate of C-sections. Med Tribune 1998; June 18: 16.
49.  Svea Gold, *When Children Invite Child Abuse.* Eugene, OR: Fern Ridge Press, 1986.
50.  Smith LH 1996, op. cit. p. 21.
51.  Conroy E. Interview, 1995.
52.  Smith LH 1996, op. cit.
53.  *New Scientist* 1991;Apr 20.
54.  Breast milk: Can it slime away disease? *Sci. News* 1992; Dec 5: 390.
55.  Smith LH. Personal communication, 1998.
56.  Mendelsohn, RS. *How to Raise a Healthy Child.* Op. cit.
57.  Merck Manual, 14th edition.
58.  Mendelsohn RS, op. cit.
59.  Mendelsohn RS. Op. cit.
60.  *JAMA* 1972;220:409.
61.  Smith LH, 1996 Op. cit. p. 34.

---

# CHAPTER SIX

1.  Rosenfeld I. Don't Worry About Vaccinations, *Parade Magazine,* 2000; Jan. 9: 10-11.
2.  Bick S, Preuschat S. Vaccine ingredients: Are they safe? *Health Naturally* 1998 (Feb/March): 15-17.
3.  Rogers SA. *Tired or Toxic?* Syracuse, NY: Prestige Publ., 1990.
4.  Murphy J. Toxic chemicals in vaccines, pp. 39-58. Role of aluminum sensitivity in delayed persistent immunization reactions. *J Clinical Pathology* 1991; 44: 876-877.
5.  Formaldehyde. *The World Book Encyclopedia.* Vol. 7, 1994: p.410.
6.  Ziff S. *Toxic Time Bomb: Can the Mercury in Your Dental Fillings Poison You?* Santa Fe, NM: Aurora Press, 1986.
7.  Huggins H. *It's All in Your Head. Diseases Caused by Silver-Mercury Fillings.* Life Sciences Press, Colorado Springs, Co., 1990. ISBN 0-943685-06-0.
8.  Miller NZ. *Op. cit.*
9.  Murphy J. *What Every Parent Should Know About Childhood Immunization.*

Earth Healing Products, 1993.
10.  Bick S, Preuschat S. *Vaccine ingredients: Are they safe?*
11.  Murphy J. *What Every Parent Should Know About Childhood Immunization.*
     Earth Healing Products, 1993.
12.  Rogers SA. *Depression. Cured at Last.* Sarasota, FL: SK Publ., 1997. P. 557.
13.  From James W. *Immunization: The Reality Behind the Myth.* Bergin & Garvey,
     MA, 1988.
14.  Plotkin SA. Development of RA 27/3 attenuated rubella virus grown in WI-38
     cells. *Int Symposium on Rubella Vaccines, London,* 1968; Symp Series
     Immunobiological Standards, V. 11. Karger, Basel/New York, 1969. Pp. 249-
     260.
15.  Beale AJ. Vaccines and antiviral drugs. *Topley and Wilson's Principles of
     Bacteriology, Virology and Immunity.* Baltimore: Williams and Wilkins, 1984. P.
     149.
16.  Hoskins JM, Plotkin SA. Behavior of rubella virus in human diploid cell strains.
     *Wistar Institute of Anatomy and Biology.* Philadelphia: Jan 16, 1969. Pp. 284-
     295.
17.  Jegede VA et al. Vaccine technology. *Encyclopedia of Chemical Technology.*
     NY: John Wiley & Sons, 1983. P. 629.
18.  Miller NZ. *Immunization: Theory vs. Reality.*
19.  Jegede VA et al, *Op. cit.,* pp. 630-631.
20.  Murphy J. *The making of a vaccine. What Every Parent Should Know about
     Childhood Immunization. Op. cit.,* pp. 25-28.
21.  Landrigan PJ, Witte JJ. Neurological disorders following live measles-virus vac-
     cination. *Jour Amer Med Assoc* 1973; 223; 13: 1459-1462.
22.  Miller NZ. *Immunization: Theory vs. Reality. Op. cit.* From Scott J. Report:
     U.S. slips in fight to cut infant mortality. Los *Angeles Times/Press & Sun
     Bulletin* 1990; March 1; p. 1A.
23.  Stewart G. *The Lancet* 1979; Aug 18.
24.  Mendelsohn RS. *How to Raise a Healthy Child; In Spite of Your Doctor.* NY:
     Ballantine Books, 1984.
25.  Cherry JD et al. Report of the task force on pertussis immunization. *Pediatrics*
     81 (Supplement) 1988: 939-977.
26.  Sprott TJ. Personal communication, 1999.
27.  Noble GR et al. *JAMA* 1987; 257: 1351-1356.
28.  Cherry JD et al. Report of the task force on pertussis immunization. *Op. cit.*
29.  Torch WC. Diphtheria-pertussis-tetanus (DPT) immunization: A potential cause
     of the sudden infant death syndrome (SIDS). *Neurology* 1982; 32; 4: A169
     (abstract).
30.  Torch WC. Characteristics of diphtheria-pertussis-tetanus (DPT) postvaccinal
     deaths and DPT-caused sudden infant death syndrome (SIDS): A review.
     *Neurology* 1986; 36 (Suppl. 1): 148 (abstract).
31.  Torch WC. Diphtheria-pertussis-tetanus (DPT) immunization: A potential cause
     of the sudden infant death syndrome (SIDS). *Op. cit.*
32.  Scheibner VS. *Vaccination.* Pp. 60f.
33.  Scheibner VS. *Vaccination, op. cit.*
34.  Griffin MR et al. Risk of sudden infant death syndrome after immunization with
     the diphtheria-tetanus-pertussis vaccine. *New Engl Jour Med* 1988; 319: 618-
     623.
35.  Bernier RH, Frank JA, Dondero TJ, Turner P. Diphtheria-tetanus toxoids-pertus-

sis vaccination and sudden infant deaths in Tennessee. *Jour Pediatrics* 1982; 101; 5: 419-421.

36. Walker AM, Jick H, Perera DR, Thompson RS, Knauss TA. Diphtheria-tetanus-pertussis immunization and sudden infant death syndrome. *Am Jour Pub Health* 1987; 77: 945-951.

37. Coulter HL, Fisher BL. *A Shot in the Dark.* NY: Avery Publ Group, 1991.

38. Kalokerinos A. *Every Second Child.* New Canaan, CT: Keats Publ., 1984.

39. Hattersley JG. The answer to crib death. *Jour Orthomolecular Med* 1993; 8; 4: 229-245.

40. Cathcart RF III. The method of determining proper doses of vitamin C for the treatment of disease by titrating to bowel tolerance [the intake at which bowel movements are loose and symptoms dramatically improve]. *J Orthomolecular Psych* 1980; 10; 2: 125-132.

41. Cathcart RF III. Lecture, 1982.

42. Sprott TJ. Personal communication, 1998.

43. Sprott TJ. Personal communication, 1999.

44. Landrigan PJ, Witte JJ. Neurologic disorders following live measles-virus vaccination. *JAMA* 1973; 223; 13: 1459-1462.

45. Denborough MA, Galloway GJ, Hopkinson KC. Malignant hyperpyrexia and sudden infant death. *Lancet* 1982 (13 Nov): 1068-1072.

46. Goldwater PN, Williams V, Bourne AJ, Byard RW. Sudden infant death syndrome: A possible clue to causation. *Med J Australia* 1990; 15:59-60.

47. Cookson WOCM, Moffatt MF. Asthma: An epidemic in the absence of infection? *Science* 1997; 275: 41-42.

48. Scheibner VS. Shaken baby syndrome. Nexus 1998; Aug/Sept: 31-34,75.

49. Cumming F. Vaccinations: A health hazard? *Sydney Sunday Herald-Sun* 1993; Apr 4: 41-42, 79.

50. Miller NZ. *Immunization: Theory vs. Reality — Expose on Vaccinations.* Santa Fe, NM: New Atlantean Press, 1996.

51. Dublin L. Health progress, 1936-1945. New York Metropolitan Life Insurance Co., 1948, page 12.

52. Sagan LA. *The Health of Nations,* NY: Basic Books, Inc., 1987.

53. Incao PF. Vaccine information. In Mercola J., *Healthy News You Can Use* 1999 (#114); Aug 22, pp. 12-14.

54. Hume ED. *Bechamp or Pasteur? A Lost Chapter in the History of Biology.* London: C.W. Daniel, 1923.

55. Cookson WOCM, Moffatt MF. Asthma: An epidemic in the absence of infection? *Science* 1997; 275: 41-42.

56. Hattersley JG, Treacy K. A Real Cure for Asthma and a Lot More. *Townsend Letter for Doc/Patients* 1998; Jan: 92-95. An update: www.angelfire.com/wa/jhattersley/content.html

57. A survey by the American College of Allergy, Asthma and Immunology (ACAAI). Reported in Mercola J. *Healthy News You Can Use.* 1999; Aug 15: p. 6. Hyperlink: www.mercola.com

58. *Lancet* 1999; 353 (9163) (May 1): 1485-1488.

59. Odent MR, Culpin EE, Kimmel T. Pertussis vaccination and asthma: Is there a link? *JAMA* 1994; 272: 588.

60. Martinez FD. Role of viral infections in the inception of asthma and allergies during childhood: Could they be protective? *Thorax* 1994; 49: 1189-1191.

61. Statement by Dr. Jane Orient to the Committee on Government Reform of the

US House of Representatives, June 14, 1999, US Centers for Disease Control and Prevention, and FDA statistics in their VAERS database.

62.  Statement in 1993 by Dr. Craig Shapiro of U.S. Centers for Disease Control and Prevention in Atlanta.

63.  Mendelsohn RS. *How to Raise a Healthy Child: In Spite of Your Doctor. Op. cit.*

64.  Scheibner VS. *Vaccination.* P. 257.

65.  Wakefield A. Murch SH, Anthony A et al. Ileal-lymphoid-nodular hyperplasia, non-specific colitis, and pervasive development disorder in children. *Lancet* 1998; 351: 637-641.

66.  Mullins E. *Murder by Injection.* The Medical Conspiracy Against America. Staunton, VA: Natl Council for Medical Research, 1988. A cancer specialist in London said he had never seen a cancer patient who hadn't gone through multiple vaccinations. Mullins gave no references; but of his statements I've checked against sources I know to be reliable, every one has been accurate.

67.  Singh VJ et al. Antibodies to myelin basic protein in children with autistic behavior. *Brain, Behavior and Immunity* 1993; 7: 1197-1203.

68.  MMR shot causes Crohn's and autism, say studies. *What Doctors Don't Tell You.* 1997; 8; 8: 9.

69.  Mercola JM. Current health news you can use. *Townsend Ltr Doc/Patients* 1998; June: 26-28.

70.  From Mercola J. *Healthy News You Can Use* #114; 1999; Aug 14: 15-17. (mercola @pol.net)

71.  Miller AL. The pathogenesis, clinical implications, and treatment of intestinal hyperpermeability. *Alt Med Rev* 1997; 2;5: 330-345.

72.  Wakefield AJ, Murch SH, Anthony A et al. Ileal-lymphoid-nodular hyperplasia, non-specific colitis and pervasive development disorder in children. *Op. cit.Lancet* 1998; 351: 637-641.

73.  Bland JS. *Funct Med Update* 1999; Aug.

74.  *Ray Peat's Newsletter,* January 1998, pp. 1-5, by Raymond Peat, PhD.

75.  Roch-Arveiller M, Giroud JP. [Biological and pharmacological effects of carrageenan] (Article in French). *Pathol Biol* (Paris) 1979 Dec; 27 (10): 615-626.

76.  Bland JS. *Funct Med Update* 1999; July.

77.  *Revista de Neurologia* 1999;May 1-15; 28; 9: 881-882.

78.  Kaplan S, Hanchette J. Vaccination policies spark debate. Olympia, WA: *The Olympian,* 1998; Sept. 21: A2.

79.  Cumming F. Vaccination: A health hazard? *Op. cit.*

80.  Duesberg D. *Inventing the AIDS Virus.* NY: Regnery, 1996.

81.  Maibach H, Hildrick-Smith G. *Skin Bacteria and Their Role in Infection.* NY: McGraw-Hill, 1965, p. 121.

82.  Moreau-Horwin R, Horwin M. Patient report: Link between rate of pediatric cancers and childhood vaccines. *Townsend Ltr Doc/Patients* Dec 1999/Jan 2000: 72-79.

83.  Legendre C, Caillat-Zucman S, Samuel D, et al. Transfer of symptomatic peanut allergy to the recipient of a combined liver-and-kidney transplant. *New Eng J Med* 1997; 337; 12: 822-824.

84.  Lyon MR. Interview on Bland JS, *Funct Med Update* 1999; Feb.

85.  Cumming F. Vaccination: A health hazard? *Op. cit.*

86.  Buttram HE. Vaccine scene 1999; Overview and update. *Townsend Ltr Doc/Patients* Dec 1999/Jan 2000; 80-82.

87.    Robinson E. Matters of Life and Death: Risks vs. Benefits of Medical Care.
88.    Mercola J. Congressional Vaccine Testimony. *Healthy News You Can Use*. #114; 1999; Aug 15: 12-15.
89.    Cumming F. Vaccinations: A health hazard? *Op. cit.*
90.    Orenstein WA, Heseltine PNR et al. Rubella vaccine and susceptible hospital employees: Poor physician participation. *JAMA* 1981; Feb. 20.
91.    Mendelsohn RS. *How to Raise a Healthy Child: In Spite of Your Doctor.* NY: Ballantine Books, 1984.
92.    Miller NZ. Immunization: Theory vs. Reality. *Op. cit.*
93.    Mercola J. E-mail message. 1999; Aug. 29. The reply to my inquiry came back in less than five hours on a Sunday afternoon.
94.    Watson E, Gardner AS, Carpenter RG. An epidemiological and sociological study of unexpected death in infancy of nine areas of Southern England. *Med Sci Law* 1981; 21; 2: 89-98.
95.    Kalokerinos A. *Every Second Child. Op. cit.*
96.    Wright AE. On the changes affected by anti-typhoid inoculation on the bactericidal power of the blood; comments on the probable significance of these changes. *Lancet* 1991; (Sept 14): 715-723.
97.    Miller NZ. *Immunization: Theory vs. Reality. Op. cit.*
98.    Message from Lendon H. Smith, MD. March 1998.

---

## CHAPTER SEVEN

1.    Schwartz PJ, Stramba-Badiale M, et al. Prolongation of the QT interval and the sudden infant death syndrome. *New Eng J Med* 1998(June 11);338;24:1709-1714.
2.    Towbin JA, Friedman RA. Prolongation of the QT interval and the sudden infant death syndrome (Editorial). *New Eng J Med* 1998;338;24:1760-1761.
3.    Schwartz PJ, Stramba-Badiale M, et al. Op. cit.
4.    *Clinical Pharmacology & Therapeutics* 1997;61;4:396-399, 401-408.
5.    Tainsh AR. Second thoughts on beri-beri. *Townsend Ltr Doc/Patients* 1998;Nov:78-82.
6.    Lonsdale D. Personal communication, 1998.
7.    Firshein RN. *Reversing Asthma: Reduce Your Medications with this Revolutionary New Program.* NY: Warner Books, 1997.
8.    Rogers SA. *Tired or Toxic?* Syracuse, NY: Prestige Publ, 1990.
9.    Kukolich MK, Telsey A et al. Sudden infant death syndrome: Normal QT interval in ECG's of relatives. *Pediatrics* 1977;60:51-54.
10.    Schwartz PJ. Cardiac sympathetic innervation and the sudden infant death syndrome. *Am J Med* 19786;60:167-172.
11.    Guntheroth WG. Sudden infant death syndrome (Crib Death). *Amer Heart Jour* 1997;93;6:784-793.
12.    Lendon H. Smith. Personal communication, 1999.
13.    Guntheroth WG. Sudden infant death syndrome (crib death). *Amer Heart Jour* 1997;93;6:784-793.
14.    Guntheroth WG. Sudden infant death syndrome (crib death). Op. cit.
15.    Rogers SA. *Tired or Toxic?* Op. cit.

15a. Schwartz PJ, Stramba-Badiale M, et al. *Prolongation of the QT interval and the sudden infant death syndrome*. Op. cit.

26.   Ravich RM, Rosenblatt P. Myocardial infarction in newborn infant. *J Pediatr* 1947;31:266-273.

27.   Clapp JF, Naeye RL. Intra-uterine myocardial infarction. *JAMA* 1961;178:1039-1040.

28.   Jaffe D et al. Coronary arteries in newborn children. Intimal variations in longitudinal sections and their relationships to clinical and experimental data. *Acta Paediat Scand Supp* 1971:219:1-27.

29.   Suzman MM. Personal communications, 1984, 1988.

30.   Jaffe D et al. *Coronary arteries in newborn children*. Op. cit.

31.   Suzman MM. Nutritional and metabolic factors in the development of coronary artery disease in early life: The possible role of dietary protein and pyridoxine. Unpub manuscript, 1984.

32.   Suzman MM. Personal communications, 1984, 1991. Forty-seven phone calls plus correspondence; interviews in Johannesburg in 1992.

33.   Rogers SA. *Sherry Rogers' Total Wellness* 1999;Sept: p.2.

34.   Guntheroth WG. Personal communication, 1999.

35.   Weninger WJ, Muller GB, Reiter C et al. Intimal hyperplasia of the infant parasellar carotid artery: A potential development factor in atherosclerosis and SIDS. *Circ Research* 1999;85:970-975.

35a.  Appleton N. *Licking the Sugar Habit;* Life-Saving Guide. 1996.

35c.  Horrobin DF. The importance of gamma-linolenic acid and prostaglandin E1 in human nutrition and medicine. *Jour Holistic Med* 1981;3;2: 118-139.

36.   Pamphlett R, Raisenen J, Kum-Jew S. Vertebral artery compression resulting from head movement: A possible cause of the sudden infant death syndrome. *Pediatrics* 1999;103:460-468.

37.   Enos WF et al. Coronary disease among United States soldiers killed in action in Korea. *Jour Amer Med Assoc* 1953;152:1090-1093.

38.   Morin RJ, Peng S-K. The role of cholesterol oxidation products in the pathogenesis of atherosclerosis. *Annals Clin Lab Sci* 1991;19:225-237.

39.   Holtz P, Palm D. Pharmacological aspects of vitamin B6. *Pharmacol Rev* 1964:113-178.

40.   Rinehart JF, Greenberg LD. Arteriosclerotic lesions in pyridoxine-deficient monkeys. *Amer J Pathol* 1949;25:481-492.

41.   Kuzuya F. Reversibility of atherosclerosis in pyridoxine-deficient monkeys. In *Atherosclerosis IV*. Eds. G. Schettler et al. Berlin: Springer-Verlag, 1977.

42.   Hattersley JG. Acquired atherosclerosis: Theories of causation, novel therapies. *Jour Orthomolecular Med* 1991;6:83-98.

43.   Ellis JM, McCully KS. Prevention of myocardial infarction by vitamin B6. *Res Comm Molec Pathol Pharmacol* 1995;89;2:208-220.

44.   Rimm EB, Willett WC et al. Folate and vitamin B6 from diet and supplements in relation to risk of coronary heart disease among women. *JAMA* 1998;279;5:359-364.

45.   Folsom AR, Nieto FJ et al. Prospective study of coronary heart disease incidence in relation to fasting total homocysteine, related genetic polymorphisms, and B vitamins. *Circulation* 1998;98: 204-210.

46.   Rudman D, Williams PJ. Megadose vitamins: Use or misuse? *New Eng J Med* 1983;389:488-490.

47.   Jaffe RM. Lecture to Well Mind Assoc., Seattle, 1990.

48. Ellis JM. *Free of Pain,* rev. ed. Dallas: Southwest Publ., 1985.
49. Gruberg ER, Raymond SA. *Beyond Cholesterol: Vitamin B6, Arteriosclerosis, and Your Heart.* NY: St. Martin's Press, 1981.
50. Hattersley JG. Vitamin B6: The overlooked key to preventing heart attacks. *Jour Applied Nutr* 1995;47:24-31.
51. Carper J. Surprising new heart threat: B6 deficiency. *USA Weekend* 1998;June 12-14:21.
52. Ellis JM et al. A deficiency of vitamin B6 is a plausible molecular basis of the retinopathy of patients with diabetes mellitus. *Biochem Biophys Res Comm* 1991;179:615-619.
53. Lewis GF, Zinman B et al. Hepatic glucose production is regulated both by direct hepatic and extrahepatic effects of insulin in humans. *Diabetes* 1996;45(2 suppl):454.
54. Bland JS. *Funct Med Update* 1999;Dec.
55. Bland JS. *Funct Med Update* 1999;Dec.
56. Maseri A. Inflammation, atherosclerosis, and ischemic events-Exploring the hidden side of the moon. *New Eng J Med* 1997;336;14:1014-1016.
57. Lipton BH. Lecture, 1994.
58. Pauling L. *Vitamin C, The Common Cold, and the Flu.* SF: WH Freeman, 1976.
59. Gardner TW, Eller AW, Friberg TR, et al. Antihistamines reduce blood-retinal barrier permeability in patients with background diabetic retinopathy. *Invest Opthalmol Visual Sci* 1991;32:1289.
59a. Ellis JM et al. A deficiency of vitamin B6 is a plausible molecular basis of the retinopathy of patients with diabetes mellitus. *Biochem Biophys Res Comm* 1991;179:615-619.
60. Witting LA et al. The relationship of pyridoxine and riboflavin to the nutritional value of polymerized fats. *Amer Oil Chemists' Soc* 1957;34:421-424.
61. Kuzuya F. Vitamin B6 and arteriosclerosis. *Daiichi Vitamin News* 1991;6:1-7.
62. Kuzuya F. Vitamin B6 and arteriosclerosis. *Daiichi Vitamin News* 1991;6:1-7.
63. Nabu M. New application and effect of vitamins, to food-antioxidation effect of vitamin B6. *Daiichi Fine News* 1989;2:1-3.
64. Zhou Y-C, Zheng R-L. Phenolic compounds and an analog as superoxide anion scavengers and antioxidants. *Biochem Pharmacol* 1991;42:1177-1179.
65. Ravichandran V, Selvam R. Lipid peroxidation in subcellular fractions of liver and kidney of vitamin B-6 deficient rats. *Med Sci Res* 1990;18:369-371.
66. Ravichandran V, Selvam R. Increased lipid peroxidation in kidney of vitamin B-6 deficient rats. *Biochem Internatl* 1990;21;4:599-605.
67. Ravichandran V, Selvam R. Increased plasma lipidperoxidation in vitamin B-6 deficient rats. *Ind J Exp Biol* 1991;29:56-58.
68. McCully KS. Chemical pathology of homocysteine. I. *Atherogenesis. Ann Clin Lab* Sci 1993; 23:477-493.
69. Gruberg ER, Raymond SA. *Beyond Cholesterol.* Op. cit.
70. Pfeiffer CC, Sohler A, Jenney CH, Bliev V. Treatment of pyroluric schizophrenia (malvaria) with large doses of pyridoxine and a dietary supplement of zinc. *J Orthomolecular Psych* 1974;3:292-300.
71. Vir SC, Love AH. Vitamin B6 levels in the elderly. *Vitam Nutr Res* 1977;47:364-372.
73. Leklem JE, Hollenbeck CB. Acute ingestion of glucose decreases plasma pyridoxal-5'-phosphate and total vitamin B6 concentration. *Am J Clin Nutr* 1990;51:832-836.

74. McCully KS. Homocysteine theory. Development and current status. *Atherosclerosis Rev* 1983;11:157-246.
76. Hattersley JG. Preventing heart attacks, strokes and sudden infant death. *Townsend Ltr Doc* 1991;Dec:982-986.
75. Becker RO. *Cross Currents: The Perils of Electropollution.* Los Angeles, CA: Tarcher, 1990.
77. Delport R et al. Relationship between maternal and neonatal vitamin B6 metabolism: Perspectives from enzyme studies. *Nutrition* 1991;7:260-264.
78. Ellis JM. *Free of Pain.* Op. cit.
79. Ellis JM. Personal communication, 1997.
80. Baldewicz T et al. Plasma pyridoxine deficiency is related to increased psychological distress in recently bereaved homosexual men. *Psychosomatic Med* 1998;60:297-308.
81. Gullette EC, Blumenthal JA, Babyak M et al. Effects of mental stress on myocardial ischemia during daily life. *JAMA* 1997;277;20:1521-1526.
83. Ellis JM. *Free of Pain.* Op. cit.
84. Ueland PM, Refsum H. Plasma homocysteine, a risk factor for vascular disease: Plasma levels in health, disease and drug therapy. *J Lab Clin Med* 1989;114:473-501.
85. Gruberg ER, Raymond SA. *Beyond Cholesterol.* Op. cit.
86. Leklem JE, Hollenbeck CB. Acute ingestion of glucose decreases plasma pyridoxal-5í-phosphate and total vitamin B6 concentration. *Am J Clin Nutr* 1990;51:832-836.
87. Suzman MM. Nutritional and metabolic factors in the development of coronary artery disease in early life: The possible role of dietary protein and pyridoxine. *Unpub. manuscript abstract,* 1984.
88. Pfeiffer CC, Sohler A, Jenney CH, Bliev V. Treatment of pyroluric schizophrenia (malvaria) with large doses of pyridoxine and a dietary supplement of zinc. *J Orthomolecular Psych* 1974;3:292-300.
89. Anderson BB et al. In *Vitamin B6: Its Roles in Health & Disease.* JE Leklem and RD Reynolds, eds., 1986:273-299,
90. Nair SSD. Prevention of cardiac arrhythmia by dietary (n-3) polyunsaturated fatty acids and their mechanism of action. *Jour of Nutrition* 1997;127;3:383-393.
91. Brown M. Do vitamin E and fish oil protect against ischaemic heart disease? *Lancet* 1999;354: 441-442.
92. Jump DB, Clarke SD. Regulation of gene expression by dietary fat. *Ann Rev Nutr* 1999;19:63-79.
93. Bland JS. *Funct Med Update* 1999;Dec.
95. Nair SSD. *Prevention of cardiac arrhythmia.* Op. cit.
94. Bland JS. *Funct Med Update* 1997;June.
97. Privitera JS, Stang A. *Silent Clots: Life's Biggest Killers.* . Covina, CA: The Catacombs Press, 1996.        (818) 966-1618. Covina, CA: The Catacombs Press, 1996.  (818) 966-1618.
96. M. Schmidt. Interview on Bland JS, *Prev. Med Update,* 1997.
98. Willis GC. The reversibility of atherosclerosis. *Canad Med Assoc J* 1957;77:106-109.
99. Privitera JR, Stang A. Silent Clots: Lifeís Biggest Killers. Op.107 Willis GC. The reversibility of atherosclerosis. *Canadian Med Assoc Jour.* 77;1957:106-109.

94.   Whitaker JM. *Health & Healing* 1998;8;11(Nov):5,6.
95. Genco R et al. Periodontal disease and risk for myocardial infarction and cardio-vascular disease. *CVR&R,* 1998;March:34-40.
96.   Crafton DB II. Three types of oral bacteria increase risk of heart attack by 300%. *Jour of Longevity* 1999;5;12:10-12.
97.   Okuda K et al. The efficacy of antimicrobial mouth rinses in oral health care. *Bull Tokyo Dental College* 1998;39;1:7-14.
98.   Kuller LH, Eichner JE et al. The relation between serum albumin levels and risk of coronary heart disease in the Multiple Risk Factors Intervention Trial. *Amer J Epidemiology* 1991;134; 1266-1277.
98a.  Willis GC, Fishman S. Ascorbic acid content of human arterial tissue. *Can Med Assoc J* 1955; 72:500-503.
99.   Gillum RF. The association between serum albumin and HDL and total choles-terol. *J Natl Med Assoc* 1993;85:290-292.
100.  Gillum R. et al. Serum albumin, coronary heart disease and death. *Amer Heart Jour.* 1992; 123:507-513.
101.  Seaton K. Is albumin the secret of health, intelligence and aging? *Health Freedom News.* 1993;July:19.
102.  J. Privitera, interview, 1992.
103.  Privitera JR, Stang A. *Silent Clots: Lifeís Biggest Killers.* Op. cit.
104.  Thomas W et al. Incidence of myocardial infarction correlated with venous and pulmonary thrombosis and embolism. *Amer Jour Cardiology* ;1960:41-47.
105.  Nieper H. Mineral transporters, *New Dynamics of Preventive Medicine,* 1974.
106.  Editorial: Is vitamin B6 an antithrombotic agent? *Lancet* 1981;June 13:1299-1300.
107.  McCully KS. The Homocysteine Revolution. New Canaan, CT: Keats Publ., 1998.
107a. Hendrix MGR et al. Cytomegalovirus nucleic acid distribution within human vascular tree. *Amer Jour Pathology* 1991; 138: 563-567.
707b. Minick CR. Atheroarteriosclerosis induced by infection with herpesvirus. *Amer Jour Pathology* 1979; 96: 673-706.
108.  Lee JR. Natural *Progesterone: The Multiple Roles of a Remarkable Hormone.* BLL Publ, Sebastapol, CA:, BLL Publ, 1993; p. 8.
109.  Sellman S. *Hormone Heresy: What Women MUST Know About Their Hormones.* Getwell International, Inc. 350 Ward Ave., Suite 106. Honolulu, Hawaii USA 96814, 1998.
110.  Cross T et al. Gas phase cigarette smoke (CS) induces lipid peroxidation in human plasma. *Free Radical Biol & Med* 1990;9(Suppl):69(abstr).
111.  Rath M, Pauling L. Solution to the puzzle of human cardiovascular disease: Its primary cause is ascorbate deficiency leading to the deposition of lipoprotein(a) and fibrinogen/fibrin in the vascular wall. *J Orthomolecular Med* 1991;6:125-134.
112.  Clark WM et al. Need for treatment of elevated plasma fibrinogen levels in cerebrovascular disease. *Heart Dis & Stroke* 1993;2:503-506.
113.  De Villiers LS, Serfontein WJ. *Your Heart: The Unrefined Facts.* Pretoria: Haum Educational, 1989.
114.  Taylor CB et al. Spontaneously occurring angiotoxic derivatives of cholesterol. *Amer J Clin Nutr* 1979;32:40-57.
115.  Luc G, Fruchart JC. Oxidation of lipoproteins and atherosclerosis. *Am J Clin Nutr* 1991;53: 206S-209S.

116. Hattersley JG. Preventing heart attacks, strokes and sudden infant death. *Townsend Ltr Doc* 1991;Dec:982-986.
117. Oster K. *The XO Factor.*
118. McCully KS. Personal communication, 1993.
119. Hattersley JG. Vitamin B6: The overlooked key to preventing heart attacks. *J Applied Nutr* 1995;47:24-31.
120. Ellis JM. Personal communication, 1993.
121. Maksymowych AB, Robertson NM, Litwack G. Efficacy of pyridoxal treatment in controlling the growth of melanomas in cell culture and an animal pilot study. *Anticancer Research* 1993;13: 1925-1938.
122. Maksymowych A, Litwack DV, Litwack G. Pyridoxal phosphate as a regulator of the glucocorticoid receptor. *Ann NY Acad Sci* 1990;585:438-451.

## CHAPTER EIGHT

1. Lee L. *Polyunsaturated fats (PUFA's).* Unpublished manuscript, 1998.
2. Statement by a representative of Protein Technologies, Inc., 1999.
3. *Myths and truths about nutrition. Wise Traditions.* Weston A. Price Foundation(SM) 1999.
4. Sally Fallon and Mary G. Enig. *The Ploy of Soy.* $10; 1-888-593-8333.
5. West B. Get ready for soy. *Health Alert* 2000;17;1:7-8.
6. Fitzpatrick M. *Soy isoflavones: Panacea or poison?* Jour Price-Pottenger Nutr Foundation 1998;Fall.
7. Mary Enig, PhD. Dr. Enig is a leading authority on fats, oils and related matters. She is widely published over the past 25+ years.
8. Sally Fallon, president of Weston A. Price Foundation and founder of A Campaign for Real Milk.
9. Moore, Thomas. *Prescription for Disaster.* NY: Simon & Schuster, 1998.
10. Soy infant formula could be harmful to infants—Groups want it pulled. *Nutrition Week* 1999;29; 46:1.
11. Sally Fallon and Mary G. Enig. *The Ploy of Soy.* Op. cit.
12. Fallon SW, Enig MG. Soy products for dairy products? Not so fast... *Health Freedom News* 1995;Sept:12-20.
13. Harman D et al. Free radical theory of aging: Effects of dietary fat on central nervous system function. *Jour Amer Geriatrics Soc.* 1976;24;1:292-298.
14. Meerson FZ et al. Effect of the antioxidant ionol on formation and persistence of a defensive conditioned reflex during peak exercise. *Bull Exp Biol Med* 1983;96;9:70-71.
15. R. Wisner, Iowa State University; U.S. Dept. of Agriculture.
16. Abe T. Infantile leukemia and soybeans: A hypothesis (editorial). *Leukemia* 1999;13:317-320.
17. *Oncol Rep* 1999(Sept-Oct);6;5:1089-1095.
19. West B. *Get ready for soy.* Op. cit.
20. Price W. *Nutrition and Physical Degeneration.* 6th ed. New Canaan, CT: Keats Publ, 1997.

21. Schauss AG. *Crime, Diet & Delinquency*. SF: Parker House, 1981.
22. Marshall RJ. No healing without quality food. *Acres-USA* 1998;Apr:24-29.
23. Pottenger E, Pottenger R Jr., eds. *Pottenger's Cats*. A Study in Nutrition (edited writings of Francis Pottenger). La Mesa, CA: Price Pottenger Nutr Foundation, 1983.
24. Price W. Op. cit.
25. Schauss AG. *Crime, Diet & Delinquency*. SF: Parker House, 1981.
25a. Cleave TL. *The Saccharine Disease: The Master Disease of Our Time*. New Canaan, CT: Keats Publ., Inc., 1974.
26. Hawk PB, Bergeim O. *Practical Physiological Chemistry*, 11th ed., Philadelpha: The Blakiston Co., 1937; Gortner RA. *Outlines of Biochemistry*, New York: John Wiley & Sons, 1929.
28. Gortner RA. *Outlines of Biochemistry*, New York: John Wiley & Sons, 1929.
29. Beyratgm G et al. *J Phys Chem* 1942;46:203.
30. Clouse RC. Compilation of recent data on mineral and vitamin values of foods, *J Am Dietetic Assoc* 1942;18:553.
31. Walters C. View from the country. *Acres-USA* 1997;May:33,7.
33. Appleton N. *Licking the Sugar Habit; A Life Saving Guide*, 1996.
34. West B. Arthritis, gum disease and raw foods. *Health Alert* 1998;15;5:4-5.
35. Lee L. Gift of Life enzymes. *Earthletter* 1994(summer);4;2:13-14.
32. Charles Walters, editor of Acres-USA. View from the Country. *Acres-USA* 1997;May:3,7.
36. Sprott TJ. *The Cot Death Cover-up?* Auckland, NZ: Penguin Environmental-NZ: 1996.
40. Foster HD. Sudden infant death syndrome and iodine deficiency: Geographical evidence. *Jour Orthomolecular Med* 1988;3;4:207-211.
41. Foster HD. Medical hypothesis: The iodine-selenium connection in respiratory distress and sudden infant death syndromes. *Townsend Letter for Doc/Patients* 1995;Dec:30-35.
42. SIDS Resource Center.
43. Lonsdale D. A general hypothesis to explain the mechanism of sudden infant death syndrome (SIDS). *Jour Advancement in Med* 1989;2;3:443-449.
44. Lonsdale D. Stopping crib death. *Townsend Ltr Doc* 1995;Feb/Mar:88-89.
45. Lonsdale D. A general hypothesis to explain the mechanism. Op. cit.
46. Lonsdale D. Personal communication, 1999.
47. Kraus JF, Borhani NO. Post-neonatal Sudden Unexpected Death in California: A cohort study. *Am J Epidemiology* 1972;95:497.
48. Valdes-Dapena MA. *Sudden Unexplained Infant Death 1970 through 1975: An Evolution of Understanding*. U.S. Dept. of Health, Education & Welfare, Public Health Service, DHEW Publication, 1980 No. (HAS)80-5255,9-10.
49a. *U.S. News & World Report* 1999;May 10. Cited by Mercola J. *Healthy News You can Use*. #123;1999;Oct. 17: 9-11. www.mercola.com
49. Foster HD. *Sudden Infant death syndrome and iodine deficiency*. Op. cit.
50. Lendon Smith, *How to Raise a Healthy Child*, NY: M. Evans, 1996. P 77.
51. William Rea, MD. Lecture, 1999.
52. Pelton R, Lavalle J, Hawkins E et al. *Drug-Induced Nutrient Depletion Handbook*, Lexi-Comp, 1999.
53. Knapen MHJ et al. The effect of vitamin K on circulating osteocalcin (bone Gla protein) and urinary calcium excretion. *Annals Internal Med* 1989;112;12:1001-1005.

54. Weber R. Management of osteoporosis: Is there a role for vitamin K? *Int Jour Vit Nutr Res* 1997;67:350-356.
55. Free Radical Research 1997;26;5:419-429.
56. Kawashima H, Nakajima Y et al. Effects of vitamin K2 (Menatetrenone) on atherosclerosis and blood coagulation in hypercholesterolemic rabbits. *Japanese Jour Pharmacology* 1997;75:135-143.
57. Martin C, Philip W et al. Effects of long-term warfarin therapy on bone mineral density (BMD) at peripheral and axial sites. *Scottish Med Jour* 1994;39:153.
58. Low DE. The evolution and dissemination of resistance: Antibiotics influence on the normal flora. *Infections in Medicine* 1999;Supp:18-23.
59. Crook WG. *The Yeast Connection Handbook*. Jackson, TN: Professional Books Inc., 1996.
60. Mendelsohn RS. *How to Raise a Healthy Child… In Spite of Your Doctor*. NY: Ballantine Books, 1984.
60a. Essential further reference in support of statement that most ear infections are viral, not bacterial. Wickens K, Pearce N, Crane J, Beasley R. Antibiotic use in early childhood and the development of asthma. *Clinical & Experimental Allergy* 1999;29:766-771.
61. Survey shows link between antibiotics and developmental delays in children. *Townsend Ltr Doctors/Patients* 1995;Oct:9.
61a. Hunter A. Food allergies and hereditary illness—Is this the solution? *Int Jour Alt Comp Med* 1999;Oct:13-18.
62. Cumming F. *Vaccination: A health hazard?* Op. cit.
63. *Diabetes Care* 1994;17:13-19.
64. Austin S. Nutrition update: New antioxidants and more. Alpha-lipoic acid may protect against radiation. *Health Notes* 1996;July:1,3.
65. Price WA. *Nutrition and Physical Degeneration*. New Canaan, CT: Keats Pub., 1945.
66. Certified Milk Magazine 1929;Jan
67. Fallon SW, Enig MG. Soy products for dairy products? Not so fast… *Health Freedom News* 1995;Sept:12-20.
68. Williams DG. *Don't let the fresh scent deceive you*. Alternatives for the Health Conscious Individual 1999(Dec);8;6:46.
69. Jinot J, Bayard S. Respiratory health effects of exposure to environmental tobacco smoke. *Reviews on Environmental Health* 1996;11:89-100.
70. Dybing E, Sanner T. Passive smoking, sudden infant death syndrome (SIDS) and childhood infections. *Human & Experimental Toxicology* 1999; 18:202-205.
70a. Ey JL et al. Group Health Medical Associates. Passive smoke exposure and otitis media in the first year of life. *Pediatrics* 1995;95:670-677.
70b. Paradise JL. Short-course antimicrobial treatment for acute otitis media. *JAMA* 1997(Nov 26);278;20:1640-1642.
70c. Culpepper M, Froom J. Routine antimicrobial treatment of acute otitis media is unnecessary. *JAMA* 1997;278;20:1643-1645.
50. A Douglass WC. What not to do for an ear infection. *Second Opinion* 1998;June:8.
72. Lipton BH. Lectures, 1994.
71. Hattersley JG, Treacy K. Overbreathing and its harm to health. *Townsend Letter Doc/Patients*. 1998;Jan:92-95. An enlarged update: www.angelfire.com/wa/jhattersley/content.html.
    Douglass WC. *Letters*. Op. cit.

73.  Hattersley JG. The negative health effects of chlorine. In press for publication in *Jour Orthomolecular Medicine*.
74.  Dayan AD. Alleve antimicrobial reduces in food: Assessment of the risk to man. *Vet Microbiol* 1993;35:213-226.
75.  West B. *Health Alert* 1997;14;3:6-8.
75a. Blate M. *Townsend Letter for Doctors and Patients*, 1997;April:36-37.
      Sahley BJ. *The Anxiety Epidemic*. San Antonio, TX: Pain & Stress Publications, 1999.
76.  Gaby AR. Gaby replies to letters concerning food allergy testing. *Townsend Ltr Doc/Patients* 1998;Apr:105.
77.  Vincent A. Marinkovich, MD. Interview on Bland JS, *Funct Med Update* 1999;Nov.
78.  Gorlick AC. A leader in natural medicine tells County Council of better treatments. *Townsend Ltr Doc/Patients* 1997;June:23.
79.  Douglass WC. Letters. *Second Opinion* 1998;June:8.
80.  Rogers SA. Dr. *Sherry Rogers' Total Wellness*, 1999 Jan. p.6.
81.  Majamaa H, Hisolauri E. Probiotics: A novel approach in management of food allergy. *J Allergy & Clinical Immunol* 1997;99;2:179-185.
82.  Galland L. *The Four Pillars of Healing*. NY: Random House, 1997.
83.  Mercola J. *Healthy News You Can Use*. #123;1999;Oct. 17:9-11. www.mercola.com.
84.  Hunter BT. The benefits of integrated medicine: review of Leo Galland, MD's The Four Pillars of Healing. In *Townsend Ltr Doc/Patients* 1998;Feb-Mar:153.
85.  Marinkovitch V. Interview on Bland JS. *Funct Med Update* 1999;Nov.
86.  West B. Allergies and skin eruptions. *Health Alert* 1998(June);15;6:5-6.
86a. *Chinese Jour Stom* 1993;28;4:197-199.
87.  *Jour Cell Biochem* 1995;22:1169-180.
88.  Luo M, Kannar K, Wahlquist ML, O'Brien RC. Inhibition of LDL oxidation by green tea extract. *Lancet* 1997;349:360-361.
89.  Breithaupt-Grogler K et al. Protective effect of chronic garlic intake on elastic properties of the aorta in the elderly. Circulation 1997;96:2649-2655. Cited in *World Research News* 1998;1st quarter:4.
90.  Weaver JC. Electroporation: A general phenomenon for manipulating cells and tissues. *Jour Cellular Biochemistry* 1993;51:426-435.
91   Beck RC. Lecture, 1996. Sota Instruments, 1-800-224-0242.
92.  Hendler, SS. *The Doctors' Vitamin and Mineral Encyclopedia*. NY: Simon & Schuster, 1990.
93.  Heinerman J. Organic chlorophyll fights infection. Personal communication, 1991.
94.  Mowrey DB. *Herbal Tonic Therapies*. New Canaan, CT: Keats Publ Inc., 1993.
95.  Jennifer Jacobs, MD. Homeopathic treatment of diarrhea in children. *Pediatrics* 1994(May); 93:719-725.
96.  Williams RJ. The expanding horizon in nutrition. *Texas Reports of Biology & Medicine* 1961; 19:245-248.
97.  Bliznakov EG, Hunt GL. *The Miracle Nutrient: Co-enzyme Q10*. NY: Bantam, 1988.
98.  Marshall RJ. *No healing without quality food*. ACres-USA 1998;Apr:24-29.
99.  Lita Lee, PhD with Lisa Turner and Burton Goldberg. *The Enzyme Cure*. Future Medicine Publishing, Tiburon, California, 1998.
100. Young JDE, Cohn ZA. How killer cells kill. *Scientific American* 1988; Jan:38-

45.
101.   Cheraskin E. The breakfast/lunch/dinner ritual. *J Orthomolecular Med* 1993; 8:6-10.
102.   Rogers SA. *Wellness Against All Odds*. Syracuse, NY: Prestige Publ, 1994.

---

## CHAPTER NINE

1.   Ott JN. *Light, Radiation and You. How to Stay Healthy*. Greenwich, CT: Devin-Adair Publishers, 1990.
2.   Hattersley JG. Full-spectrum light: Energy and health builder. *PPNF Health Journal* 1995; Winter: 3-5.
3.   Wendel H. *Light - Medicine of the Future*. Seminar, Ruhpolding, Germany, Oct. 22, 1996.
4.   Thalen B-E et al. Light treatment in seasonal and nonseasonal depression. *Acta Psychiatr Scand* 1995; 91: 352-360.
5.   Sandyk R. Successful treatment of multiple sclerosis with magnetic fields. *Int J Neuroscience* 1992; 66: 2377-2350. Later refer in PMU 1996 Dec.
6.   Sandyk R. Chronic relapsing multiple sclerosis. A case of rapid recovery by application of weak electromagnetic fields. *Int J Neurosciences* 1995; 82.
7.   Sandyk R. Reversal of alexia in multiple sclerosis by application of weak electromagnetic fields. *Int J Neurosciences* 1995; 82.
8.   Grimes DS. Sunlight, cholesterol and coronary heart disease. *Quarterly J Medicine* 1996; 89: 579-589.
9.   Foster HD. The geography of schizophrenia: Possible links with selenium and calcium deficiencies, inadequate exposure to sunlight and industrialization. *J Orthomolecular Med* 1988; 33: 115-140.
10.   Sandyk R. Magnetic fields in the therapy of Parkinsonism. *Int J Neuroscience* 1992; 66: 141-171.
11.   *The politics of sunlight. What Doctors Don't Tell You* 1995; 5; 12: 12.
12.   Garland FC et al. Occupational sunlight exposure and melanoma in the U.S. Navy. *Arch Environmental Hea*lth 1990; 45: 261-267.
13.   Beral V et al. Malignant melanoma and exposure to fluorescent lighting at work. *Lancet* 1982; Aug 7: 290-293.
14.   Kennedy AR et al. Fluorescent light causes malignant transformation in mouse embryo cell. *Science* 1980; 207: 1209-1211.
15.   Ott JN. Interview on Bland JS, *Prev Med Update* 1991; Jan
16.   Beral V, Ramchara S, Faris R. Malignant melanoma and oral contraceptive use among women in California. The Walnut Creek Contraceptive Drug Study. *U.S. National Institutes of Health, vol. III*, 1986, pp. 247-252.
17.   Sunlamp use linked to melanoma. Sci News 1994; 146: 296.
18.   Jablonski NG. A possible link between neural tube defects and ultraviolet light exposure. *Med Hypotheses* 1999; 52; 6: 581-582.
19.   Rogers SA. *Tired or Toxic?* Syracuse, NY: Prestige Publ., 1990.
20.   Ott JN. *Light, Radiation and You. How to Stay Healthy*. Op. cit.
21.   US EPA. Inert ingredients of pesticides. *Rachel's Environmental and Health Weekly #469*.
22.   *Journal of Pesticide Reform* 1995; Fall.

23.   Rogers SA. *Northeast Center for Environmental Medicine*. 1993; Nov.
24.   The quiet health threat - Pesticide-treated foods. *Jour of Longevity* 1999; 5; 7: 30-32.
25.   Kierman V. Chemical in fluoridated water may foster violent behavior and cocaine use, scholar says. *Academe Today* 1998; Sept. 8.
26.   Judd GF. *Good Teeth Birth to Death*, 6615 W. Lupine, Glendale, AZ 85304-3136. p.12.
27.   Glasser GC. Fluoride and the phosphate connection. *Earth Island Jour special report* 1998: 14-15.
28.   Hattersley JG. The case against fluoridation. *Jour Orthomolecular Medicine* 1999; 14; 4185-197.
29.   Glasser GC. Fluoride and the phosphate connection. *Earth Island Jour special report* 1998: 14-15.
30.   Kierman V. Chemical in fluoridated water may foster violent behavior and cocaine use, scholar says. *Academe Today* 1998; Sept. 8.
31.   London Telegraph 1998; March 8. Reported in Douglass WC, *Second Opinion* 1998; Aug: 7.
32.   Hazeltine W. *Lancet* 1969; 2: 4-6.
33.   Robinson AB. Intrinsic mutations. *Access to Energy* 1997; 24; 5: 3-4.
34.   Wald MW. Hanford exposure admitted. *Seattle Post-Intelligencer* 2000; Jan. 29: A!, A8. From *The New York Times*.
35.   Gerber M. *On the Homefront*. 1992.
36.   Kendall GM et al. Mortality and occupational exposure to radiation; First analysis of the National Registry for Radiation Workers. *Brit Med Jour* 1992; 304: 220.
37.   Voelz GL, Lawrence JNP, Johnson ER. Fifty years of plutonium exposure to the Manhattan Project plutonium workers: An update. *Health Physics* 1997; 73; 4: 611-618.
38.   *USPHS Toxicological Profiles on Fluorides* Sec. 2. Health effects. Death, Keplinger 1969.
39.   Global Liars. *Access to Energy*. 1997; Dec; 25; 4: 1-4.
40.   Discarding the truth. *Access to Energy*. 2000 (Jan); 17; 5: 3-5.
41.   Bogen KT. A cytodynamic two stage model that predicts radon hormesis (decreased, then increased lung-cancer risk vs. exposure). Lawrence Livermore National Laboratory, Univ of California, Preprint UCRL-TC-123219. Based on data of Cohen BL. Test of the linear-no threshold theory of radiation carcinogenesis for inhaled radon decay products. *Health Physics* 1997; 68: 157-174.
42.   Cohen BL. Test of the linear-no threshold theory of radiation carcinogenesis for inhaled radon decay products. *Health Physics* 1991; 68: 157-174.
43.   Kendall GM et al. Mortality and occupational exposure to radiation; First analysis of the National Registry for Radiation Workers. *Brit Med Jour* 1992; 304: 220.
44.   Robinson AB. Cancer postponement with radon. *Access to Energy* 1997; 24; 6: 1-3.
45.   Bogen KT. Op. cit.
46.   Hileman B. Fluoridation of water. *Chem Engr News* 1988; Aug 1: 26-42.
47.   Sugahara T, Sagan LA, Aoyama T. Low dose irradiation and biological defense mechanisms. Amsterdam: *Excerpta Medica*, 1992.
48.   Calabrese EJ. *Biological effects of low level exposures to chemicals and radiation*. Boca Raton, FL: Lewis Publishers, 1994.
49.   Shadley JD, Wolff S. Very low doses of X-rays can cause lymphocytes to

become less susceptible to ionizing radiation. *Mutagenesis* 1987; 2; 95-96.

50.   Wolff S. Low dose exposures and induction of adaptation. In: Sugahara T, Sagan LA, Aoyama T. *Low Dose Irradiation and Biological Defense Mechanisms*. Amsterdam: Excerpta Medica, 1992.

51.   Cohen BL. Test of the linear-no threshold theory of radiation carcinogenesis. Op. cit.

52.   Robinson AB. *Access to Energy*. 1999; Mar: 3-4.

53.   Discarding the truth. *Access to Energy* 2000(Jan); 27; 5: 3-4.

54.   Smith BL. Organic foods vs. supermarket foods: Element levels. *J of Applied Nutr* 1993(Mar); 45: 35-39.

55.   Smith BL. Personal communication, 1995.

56.   Worthington V. Effect of agricultural methods on nutritional quality: A comparison of organic with conventional crops. *Alternative Therapies* 1997; 4: 58-63.

57.   Profet M. *Protecting Your Baby-to-Be*. Preventing Birth Defects in the First Trimester. Reading, MA: Addison-Wesley Publ, 1995.

58.   Profet M. Pregnancy sickness as adaptation: A deterrent to maternal ingestion of teratogens. In Barkow J, Cosmides L, Tooby J (eds): *The Adapted Mind*. NY: Oxford Univ. Press, 1992: 327-365.

59.   Hulda Clark, PhD, ND. *The Cure for All Cancers*. www.naturalearthdirection.ow/markets/product/itm00255.htm.

60.   Klinghardt DK, Williams LL. Isopropyl alcohol and other toxic solvents: A historical literature review.

61.   Schuldt H. The cure of cancer based on bio-energetic analysis. *Townsend Ltr Doc/Patients* 1999; Oct: 86-88.

62.   Lam F, Tsuei J. *Amer Jour Acupuncture,* 1983; Mar.

63.   Schuldt H. *Townsend Ltr Doc/Patients* 1997; Dec: 84.

64.   Fuchs NK. The pesticide and breast cancer connection. *Women's Health Ltr* 1994; Jan.

65.   Peat R. *Ray Peat's News*letter. 1995.

66.   Hulda Clark books: See Sources of Information.

67.   Feshback M, Friendly A. Jr. *Ecocide in the USSR*. NY: Basic Books Div of Harper Collins Publishers, 1992.

68.   Morgan D, Roan CC. The Metabolism of DDT in man. Essays in Toxicology. 1974:39-96.)

69.   Uzbekistan: No more caviar. *Economist* 1994; Oct. 15.

70.   Uzbekistan: No more caviar. Op. cit.

71.   Feshbach M, Friendly A. Jr. Idem.

72.   Joseph Hattersley wrote (June 18, 1998) to Dr. Murray Feshbach for information and references on the matter. No reply has been received.

73.   The paper is summarized in *Access to Energy*. 2000; Jan.: 4.

74.   Chris Carson. Interview 2000; Feb. 19.

75.   Rogers SA. *Depression...Cured at Last*. Sarasota, FL: SK Publ., 1997.

76.   Philip Dickey, PhD. Lecture, 1999.

77.   Rogers SA. *Total Health in Today's World*. 1997; 1; 4: 6.

78.   Buteyko KP, Genina VA. The theory of discovery of deep respiration (hyperventilation) as a main cause of allergic, bronchial-vascular-spasmodic and other diseases of civilisation. Tez. Dokl. Vsesoyuzn. Conf. Moscow, 1986 (Report Thesis from All-Union Conference, M.)

79.   Hattersley JG, Treacy K. Overbreathing and its harm to health. *Townsend Letter Doctors and Patients*. 1998; Jan: 92-95. An update is posted at

www.angelfire.com/wa/jhattersley/content.html.

80.  Courtney R, Eucapnic asthma and the role of hyperventilation in human health. *Australian J Osteopathy* 1997; 7; 1: 14-17. P. 17.

81.  Bowler SD et al. Buteyko breathing techniques in asthma: A blinded randomized controlled trial. *Med Jour Australia* 1998(Dec 7/21); 169: 575-578.

82.  Hattersley JG, Treacy K. *Overbreathing and its harm to health.* Op. cit.

83.  Riordan PJ. Dental fluorosis, dental caries and fluoride exposure among 7-year-olds. *Caries Res* 1993; 27: 71-77.

84.  Pendrys DG et al. Op. cit.

85.  Pope TP. Health journal. Some young children get too much fluoride in caring for teeth. *Wall St. Jour* 1998; Dec. 21: B1.

86.  Pendrys DG, Katz RV, Morse DE. Risk factors for enamel fluorosis in a fluoridated population. *Am J Epidemiology* 1994; 140: 451-471.

87.  Sherrell D. Rethinking fluoridation. *Earth Island Jour* 1998; Spring: 40-41.

88.  Cheng YX. IQ of children in areas of high fluorine content. *Chin J Control Endemic Disease,* Supplement 1991 [in Chinese].

89.  Li XS, Zhi JL, Gao RO. Effect of fluoride exposure on intelligence in children. *Fluoride* 1995; 20; 4: 109-192.

90.  Spittle B. Psychopharmacology of fluoride: A review. Int Clin Psychopharmacology J 1994; 9: 79-82.

91.  Czerwinski E, Lankosz W. Fluoride-induced changes in 60 retired aluminum workers. *Fluoride* 1977; 10: 12-16.

92.  Hattersley JG. The case against fluoridation. *Jour Orthomolecular Med* 2000; 14; 4: 185-197.

93.  Rapaport I. Studies in the 1950s. Cited by Foulkes RG. *Health Naturally* 1994 (June/July): 7-11.

94.  Lee L. *Earthletter* 1993; winter.

95.  Clear and present danger. *The Guardian* 1997; June 7: 27-30.

96.  Schuld A. Personal communication, 1999.

97.  Huggins HA, Levy TDD. *Uninformed Consent. The Hidden Dangers in Dental Care.* Charlottesville, VA: Hampton Roads Publ., 1999 1 (800) 766-8009 or (804) 296-2772).

98.  Drasch D et al. Mercury burden of human fetal and infant tissues. *European Jour Pediatrics* 1994; 153; 8: 607-610.

99.  Vimy MJ et al. Maternal-fetal distribution of mercury (203Hg) released from dental amalgam fillings. *Am J Physiol* 1990; 258: 939 945.

100. Whitaker J. *Health and Healing* 1993; Oct.

# INDEX